GOLF
FOR BEGINNERS

GOLF
FOR BEGINNERS

by **Mac Hunter,** PGA Professional

**Photographs by
Jack Scagnetti**

GROSSET & DUNLAP
A National General Company
Publishers   New York

Cover Photo by Simone Zorn

Contents

Foreword

Golf is one of the few competitive sports one can enjoy for a lifetime. It is a game that one can begin vigorously at an early age and continue with interest, enthusiasm and enjoyment on into the retirement years. Its appeal is universal, engaging all walks of life, creeds, colors, religions, ages and sex.

It's a very peculiar game: to the onlooker, there's no question that it must appear to be one of the simplest, if not silliest, games ever conceived. But those who learn to play and learn to appreciate it, will in turn reap everlasting pleasures.

I have had the happiness of knowing Mac Hunter for many years, and have always felt his understanding and forthright approach to the game—both as a friend, player and teacher—to be sensible and sound. He is well-qualified to author this book on golf for beginners.

The golfer who will not take time to go to a professional for a lesson can, in my opinion, supplement desire for the game with study of this book's content. I am certain anyone who feels that "seeing is believing" will benefit tremendously from the more than 100 pictures this book offers. Then again, I know there are not one or two, but many refreshing thoughts waiting inside, just for you, that will both reduce your score and discourage opponents.

—*Gene Littler*

Introduction

Mac Hunter, the former head professional at the Riviera Country Club in Pacific Palisades, is now a consultant with the Los Angeles Athletic Club, owner of the Riviera.

He is the son of the late Willie Hunter, extraordinary Scottish professional of international fame.

Mac began his golfing career at the early age of ten by winning the Inglewood City Junior. In 1946, he defeated Arnold Palmer in the finals of the National Junior Championship. In 1949 he won the California State Amateur and climaxed the most thrilling match in the history of this Championship when he defeated Gene Littler after 39 holes of strenuous, if not spectacular, play. That same year he won the Mexican National Amateur Championship.

In 1951, he became the professional at Riviera, where he has been for 22 years. During this span he has played in eleven U.S. Opens, six PGA Championships and two British Opens. In 1968 he defeated Tommy Jacobs in the finals of the Southern California PGA Championship. He was Southern California's leading money winner for the years 1953, '54, '56 and '68. As recently as 1972, he finished tenth behind Jack Nicklaus in the Bing Crosby National Pro-Am. Besides having made 8 holes in one, he still holds course records at Tamarisk Country Club, Palm Springs (64); Riviera Country Club (65), and Westchester Country Club (West Course), New York (64).

He served as an officer of the Southern California PGA for six years, from 1959-1965. In 1962 he was voted Southern California's Outstanding Golf Professional. Mac is readily recognized as one of the country's foremost golf instructors, an outspoken exponent of the game, and certainly one of the most versatile club professionals.

He is forty-four years old and has a son, MacGregor, who in 1972 became the youngest golfer (age sixteen) to win the California State Amateur Championship.

Equipment

Knowledge of golf equipment will help you to play better golf and make your game more enjoyable. I could offer no better advice than to urge you to consult a PGA professional for all information regarding the equipment best suited for you. The plain truth is that the man behind the counter in a department store is not as qualified as a professional to appraise and to fit your needs.

What you buy in equipment will depend on two things: (1) how often you plan to play golf, and (2) your budget.

Clubs

For those just learning to play, it's advisable to first purchase an inexpensive starter set or a good used complete set of clubs picked out by a PGA professional. A starter set usually consists of five irons (3, 5, 7, 9 and putter) and two woods (1 and 3). This gets you into the game without cutting too deeply into the budget. Or you could begin with a used set of clubs provided they're selected for you by a qualified pro. Remember all the golf equipment in the world won't help you to play unless you also have good instruction—and as much of this as you can afford.

Once you have played awhile and made your decision to play golf regularly, it's a good idea to move into a better set of clubs in a medium price range. This intermediate set should necessarily be more complete and of better quality. It should include the eight irons (2 through 9), a sand

A PGA professional is best qualified to recommend and fit all types of golf equipment.

wedge, a pitching wedge, a putter and four woods (1, 3, 4 and 5). These clubs are completely swing-weighted. They are manufactured on the basis of the average size and physical characteristics of men, women and juniors.

(Swing weight is the weight you feel when you swing the club—the proportion of the weight in the clubhead as related to the shaft and grip. Total weight is the dead weight of the club. PGA pro shops have scales to measure both the swing weight and the total weight of the clubs.)

Players who play regularly and who can afford it will want to buy a matched swing-weighted set. It will cost at least twice as much as an intermediate set but will be well worth the investment in the long run.

Manufacturers of golf clubs use letters and numerals to designate swing weights. Golfers who are capable of hitting a ball more than 200 yards will generally use a D-0 to D-4 weight. C weights are generally right for women or senior players. Of course there will always be some exceptions to this generalization.

In addition to specific swing weight, a matched set of clubs requires graduated shaft lengths and uniform flexibility of shafts. Flexibility, or shaft flex as it is commonly called, is the amount of stiffness built into a shaft. A club shaft bends during the backswing and downswing. How much it bends is determined by the speed of your swing, the swing weight of the club, the shaft flex and strength of the swinger. Fast swingers usu-

The basic wood set includes a driver, 3-, 4- and 5- wood. The 2- wood and 6-, 7- and even 8-woods are not uncommon, but are considered auxiliary clubs.

ally use a stiffer shaft because they are able to generate sufficient power to move the shaft. Slower swingers are advised to use a more flexible shaft to add controlled clubhead speed at impact. There are several variations of shaft flexibilities: extra stiff, stiff, medium, flexible and soft.

Selection of the proper flexibility is very important to your swing. Hitting a ball straight requires that you control the clubhead at all times. If your shaft is too flexible for the speed of your swing, it can cause you to either hook or slice. Hand and wrist action is supplemented by this bending of the shaft. The average male golfer uses a medium shaft. Club manufacturers say the ideal shaft should be as light as possible. With the advent of lighter shaft materials, they have found it is possible to lighten the total weight of the club while increasing the weight in the clubhead. This has been a plus for added distance.

In recent years, manufacturers have come up with new materials to lighten shafts. In the late 1960's, aluminum shafts appeared on the market and attracted considerable attention. They were soon replaced in popularity by *lightweight* steel because most players liked the feel of steel better. *Stainless* steel shafts never worked out because they wouldn't consistently spring back to their original position after impact.

In 1972, a few manufacturers introduced shafts made of graphite or carbon. The shafts are lighter than steel and are advertised as providing as much as 20 to 30 yards more distance. However, the initial introductory price is $100 per club. Some tour pros, notably Gay Brewer, have used them with success.

Shaft length should also be considered when buying clubs. Height alone does not determine shaft lengths. Arm length is a major determining factor as well as the length of your legs, torso and how you stand to the ball. Another consideration is your type of swing. An upright swinger (usually a tall player) often needs less length in the shaft because he stands closer to ball at address. A flat swinger (usually a short man) moves his clubhead in a more horizontal plane and, generally, needs more shaft length.

The grip on the club should fit firmly in your hands to give better control. Use a grip that provides traction. Grips must not slip in any weather and should shed or absorb moisture easily. Rubber grips are the most popular today because they are easier to put on and are cheaper. With the possible exception of very humid climates, they will keep the hands from slipping.

Leather grips have an advantage in that they absorb moisture and can be used anywhere. Slip-on leather grips have become available in recent years but they require more care. If not maintained, they become hard and slippery.

Another factor to consider in golf club selection is the loft of the clubhead. Loft is the angle between the face of the club and an imaginary vertical line from the sole of the club. Manufacturers are usually uniform in their loft angle, although there can be some variation among clubmakers. Loft is usually specified in manufacturers' catalogs. A player who is having trouble getting the ball airborne can order more loft on his driver. The standard loft angle for the No. 1 wood is 11-13 degrees.

Average players are advised to use a loft of 12 degrees (half sizes are available from some club-makers).

Still another factor to consider in club selection is the lie, which is the angle between the center line of the shaft and the horizontal. A player with unusual physical characteristics or stance may sometimes have to adjust the lie of his clubs. The sole of the club should be almost flat on the ground with the toe up about a quarter-inch as the player assumes his normal stance at address. The ball will veer off from either the toe or heel if either is excessively raised. Most pro shops today have a machine to adjust a club's lie.

Finally, club selection is a matter of personal taste. A player has to like the look and feel of his clubs if he is going to feel comfortable and confident with them.

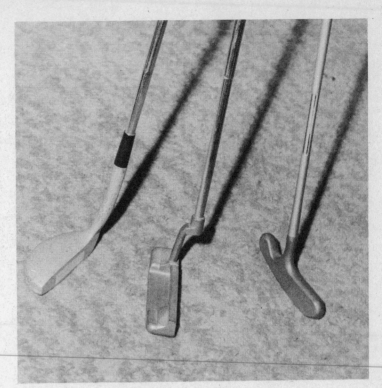

There are a great variety of putters available. Shown here are three of the most popular models.

Gloves

Wearing a glove is virtually a must for playing golf. A glove helps a player to have a firm grip on the club and to lessen the chances of slipping. A glove is also a necessity for those whose hands sweat freely. Likewise, tender skin would warrant the use of a glove for added protection. A glove should be thin-skinned in order for the hand, especially the fingers, to feel the movement of the club throughout the swing. A glove must fit snugly. A little-known fact is that gloves in their most natural state afford the best tackiness for grip. Gloves of such colors as white, red, blue and yellow require more paste in them to make the color stay. If you question the truth of this, purchase a glove in its natural state, tan or brown, and compare its feel and durability with that of a white glove to determine which contains the most paste.

Golf Bags

A good golf bag will not only provide protection for your clubs but through its several built-in conveniences it will also add to the pleasure of your game. It's better to pay a few dollars more to buy one that provides plenty of room for all your clubs than to have a bag that is too small and results in the clubs being jammed and eventually damaging the grips. Plus it is an annoyance having to push a club in and to struggle pulling it out. Buy a bag with enough pocket space to store such useful items as an extra sweater, rain

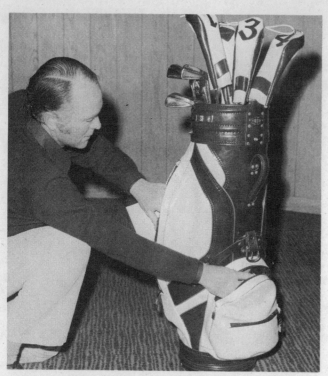

Select a golf bag that fits your needs. Pockets provide space for sweaters as well as balls and tees.

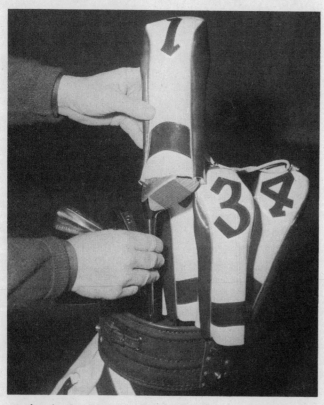

Individual covers for your woods usually blend with the bag and prevent unnecessary nicks and scratches.

gear, gloves, balls, tees and any other personal items you might need. And be sure to invest a few more dollars to protect your wood clubheads against scratches with a sturdy set of hood covers.

Shoes

When selecting golf shoes, look for shoes that will give you good support. During the golf swing your body puts a tremendous strain on a pair of shoes. Comfort and service are far more important than looks. Buy a shoe for these qualities, and you will never be sorry.

Golf Balls

Beginning golfers and other high-handicap players should use balls with a regular compression (80-90 range). Only experienced players with a strong swing should use 100 compression balls. It might be noted that even among the touring pros only a small percentage use the 100's.

Clothes

Selection of clothes for golf is a personal matter. The primary requirement is to wear something comfortable and free enough so you can swing easily. You will do well to consider dressing according to the weather. Almost any PGA Pro shop is stocked with a good variety of handsome styles in an array of beautiful colors. Women should check out the rules of their local golf course as to what women are permitted to wear before investing in a golf wardrobe. Some courses prohibit women players wearing shorts or some types of shorts.

How to Take Lessons

Everyone needs to take lessons, regardless of whether he is a beginner or an intermediate golfer. Even Jack Nicklaus takes lessons from his golf pro before he starts on the winter pro tour or whenever he feels that his swing needs attention. Arnold Palmer sees his father, Milfred (Deacon) Palmer, a golf pro, whenever he feels that some phase of his game needs sharpening. Tour pros consult other tour pros. Deane Beman, Gene Littler, Phil Rodgers and Gardner Dickinson are among the pros most often sought by fellow tour pros for lessons.

No matter how good a player you are, you need an observant eye to check your swing. My father, the late Willie Hunter, checked my swing regularly. I recently had tour pro Gene Littler look at my son MacGregor's swing just before he won the California State Amateur in 1972.

Before scheduling golf lessons, seek out the best instructor in the area where you live. The fee for good instruction is not high by any professional standards, but no matter what the fee, it's always well worth the money. You'll learn faster and you'll learn correctly. Depending upon the professional and the area you select, a half-hour lesson will run between $5 and $12. Country club teaching pros will usually charge more than those at public courses.

Someone who plays the game well competitively and teaches is apt to be a better teacher than someone who is solely a player or teacher. I don't mean to imply playing pros make better teachers than club pros. One who has played well has generally had much instruction himself and has put it all together in competition. Generally speaking, tour pros don't always make good teachers because they are too used to looking at only the fine points of a swing and lack the patience to start beginners. Adjustments they make may be too startling or drastic whereas a club pro, working with pupils constantly, will understand the limitations of a person far better and make the same adjustments gradually and without confusion.

If you're on a budget and cannot afford $75 to $100 for lessons, look into group lessons. They will cost anywhere from $2 to $3 per lesson and usually include the rental of a bucket of balls. You cannot expect to become a super player from a clinic or group lesson, but you can learn the fundamentals. Neither can you expect to get out of a clinic or group what you would get from private instruction.

Taking a special series of lessons at a package price is okay but is not favored. In this arrangement, some pros give out a book with a coupon entitling pupils to lessons and the use of a bucket of balls. A pro in this setup may lose interest in a specific pupil if he has 10 to 30 people signed up for a series.

The main complaint with series is that the pupil feels that he owns the pro's time. The pro should have the prerogative to say "no lessons" on a certain day to any pupil. No one can possibly be in the right frame of mind to teach every day.

Actually, there are two kinds of instruction: teaching and coaching. An instructor can usually teach a pupil enough basics to be-

Seek out a teaching pro who is knowledgeable, easy to talk to and who can motivate you.

gin to play after a dozen lessons. Thereafter, the instructor becomes a coach. Once this initial learning period is passed, a student should continue to take lessons periodically and to be coached in developing his game. In the initial lessons, the instructor can only give the student a solid foundation on which to build a sound game. He can teach him the grip, stance and address, alignment, balance, backswing, etc. Thereafter, the instructor will coach the student.

Seek a teaching pro who motivates you, one with whom you can communicate and one who gives you a full 30 minutes of his time. Start with a one-hour lesson that includes orientation rather than

Youngsters who take lessons at an early age are a good bet to develop into good players. Youth imitates. Age reasons.

just hitting balls. There should be a discussion regarding clubs and what's involved in lessons. Thereafter, lessons should be limited to a half-hour. Taking more than half an hour is usually a waste of time. A person can only absorb so much. Thirty minutes of *concentrated* instruction can be more beneficial than an hour when your mind is wandering and you are tired.

If you have the time, take two half-hour lessons a week and schedule at least a dozen such lessons. A beginner seldom progresses when taking only one half-hour lesson once a week. After you have taken a dozen lessons, schedule a lesson once a week or twice a month. Even after you have improved, you should continue to take a periodic checkup lesson.

When you have progressed with your game to a state where you feel you have a basic knowledge of the swing and can chip and putt, take a playing lesson. A playing lesson is more expensive, but you will get your money's worth. The pro can teach you etiquette, what's expected on the course, how to play trouble shots: such as uphill, sidehill or downhill lies, sand shots, hitting over and under trees and golf course strategy. You will get a better perspective of the game and discover that you will have to go back to the lesson tee for more practice.

Many instructors today use visual aids to help the pupil analyze his swing. Sequence cameras with instant film development are popular as well as video tape with instant replay.

Good Golf Starts
with Grip and Stance

Grip

A beginning golfer is destined to remain a duffer unless he learns a good grip at the outset. Persistence in this least interesting component of a sound swing will reap abundant dividends as knowledge of the game progresses. It's an often said truth: "Good golf starts with a good grip." But, alas, too many golfers have become confused with too many tedious details about the proper placement of the hands on the club. The grip can be, and should always be, the one most natural to you.

To illustrate a proper grip, one may stand relaxed with hands limp at the sides. In so doing, note that both hands tend to toe in (face) toward each other. If you stand with your hands in any other position, it would be unnatural. Set the club in the left hand so that the left thumb is placed just slightly off-center to the right. This enables the right hand to meld with the left so that the right thumb assumes the same position on the other side of the handle. No matter how you swing, your hands, if you will just let them, will always have the tendency to return at impact to this most natural starting position. Your grip should be firm but never tense. (I might suggest that the only shot in golf that requires you to grip the club tightly is the intentional slice.)

Somewhat more pressure can be applied by the last three fingers of the left hand and the two middle fingers of the right hand. There should be a feeling that the hands

Standing relaxed, thumbs tend to toe-in naturally toward each other.

Hold club in left hand so the left thumb is placed just slightly off-center to the right. There should be very little gap between thumb and forefinger.

are melded together to form a single unit.

By far the most popular grip in use today is the overlapping grip. It is characterized by overlapping the little finger of the right hand with the forefinger of the left hand. This grip is favored because it tends to knit the hands closely together so that they may do their job as a single unit.

It is important to keep the finger pressure on the club constant throughout the swing. A little tip that seems to help firm up the grip is to set your grip while holding the clubhead in the air about an inch above the ground. If you sole the clubhead on the ground it tends to relax and loosen the fingers; in so doing, the grip is often altered enough to create a flaw in the swing.

Grip should be firm but never tense. Right thumb rests slightly to left side.

Most popular grip is the overlapping. Little finger of right hand overlaps forefinger of left hand. Grip becomes compact unit.

Interlocking grip has little finger of right hand interlocking index finger of the left. Gene Sarazen and Lloyd Mangrum use this grip.

Full 10-finger (baseball) grip is used by few. Tour pros Art Wall and Bob Rosburg use it.

Weak right-hand grip (held over) may cause clubface to open at contact, resulting in slice.

For better control, grip the club a couple of inches below the end of the handle.

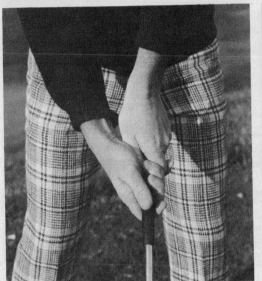

Strong right-hand grip (held under) may cause clubface to enter hitting area in a closed position, resulting in hook.

At top of backswing: Left wrist is in near line with left arm. Grip must remain firm but never tense. Firm pressure should be applied by the last three fingers of the left hand and the two middle fingers of right.

Stance

A proper stance is the next most vital ingredient of the golf swing. Without a correct stance, your swing will have to undergo constant change which, in turn, will produce unlimited off-line shots. The stance refers to the positioning of your body to the ball in relation to the target. The stance covers the positioning of the feet, hands and arms, hips, shoulders and weight.

Start by aligning your feet, hips and shoulders on an imaginary line that parallels your intended line of flight to your target. The alignment of the head, feet, hips and shoulders remains almost the same for all shots regardless of the club you're playing. Position the ball approximately 2 inches inside the left heel. Hold your hands up and advance them slightly forward toward the target, thus establishing a straight line that goes from the ball along the shaft to the left shoulder. Spread your feet so that the distance from heel to heel approximates the width of your shoulders. There should be a feeling that your feet and legs are so firmly set no one could move you from this position of address without a hard push. Your weight should be balanced from the balls of your feet back slightly toward the heels and centered toward the instep of your feet. The left knee may be slightly flexed and turned inward toward the ball. When swinging this will enable you to transfer weight more fluidly from one foot to the other. Your left foot can be opened out about 4 degrees or a little less toward the target. Your right foot may be more square or set at a right angle to the intend-

In assuming stance, grip the club in right hand. Stand slightly behind and open to the hole, mentally visualizing the line of flight as you sight towards your target.

ed line of flight. By setting your right foot in this position, it will help to restrict a sliding or swaying action off the ball while it forces your shoulders to do the hard turning work of the backswing. By having your left foot open, it will enable your left hip to get out of the way sooner at the finish of the shot, induce a freer swinging clubhead and a fuller finish after the hit.

When assuming your stance get the feeling that the part of your body from the waist down is about to sit down—the buttocks should protrude and the upper body

Waggling the clubhead over or behind the ball is a good preliminary action to release tension and establish a tempo for the swing. It also lets you size up the shot and clear your mind.

Spread your feet so that the distance between approximates the width of your shoulders. Both knees should be slightly flexed and twisted inward toward the ball.

should stay almost erect. Stand at a distance from the ball that enables you not to feel cramped or forces you to stretch for it. Lower your right shoulder and relax the right hip and right hand while raising your left shoulder, arm and hand.

The position of your hands as you address the ball should be straight on to slightly forward of the ball and the back of the left hand should face the target. The hands, regardless of the club being played, should never fall behind the ball. The position of the hands changes slightly when you move

from the longer clubs to the shorter clubs.

Under no circumstances should your head be forward (toward the target) of the ball at address. Positioning your head just slightly behind the ball will give you the feeling that all your power will be reaching out toward the ball as you move into the hitting area. Your head must remain constant. If your head moves to the left or right, up or down, forward or backward, it changes not only your balance but also your swing plane and any variety of swing faults will occur.

Buttocks should protrude with upper body staying almost erect. Stand at a distance from the ball so that you neither feel cramped nor too far from the ball.

Once you have assumed a comfortable stance, there are certain preliminary actions you might take to release tension and to establish a tempo for the swing. The first of these is to waggle your club over or behind the ball. This is an individual mannerism, a spontaneous movement or expression of one's self. Ben Hogan uses a quick, short waggle. Arnold Palmer cocks his wrists before he waggles. Jack Nicklaus uses a slow, deliberate waggle. Whichever waggle is employed, it relaxes the body and keeps it in motion. If the whole body is static over the ball, tension sets in and you are apt to experience a jerky motion during the takeaway—thus destroying any chance of rhythm even before the swing starts. Following the waggle and just before the start of the backswing make a forward press. This is a gentle movement of the hands and lower body toward the target. The forward press not only releases tension but it also appears to move everything into a perfect left-side alignment so that everything can flow evenly and in unison on the backswing.

Hands may be from four to six inches away from lower body when addressing the ball.

Square stance. Both feet are set evenly
to the intended line of flight.

Closed stance. Right foot is drawn back
from the intended line of flight.

Position the ball just inside the left heel for tee shots with a driver.

The Basic Swing

Start your backswing by rotating your shoulders in a smooth, unhurried and even motion to the right. Extend your left arm and hold it straight. At the beginning of the takeaway, start the club low and keep it fully extended as you continue to turn your shoulders as far as your muscles will permit. Your shoulders will be turning against your hips, right leg and right foot which must hold firm and resist the steady pressure of your turning shoulders. The coiling and uncoiling of the body's muscles provide the power in your swing. It's as if your muscles were strips of elastic bands. Your muscles perform an action much like that of a modified slingshot. The key to remember is that the farther and tighter you stretch your shoulders and back muscles against those of your resisting right side, the greater the uncoiling action so vital to producing power. Because of the stretched elasticity of the shoulder and the back muscles at the top of the backswing, the necessary guidance to return the clubhead correctly to its original position will result.

By turning the shoulders properly against the hips and the right side, the slightest lateral nudge of your hips toward your intended target will pull the right shoulder down and under following the lead of the hips in the correct

Takeaway starts by extending the club low and keeping it fully extended. Extend the left arm and hold it straight.

In the backswing, shoulders coil against hips, right leg and right foot.

path. In the downswing, the hips pull the shoulders under and after them—the arms and elbows take their lead from the shoulders—closely followed by the hands and then the clubhead. The uncoiling action is completed at impact. It is important to have a full extension of the left arm at impact in order to attain full power. The sequence of body movements in the downswing are universally agreed upon by teaching professionals: hips, shoulders, arms, hands and clubhead. Getting them to move smoothly with perfect timing cannot be achieved without a proper stance and address or without a properly coiled backswing.

Turn your shoulders as far as your muscles will permit. The lower body must hold firm and resist steady pressure of turning shoulders. Head is center post and remains still as you coil body around it.

On the downswing, hips pull the shoulders under and after them. Arms and elbows take their lead from shoulders, closely followed by the hands and then the clubhead. Uncoiling action is completed at impact. Full extension of the left arm at impact is vital to attain full power.

Head remains still after impact as clubhead extends towards target.

Left hip is almost completely out of way a head starts to move nearing finish of swing.

ollow-through is proper when hands finish high over shoulders.
Veight has been transferred to left side. Right foot is free and only
alancing on the toe.

Correct: Left wrist and arm are on plane. Shoulders are fully coiled against resisting hips.

Incorrect: Broken plane. Club picked up as left shoulder moved too far under. Shoulders are not coiled against hips, creating weak power position for downward thrust.

Arc and Plane

After you have learned the basic fundamentals of proper grip, positioning of the hands at address, stance and weight distribution, a knowledge of the arc and plane of the swing will help you to be a better player. The *arc* is the moving extension of the outstretched left arm and the club as they move in an almost complete circle about you. The *plane* of the swing is the angle on which your arc swings and approximates the assumed angle of the club and left arm at address.

There are a couple of fallacies about the arc and plane that must be destroyed before you can find your own arc and plane. First, the club and hands do not travel straight up from a position somewhere at a right angle to your right side. The hands and club do go up, but they go back on a 45-degree angle as they rise to the top of the backswing. The real key is to toss the hands *back* as well as up. Secondly, the left shoulder does not move *under* as much as many magazine articles, golf books and teachers would lead you to believe. The key here is to rotate the shoulders only slightly under as they move around. You must have those two key thoughts clear in your mind before you can improve your swing.

An illustration of some points that are vital to getting into a proper arc and plane of the swing will be helpful here. If I were to stand up straight with my arms held horizontally out to either side, and then were to turn them horizontally around as far as they could be turned; and if the rest of my body, from the hips down to my toes, were to resist this turning action, then I would feel the tightening of my muscles, first in my back and then all the way down to my feet. First the shoulders tighten against the resisting hips, then continue coiling on down against the resisting legs, feet and toes. All muscles would become taut, like the winding of a giant spring.

However, if you overturn your hips, you will overturn your shoulders and the coiling action is lost. Moreover, if you sway by working your left shoulder under too much, your hips correspond by moving laterally, and the coiling is lost.

Only when those muscles from your hips on down resist can you coil your backswing properly. Your feet and legs should be firmly set, planted as if you were going to spring up in a quick jump. Golfers who overswing usually do so because they have worked the left shoulder under too much or overturned the hips. It is physically impossible to overswing if your hips are resisting your shoulder turn.

When you turn your shoulders against the resistance of the lower half of the body (from the waist down), while swinging the club along the correct plane with the fullest extension of the left arm—without moving off the ball—only then can you attain a strong position at the top of the backswing. From that position of strength, where the shoulders are tightly poised and coiled, any movement of the hips laterally transferring weight to the left heel will pull your shoulders and hands down and around into the hitting position. This coiling and releasing action can be compared to that of a strong fast-ball pitcher who coils with a full shoulder turn in his windup and then shifts his weight mightily to the left heel before delivering the pitch.

Clubhead speed determines the distance that you will hit your ball. Fast hand action is vital in attaining that speed. You must have a very strong shift from the right side to achieve fast hand action. You cannot have a strong shift without a good shoulder turn against a resisting hip turn. Such a windup can only come from a sound grip, solid stance and perfect balance at address continuing throughout the swing. Your shoulders, forearms, and hands help swing the club back on the angle of plane to a point well above waist-high. From there, the hands and arms toss the clubhead gently up and back into the proper position. You reach this backswing position when your shoulders can turn no further against your resisting hips, legs and feet. To go beyond that is not easy as well as unnecessary since it places you out of the position for a good return.

Your physical characteristics will determine the limitations of your backswing. Each golfer must set up his swing to match his own physical characteristics. Short or fat golfers will swing on a flatter arc than a tall, thin player. Lightweight golfers, like Ben Hogan, during his prime, or Chi Chi Rodriguez, can get as much distance as men much heavier and taller simply because they coil properly.

Most photographs used in magazine articles are taken with camera angles straight on or at right angles to the side of the golfer. Pupils studying such pictures find it difficult to relate what they see in the photographs to what they wish they could see while trying to hit a shot. However, views taken at a 45-degree angle approximate the correct angle of the swing or plane over which your club must travel. By visualizing your plane, you can easily improve your game. Many good golfers admit that they really did not start playing well until they saw and came to know their own plane. Most golfers incorrectly picture and then transcribe their arc around themselves on the ground where they stand. The accompanying photographs, illustrated from the angle of 45 degrees or in the angle of the swing plane, should be studied carefully.

LOOKING DOWN ON SWING PLANE

LOOKING UP ON SWING PLANE

SIDEVIEW OF SWING PLANE

In the takeaway, the left arm is extended and shoulders are turning on plane.

Approaching the top of the backswing, left arm is on plane, with hands and arms tossing the clubhead up and back on plane as they near completion of backswing.

Top of backswing: Right side is firmly aligned. Shoulders are fully coiled to 90-degree angle against hips, which have turned no farther than 45 degrees.

SIDE VIEW OF SWING PLANE   LOOKING UP ON SWING PLANE   LOOKING DOWN ON SWING PLA

Start of downswing: Hips lead the way, transferring weight to left heel. Shoulders drop under on a slightly more vertical plane.

SIDE VIEW OF SWING PLANE   LOOKING UP ON SWING PLANE   LOOKING DOWN ON SWING PLANE

Impact approximates address position with club on plane. Shoulders are square to the target. Left hip is moving out of the way. Head is held steady.

SIDE VIEW OF SWING PLANE   **LOOKING UP ON SWING PLANE**   **LOOKING DOWN ON SWING PLANE**

Immediately after impact, head remains steady. Shoulders are still on plane. Hands and arms are swinging clubhead toward the target. Left hip is moving out of way.

SIDE VIEW OF SWING PLANE   **LOOKING UP ON SWING PLANE**   **LOOKING DOWN ON SWING PLANE**

Finish: Shoulders are still on plane. Weight is fully transferred to left heel. Body is slightly more erect as it faces the target.

Fairway Woods

Beginning golfers sometimes have difficulty with fairway woods. This is often caused by a misunderstanding of how the fairway wood should be used. Fear of mishitting a shot causes apprehension and tension that in turn creates a negative approach to its use. This apprehension eventually may lead to discarding the woods in favor of irons.

Once a player has gained the basic knowledge of how to use fairway woods, at least enough to get the ball airborne with reasonable accurary, he will them quickly gain the confidence necessary to continue playing them successfully. Probably the most prevalent faults of beginners with fairway woods is the attempt to elevate the ball by raising the body in the hitting zone (imme-

diately before impact). Contrary to popular belief, the downswing is far a more descending blow than has been said. This, coupled with the loft on the fairway wood's clubface, is all that is required to get the ball airborne. Hit down, not up, with the fairway wood, and you, too, will enjoy watching the ball take off in flight.

The 2-wood, offered as an optional club in a set by all manufacturers today, should only be used when you have an excellent lie in the fairway because it has less loft than the other fairway woods. Positioning of the ball with the 2-wood is similar to that of the tee shot with a driver except that the ball is played off the left heel instead of the instep. This position enables you to strike the ball almost at the bottom of the

Play the 2- or 3-wood just off the left heel, but no more than a couple of inches to the right of where you would play a tee shot with a driver. It's okay to take a divot with a fairway wood.

Your ball should have a good lie before using a 2-wood or 3-wood on the fairway. Check your alignment and set your legs strongly before starting the swing.

swing's arc and results in the ball being swept from the turf with only a slight scarring of the ground.

Whether pro or weekend player, golfers find more use for the 3-wood on the fairway than for any other wood. It gets the ball sufficiently airborne while still generating plenty of distance. The shaft length is less than an inch shorter than that of a driver, and therefore provides the same long swinging arc so vital for distance. Like the 2-wood, the 3-wood requires a good lie before it should be used. The swing with a 3-wood is quite similar to that used with the driver or 2-wood. The slightly shorter shaft makes it easier to control than the driver and requires standing just slightly closer to the ball. Play the ball to the right of the

left heel, about two inches to the right of where you would play a tee shot with a driver. This position enables the clubhead to strike the ball before reaching the lowest point on the swing's arc. It should be a full, free and unhurried swing. Do not attempt to punch down on the ball or to use a short, choppy swing. But, make no mistake, the ball must always be struck a descending blow. The same can be said of each successive fairway wood (4, 5, 6, etc.) as loft increases and club length decreases.

Golfers shooting scores of 90 or more will find the 4-wood even more useful than the 3-wood. The 4-wood has a rather small head, a thin face and greater loft—all of which combine to force the ball up more quickly than the 2- or 3-

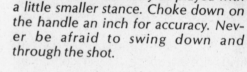

The 4- and 5-wood may be played with a little smaller stance. Choke down on the handle an inch for accuracy. Never be afraid to swing down and through the shot.

wood while still achieving distance.

The 4-wood is perhaps the most versatile of the woods. It is an ideal club to hit a long shot out of the rough or from any other poor lie. Because of the knob-like design of the clubhead, it doesn't tangle in the grass like an iron club but rather it spreads out the grass as it glides through it. The 4-wood is also a good club for hitting a ball from hardpan (bare ground). This type of shot requires that you keep a steady head over the ball while picking it off the ground cleanly.

The 4-wood can also be used from a fairway bunker whenever distance is needed. Hitting from sand with any wood requires very solid footing. Dig your feet firmly into the sand to establish a good foundation; then swing well within yourself making certain to hit the ball cleanly and precisely at the base of your swing's arc.

The shorter shaft of the 4-wood requires you to stand closer to the ball, making sure that the sole of the clubhead is laid flat or flush to the ground at address. The ball should be positioned a couple of inches inside the left heel for normal shots from normal lies. Use the same swing used for all full wood shots and make an effort to keep the head completely still while focusing your eyes on the ball throughout the swing. Your follow-through should be low and extended after the hit and finish with your weight on the outside of your left foot well towards the heel.

Another club the higher handicap player will find quite useful is the 5-wood. It is considered an auxiliary club but has been finding its way into an increasing number of golf bags in recent years. While the popularity of the 2-wood has been decreasing because of its limited use, the 5-wood has gained in popularity because of its versatility. It's the perfect club when you want to get a ball up quickly or make it land softly on the green. The extra loft makes that possible while the shorter shaft makes it easier to control. Golfers who have trouble with long irons, particularly the 2- and 3-iron, may gain a friend in the 5-wood.

The same golfers who find the long irons or mid-irons difficult to use are also turning to the Nos. 6-, 7- and 8-woods to replace them. A popular specialty wood club is the Ginty. It has a shaft equal in length to the 4-wood but has a head and loft angle similar to a 7-wood. A relieved sole at the toe and heel of the club insures minimal ground contact on bad lies and makes it ideal for use in the rough or divot holes. Good players can hit 180 to 200 yards with a Ginty.

One of the most common errors high-handicap players make in using the fairway woods is that they swing too hard, seeking power when power is not essential. Because of the longer shaft length of the fairway woods, compared with the mid-irons, a longer arc is created, thus increasing clubhead speed—and clubhead speed is one of the primary requirements for distance. Never force the fairway shot—swing the ball away.

There's no question that learning the average distance you can hit a fairway wood will make club selection easier. However, elements other than distance sometimes determine which club you should use. If you have a poor lie and are a 3-wood distance to the green, it is better to use a 5-wood or even an iron to make sure you get the ball up than to hit away with the 3-wood and miss the shot entirely.

Golf Club
Specifications
LENGTH SPECIFICATIONS

IRONS	Long Length	Standard Length	Ladies' Length	Jr. 10-14 Length	Jr. 5-9 Length
1	40	39	—	—	—
2	39½	38½	37½	—	—
3	39	38	37	35	32½
4	38½	37½	36½	—	—
5	38	37	36	34	31½
6	37½	36½	35½	—	—
7	37	36	35	33	30½
8	36½	35½	34½	—	—
9	36	35	34	32	29½
Pitching Wedge	36	35	34	—	—
Sand Wedge	36	35	34	—	—
Putter	36	35	34	32	29½
WOODS					
1	44	43	41½	38½	35½
3	43	42	40½	37½	34½
4	42½	41½	40	—	—
5	42	41	39	—	—
7	—	41	39	—	—

LIE AND LOFT SPECIFICATIONS

IRONS	Lie Men's	Lie Ladies'	Lie Jrs.	Loft Men's	Loft Ladies'	Loft Jrs.
1	56.0°	—	—	18.0¾	—	—
2	56.7°	—	—	21.0°	—	—
3	57.5°	58.4°	61.5°	24.3°	24.3°	25.0°
4	58.2°	59.1°	—	27.8°	27.8°	—
5	59.0°	60.0°	63.0°	31.5°	31.5°	33.0°
6	60.0°	61.0°	—	35.3°	35.3°	—
7	60.9°	61.9°	65.0°	39.2°	39.2°	41.0°
8	61.7°	62.6°	—	43.3°	43.3°	—
9	62.6°	63.5°	66.5°	47.5°	47.5°	48.5°
PW	62.6°	63.5°	—	51.6°	51.6°	—
SW	62.6°	63.5°	—	56.7°	56.7°	—
Putter	—	—	—			
WOODS						
1	55.0°	55.5°	56.0°	11.0°	12.5°	13.0°
3	55.6°	56.0°	57.0°	16.5°	16.5°	19.0°
4	56.0°	56.5°	—	19.2°	19.2°	—
5	56.3°	57.0°	—	22.0°	22.0°	—
7	57.0°	57.5°	—	27.5°	27.5°	—

Irons

The basic set of irons consists of at least eight clubs (2 through 9). Altogether, there are 13 distinct irons manufactured and marketed today. In addition to the numbers 1 through 9, there are the pitching wedge, sand wedge, utility wedge (a combination of a pitching and sand wedge) and a chipper (about the loft of a 5-iron but short in length like a putter).

Few players are skillful enough to use the 1-iron (one of the reasons it is not included in the basic set). Even among the touring pros, only a few have sufficiently mastered its use to warrant discarding a wood in order to include it in their set. Arnold Palmer and Jack Nicklaus stand out as two of today's players who have been able to put it to good use. The 1-iron is primarily used as a driving iron or

for keeping the ball low when shooting into the wind.

Today more and more players are discarding the 2-iron for a 5- or 6-wood. Beginners and other unskilled players will find the 1-, 2-, 3-irons the most difficult to master and the 6-, 7-, 8-irons the easiest.

Before learning how to use your set of irons, let's first examine a few of their characteristics and how they were designed to be used. First you should know that the higher the number of the club (9-iron, for example), the shorter the shaft. Secondly, the higher the number, the greater the degree of loft angle to the clubface and the more upright the lie of the club.

When you hear someone say "That club has no loft on it" or "It has too much loft," they are talking about the visual degree of loft on the clubface if one looks down on it when it is properly soled to the ground. The sand wedge has the most loft. It is usually the shortest club in the set and the heaviest. The 1-iron is the straightest-faced iron or the least lofted and is the longest of any iron made. The more loft the less distance the club is capable of striking a ball. The less loft the farther the ball can be hit.

The lie of a club approximates the angle the shaft makes when resting correctly in your hands at address. If you are a tall man with short arms, you will need a set of clubs with an upright lie. If you are a short man with long arms, you will need a flat-lying set of clubs. Generally speaking, all clubs come with a standard lie that fits the average-sized person. Exceptionally tall or short people should be fitted with custom clubs to suit their particular physical characteristics (see the table showing the variation of clubface loft, lie degrees, and the club length).

There's actually little difference between the swing of one iron and another. The swing becomes fuller with long irons and diminishes with the short irons. The long irons are generally considered the 1-, 2-, 3-, 4-irons; the 5 and 6 are known as mid-irons, while the 7, 8, 9 and wedge are the short irons.

The long irons are characterized by a full free-flowing swing which tends to sweep the ball from its lie. The short irons require a short, upright and decidedly more downward swing. The mid-irons allow a swing somewhere between the two.

Short irons are used exclusive-

Irons numbered 2 through 9, pitching wedge and sand wedge (left to right) show how loft increases as shaft length decreases.

ly for accuracy. Long irons are for accuracy plus distance. Short irons are capable of stopping a ball faster; such quick stopping is referred to as putting "backspin" on the ball.

The irons may all be comfortably and correctly played from approximately the same address position, about three inches inside the left heel. The purpose for playing each iron from the same position is to maintain a consistency in your swing pattern or swing plane. This, by no means, is meant to indicate that good golfers, with the many varied

Stance is closed for the long irons; that is, the right foot is dropped just back of the intended line of flight. Ball is played toward the left heel. Left shoulder, arm and club are in straight alignment.

Stance is square for the mid-irons—both feet square to the line of flight and not quite so far apart as with long irons. Weight is evenly distributed.

Stance is open for short irons—left foot is pulled back from the line of flight. Body quarter-faces the target. The ball may often be played back toward the right foot.

shots they are expected to play, will never vary their address to the ball. They most assuredly alter their address position, depending on the circumstances surrounding each shot. But usually all straight-forward shots are addressed with the club positioned just inside the left heel.

The stance is more closed for the long irons; that is, the right foot is dropped just back of the intended line of flight. For the mid-irons, the stance is square: both feet square to the line of flight. The short irons are best executed with an open stance: the left foot pulled back from the line of flight.

Naturally, because of the shorter shaft length of the short irons, you will have to stand closer to the ball. The weight is distributed more to the left foot, but as you move from the address of the short irons to the mid-irons and then to the long irons, the weight shifts very slightly from the left side to the right side. The movement of weight from one foot to the other is a very sensitive matter of feel. A very slight transfer of weight to one side or the other will greatly alter your swing pattern.

Slightly withdrawing the right foot from the line of flight when playing the long irons will enable the right side to turn easily out of the way on the backswing. Likewise, withdrawing the left foot when using the short irons helps the left side to get quickly out of the way on the downswing. Each slight adjustment of the feet will have an effect on the swing and,

With the long irons the backswing approaches the horizontal. Shoulder turn is full. Arms are extended and high.

Mid-irons call for a three-quarter backswing. Distance is not a requisite—smoothness is key. Strike the ball a descending blow.

ultimately, on your ability to control the ball.

The grip with all irons is firm—never tight. Most missed shots, where you feel your grip has come undone somewhere during the swing, are caused by an overly tense or tight grip on the club. (One seldom grips the club too loosely.) Tension makes the club break away from the fingers at the top of the swing.

For several reasons, long irons are more difficult to control than shorter clubs. Primary is the knowledge that the long iron should hit the ball a considerable distance. This little bit of knowledge usually makes one press or try harder to produce distance; trying or forcing adds tension to the grip which, in turn sends ten-

sion throughout the body, causing a missed shot. Secondly, long irons are tougher to use because of their design. The straighter loft of a long iron makes it harder to get the ball airborne and the longer shaft results in a wider arc in the swing. The wider the swing the more chance for body error. Unfortunately, most golfers are instinctively aware of these difficulties and inhibit themselves even more by the fear of a mis-hit.

When the beginning golfer learns that a smooth, easy swing with the long irons provides as much control as with the short irons, confidence then replaces fear and long irons become easy. The beginning golfer soon realizes he will not hit a 9-iron very far, so naturally he doesn't try to hit it hard. The result is that the swing becomes easier and smoother.

The swing with long irons is basically the same as with fairway woods. The beginner usually commits the cardinal sin of trying to help the club do its work by raising the body too soon at impact. The correct way would be to swing the club freely and allow the clubhead to do its job of elevating the ball. Forget distance and concentrate on rhythm.

One of the biggest problems most beginners have with their irons is judging distance. Few have any idea how far they should and can hit with each club. The average golfer will vary from 5 to 10 yards between clubs. With so little difference in the distance reached between one club and another, it is wise to move up one club when in doubt, i.e., if you think you can reach your target with a forced 5-iron, take a 4-iron and hit it smoothly. Never press the shot. I've heard Jack Nicklaus say that if he likes a club for a certain shot, yet thinks it may be on the strong side, he chokes down an inch or two on the grip and hits it just as hard.

Any head movement during the shot is deadly. This doesn't just mean lifting the head up. It means any head movement—forward, upward, backward, down or to the right or left. Any head movement off the ball will produce some degree of a missed shot.

Short iron shots employ to half- to three-quarter swing. An effort must always be made to be smooth and within yourself. Never swing all out. Strike the ball first.

Pitching and Chipping

All good players have one thing in common. They are adept at the short game, that is, from 100 yards out into the green. This is where strokes are earned and saved. It's where you can make up for an erratic tee shot or a poor approach shot. Play around the greens is done with strokes known as pitching and chipping.

Pitch shots, which are usually executed with a high-lofted club, travel most of the way to the pin through the air (anywhere from 100 yards out to within 10 yards of the edge of the green). Chip shots are similar to long putts except that they travel in the air for just the first few feet. They can be made anywhere from the apron of the green to 80 yards out.

There is a variation in chipping techniques. Some players advo-

cate use of a 5-, 6-, 7- or 8-iron or a pitching wedge, changing clubs according to the contour of the green, distance to the hole and to the type of shot. Others favor the use of one club only. I use only the pitching wedge around the green. There are quite a few pros, who, like myself, advocate only the use of a wedge for both pitching and chipping. The pitching wedge, although one of the most lofted clubs in the bag, can be used for lower trajectory shots by merely toeing the clubface in (closing the face) and playing the ball back toward the right foot. Those who use only one club around the green do so because they become accustomed to the club and know what it will and won't do. There's no worry about club selection and it gives the player a more positive mental approach to the impending shot. If you vary the use of the clubs around the green, there is always the problem of indecision as to which club to use.

Most beginners can learn to use two clubs with security, the pitching wedge and the 7-iron. The 7-iron is used for a fast, running type shot, and the wedge is used for a higher trajectory shot that will stop quickly.

Whether you chip or pitch to a green depends on a variety of conditions. The shot must be analyzed to determine whether the green is hard or soft, fast or slow, sloping away or toward you, whether the grain is with or against you and, of course, how much green there is to hit onto.

The type of lie also helps determine the type of shot you'll play: Is it uphill, downhill, into the wind, with the wind, out of the rough, in the sand, on the fringe of the green, over or under a tree? There is no one shot to handle all these circumstances. As a player becomes more advanced in the techniques of the short game, he can play all types of shots.

The stance for short shots is open with the body assuming a quarter-turn toward the hole. Your feet should be about 6-10 inches apart at the heels, your weight predominantly toward the left foot. The closer you are to the green the more your weight should be toward the left side and the inside of your feet. The shorter the shot the narrower your stance. The farther you are from the green the less weight should be on the left side. Your hands must be slightly ahead of the ball, playing the ball just slightly back of the center of the stance. Your clubface remains squarely aligned to the hole. Your

Whether you chip or pitch to a green depends upon green conditions. Is the green fast or slow, soft or hard, sloping away or toward you, is the grain with or against you?

arms should hang comfortably from your shoulders and you should have a firm but delicate grip, with no tension, for short shots. It's more "feel" than anything else. Use your right index finger as you would when triggering a gun—squeeze lightly but never hard. Your left hand should be firmer than your right. The closer to the hole the shorter the grip. As you get within 20 yards of the green, you may grip down almost to the end of the handle.

Think of the pitch and chip strokes as similar to lagging pennies to a line or throwing a ball underhanded. Your eye takes in the distance and then transmits to the brain and hand how hard you need to throw. If you trust your eye in pitching pennies or throwing a ball underhanded, then trust your eye when playing a pitch or chip shot.

Clubface should be squared to the flag. Arms should hang comfortably from your shoulders. Grip should be firm but delicate.

Wedge is best club to use out of the rough when there's a short distance to the green.

Stance for short shots is open with body assuming quarter-turn toward the hole. Feet should be six to ten inches apart at the heels. Hands are forward toward target. Weight is on left side.

In making a pitch or chip shot, your follow-through should approximate the same height and position as the backswing. If you take the club back waist-high, finish up waist-high. If you take too long a backswing, there is a tendency to slow the clubhead coming through the ball and thus lose control of tempo and direction. This is a bad fault among beginners. The correct swing is with your clubhead accelerating through the shot, giving the feeling of a more decisively controlled shot.

Shots of 50 yards or less are usually executed with what can be called a pendulum-type swing where the clubhead goes no higher than the waist on either the backswing or follow-through. Body movement is kept at a minimum because the body serves only as a source of balance instead of power.

To avoid the possibility of a bad bounce it is usually best to try to hit approach shots onto the green on the fly. However, there are many conceivable instances where it is necessary to make the ball hit off the green first, bouncing once or twice before rolling onto the green.

The world's best players hit an average of 14 to 15 greens a round in regulation strokes, and yet more often than not shoot under

Wedge will get the ball up quickly over a tree. Play the ball more forward toward the left foot, with hands behind the ball.

Hitting over a bunker guarding a green sometimes requires a high trajectory shot. Play the ball more forward and with your hands behind the ball for added loft. Swing slowly and evenly.

Shots of 50 yards or less are executed with a pendulum type swing. The clubhead goes no higher than the hips on the backswing and finishes in much the same position on the follow-through.

par because they employ their wedge or other chipping clubs skillfully around the greens. Seldom does even a Jack Nicklaus, Lee Trevino or Gary Player hit all 18 greens in regulation.

It is even more important for beginners to learn the fine technique of the short game because they will be required to make more pitch and chip shots per round than a scratch or low-handicap player. Good players will get down in two strokes more times than not from anywhere within 60 yards of the green. They do it because they have acquired a touch and feel for these shots. A beginner can only acquire such skill by learning a sound technique and then applying lots of practice.

As a player becomes more skillful, he can learn to put backspin on his shots to the green. Backspin is the backward spin of the ball while it is in the air after it has been struck. It can be imparted by any club but is done best with the wedge because it hits the ball with a higher immediate trajectory. You might compare backspin on a wedge shot to that of a billiard shot. The ball in either case is struck nearer the top-back with a sharp descending blow causing it to spin in reverse (backspin). The average beginner can't do it except by accident. It must be executed with a swing that comes down at precisely the right time at precisely the right place on the ball.

In playing the wedge, think of it as a "scoring" club. It is not designed for distance. Too often the beginner tries to get too much out of this club. The beginner would do well to not use the wedge for anything over 100 yards. Even the pros seldom use a wedge for more than 120 yards.

Closed clubface is shown from two angles. It is used for majority of short shots around the green.

Open clubface is shown from two angles. It is used for high trajectory shots when the ball must be laid down softly.

Sand Shots

For beginning golfers, the most feared shot is the sand shot. The idea of a ball lying in a bunker is a horrifying experience. If they don't know how to get the ball up and out, the psychological effect alone is enough to make them tense and nervous. With just a little bit of knowledge, most golfers can learn to knock the ball out and onto the green. With a little practice, they can become near experts.

It is most important to be relaxed when you enter the bunker. Relaxation should be to the point that you are almost limp. When you have this degree of relaxation, the club, with all its weight, will virtually swing itself. All you have to do is start it.

If you go into the bunker with a tense feeling, anticipating failure, you will probably hit the sand "too far behind," "top" the ball or hit it so "clean" that it flies across the green. Tension will usually cause a player to shorten his backswing considerably, thereby forcing and, ultimately, ruining this shot.

Depending on such factors as the lie of the ball, the texture of the sand, the distance from the green and the lip height of the bunker, hitting a sand shot can involve a blast shot, full iron shot, full wood shot, pitch, chip or even a putt. Since all the shots, except those using a wedge in the bunker, are described elsewhere, I will concentrate on the use of the sand wedge in the bunker because the majority of your shots from sand will be of this type.

The best club to use for hitting

Always set your feet firmly in the sand to insure good balance.

Under the rules of golf, the clubhead must not touch the sand when addressing the ball.

out of a bunker is the *sand* wedge which has a heavier clubhead than any other iron. It has a flange on the bottom which provides bounce so that the clubhead doesn't dig into the sand. It is also the most lofted club in the bag and, therefore, will get the ball up the quickest. Under the rules of golf you cannot touch the sand with your club once you have assumed your address position over the ball.

Take your stance by adjusting your feet firmly into the sand for a solid foundation. The rules do not allow you to test the texture of the sand or to artifically build up stance position with your club. A good way to determine, within the rules, the sand texture is to dig your feet securely into the sand.

The texture of the sand usually

Play the ball forward of the center of your stance (more toward your left heel). Weight should be evenly distributed when playing a normal sand shot.

Depending upon the situation and how far you must carry the ball, you may hit anywhere from immediately behind the ball to two inches behind. Sand cushions the ball as you explode both toward your target.

determines how far you will hit behind the ball. You should hit a bit farther behind the ball if the sand is dry and powdery, taking more sand. However, if the sand is wet or heavy, take less sand. Depending on the situation, and on how far you want to hit the ball, it can be struck anywhere from just behind to within four inches of the ball. There is no set rule for how much of a swing you should take.

I visualize the ball as an egg in a frying pan with the white around the yolk as the amount of sand I will take. Explode a consistent amount of sand but vary the strength of the stroke according to the distance you want to hit the ball. Open your clubface slightly if the ball isn't too deeply buried. Then give it a good healthy swing. A ball that is buried

Lay the face open for most shots. Concentrate on remaining relaxed and loose. Follow through!

A three-quarter- or half-swing will usually do the job when you are near the flagstick. Stay loose and swing the clubhead.

Always swing the clubhead. Allow the clubhead to freely (with abandon) strike the sand and ball, carrying both toward the target.

Accentuate the finish of the shot, keeping the club going through toward the target. Many a sand shot has been saved by learning this.

Most players come up short when playing an uphill lie. Remember to hit harder than normally.

In a downhill lie, play the ball more toward your right foot (high foot). Swing along the contour of the sand whether uphill or downhill. This is one of the most difficult shots in golf.

will naturally require you to take more sand. If the ball is really embedded below the surface, then close the clubface and swing as hard as you can. The ball generally pops out.

Your weight should be evenly distributed when playing a normal sand shot. Play the ball forward of the center of your stance and toward your left foot. Take a fuller swing than you would with a pitch or chip shot. Never allow the club to stop at the ball. Accentuate the finish of the shot, keeping the club moving on through towards the target. A smooth, rhythmic swing is vital.

A hard swing is seldom needed in the bunker. A three-quarter swing will usually get the job

done whenever you are in the near vicinity of the flagstick. Your swing is a bit harder than a wedge shot of equal distance off turf. The distance you want to hit the ball will determine the length and the strength of the swing.

A common mistake by beginners is that they try to help the ball up and out by using a scooping action. Instead, they would do well to swing gently down, letting the wedge glide under and through the ball. The sand will force the ball up and out onto the green.

Your address position and weight distribution will vary when playing a lie on an uphill or downhill slope. Lean your weight on your left foot (the high foot) when play-

Chipping out of the sand is okay, provided the lie is good and the bunker has no lip.

A wood in the bunker is permissible if you have a good lie, the trap is not steeply banked, and the green is distant. Set your feet firmly and hit the ball cleanly.

ing an uphill lie and play the ball off the left foot. In a downhill lie, play the ball more toward your right foot (high foot). It is important that your swing follows the contour of the sand when playing either of these shots.

Choke down on your club and stand farther away from the ball if it is a sidehill lie where the ball is higher than your feet. If the ball is below your feet in a sidehill lie, use the full length of the club and crouch down closer to the ball.

If you have a good lie in a fairway bunker and still have quite a distance to reach the green, it is okay to use any club that you think you can control sufficiently to cover as much of this distance as possible. When going for dis-

tance, it is important to hit the ball cleanly, not taking any sand until after the ball is struck.

Practice sand shots regularly to gain confidence. The more success you have with the execution, the more you will establish confidence and increase your ability as a good sand player. Mastering the sand shot will knock several strokes off your game. You will also save strokes because this same confidence will enable you to take more chances on approach shots to greens guarded by bunkers. Just knowing that if the ball should land in the sand, you can easily get it out and onto the green will enable you to go for the flagstick in situations where a poor bunker player would play safe.

Putting

A player can hit erratic tee and fairway shots but still break 100 if he is putting well. Putting strokes account for at least half of the total score in a round of golf and it is the one phase of the game where a player can demonstrate individuality.

There are many stances and types of putters from which to choose. The best-selling putters are the Bull's Eye, any of the center-shafted putters and the Ping putter, known for toe-heel balance. All major club manufacturers now produce a variation of these putters. Basically, there are two types of putters: the mallet and the blade. From these come many similar types in design, weight, thickness and size. Before buying a putter, swing it back and forth several times to feel the grip and its balance; then ask your pro to let you try it on the practice putting green. The putter should have a feeling of balance throughout your putting stroke. Whether you use a heavy putter or a lighter model is a personal matter. The head usually accounts for almost two-thirds of the overall weight of a putter (normal weight is 15 to 18 ounces). Players who like to feel the blade when putting use a heavier putter. Those who want a more delicate feel use a lighter model.

The lie will vary from one putter to another. The lie angle of a putter is the angle formed where the shaft meets the sole of the putter when it lies flat on a level surface. Putters may be purchased with any degree of lie. Usually, a tall man requires a putter with a

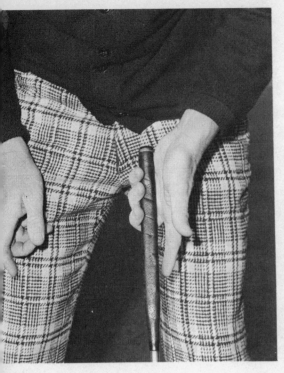
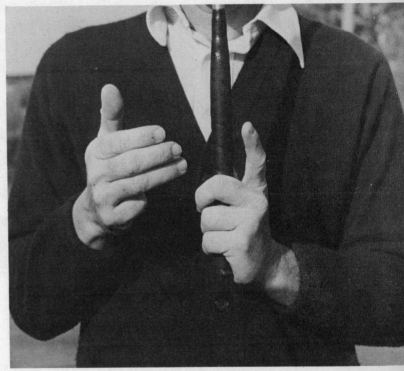

Reverse overlap grip is most popular for putting. Place putter in the last three fingers of the left hand.

more upright lie, a short stout man is usually best fitted with a flat lie so that he can bend over. Your height isn't the only determining factor in lie selection. A lot depends on whether you stand erect or crouch to the ball.

Most professional golfers use the reverse overlap grip when putting. Exceptions are rare (Bob Rosburg, a former PGA champion, and Art Wall, a former Masters champion, both pro-tour veterans, have managed to use the 10-finger grip with success). The reverse overlap grip places all of the fingers of the right hand on the putter handle but only the last three fingers of the left hand. The palms of the hands face each other with both thumbs on top of the shaft. In using this grip, the palm of the right hand is allowed to stroke along the intended putt line towards the cup. Your left hand should be firm but not rigid. This method keeps the putter face square to the target as it moves along the putt line towards the cup.

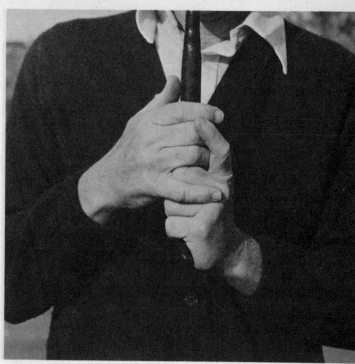

Insert three fingers of the right hand.

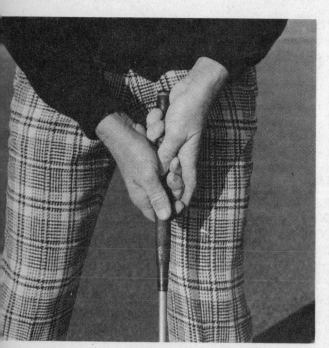
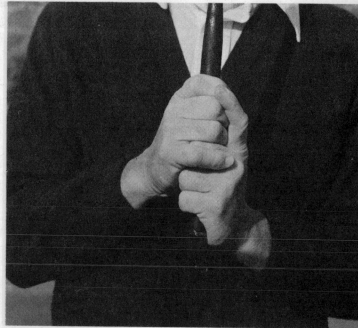

Open wrists by facing in opposite directions. This locks them in place.

Weight distribution in the stance is a personal matter. It can vary: equally on both feet, primarily on the left foot or towards the right foot. The most popular distribution among pros is with the weight toward the left side. Usually the ball is played wherever the distribution of weight is centered; thus, if a player's weight is toward the left side, he will play the ball off his left foot.

The most important thing about the stance is that your eyes must always be directly over the ball. This will give you a truer line on your putt. In addition, it will decrease the likelihood of opening and closing your putter head as it's swung back and through (eliminating pushing or pulling the putt). There is no outstanding player I could cite today who does not assume a position upright enough to center his head and eyes directly over the ball at address.

Ball is played wherever the distribution of weight is centered. If player's weight is toward the left side, he will play the ball off his left foot. Hands work best when aligned slightly ahead of the ball.

Eyes should be directly over the ball for a truer stroke. There's less chance of opening and closing the putterhead as it's swung back and through.

Many good putters place the putterhead in front of the ball while aligning and measuring the putt. This simple movement releases tension.

The whole body (except head) presses toward the target at address.

Whether you putt with your feet close together or use a wide stance is again a personal matter. The important thing is to be stable from your hips down. There should be no movement of the lower body from right to left when stroking the ball. A player's physical characteristics may sometimes determine whether he is more comfortable with a narrow or wide stance. For some players a narrow stance provides more of a pendulum feeling with the putter while other players use a wider stance to make them feel more stable. Still other players lock their knees together to achieve this same feeling of stability.

Probably the most deadly putting fault committed by beginners is head movement before impact. The eyes must remain fixed over the ball. Concentrate on holding your head absolutely steady.

The key to a good putting stroke is taking the clubhead back slow and smooth, keeping the blade low to the green and as square as possible to the intended putt line. A quick choppy stroke is usually the result of taking the putter too far back. A good way to improve the technique of taking the putter head straight back and through the ball is to alter your

grip by rotating both hands in opposite directions. Move both thumbs from their normal grip position on top of the shaft to the opposite side of the putter until they oppose each other and the fingers down to the first knuckle on both hands are visible. This simple adjustment places the wrists in a more locked position that still gives enough freedom for movement while placing an emphasis on the togetherness of the hands. You will find that your hands can now work as a compact unit while stroking the putt.

The hands should be slightly ahead of the ball at address. Never pass the left hand with the right hand on the return stroke. Your backstroke can be slightly shorter than your forward movement or vice versa.

I advocate a minimum amount of wrist action in the putting stroke, particularly for short putts of five feet and under. A light touch is needed on fast greens or downhill putts where a wristy, unwieldy stroke could cause you to lose control of the stroke. A firm, short stroke with little wrist movement will put overspin on the ball. There may be a slight wrist break going back on longer putts but the wrists should be firmed up at impact. Allow the back of the left hand and elbow to pass smoothly through.

On long putts of 25 feet or more, concentrate as much on distance as on accuracy. Treat the distance of each putt as though you were going to lag, or bowl a ball to the cup. Your hands and arms will stroke the putt according to the distance the eyes see and transmit back to the hands.

There is only one way to learn how to judge distance accurately and that is to constantly practice putts of different sizes. The putt that should be practiced the most is the short putt (five feet and under). You will generally have to play this shot from 14 to 18 times in a round. The best way to insure making crucial 3- to 5-foot putts is to shorten your backswing, keeping the putter blade low and straight back. Stroke short putts firmly so they won't be affected by spike marks or other defects around the cup.

Bob Rosburg, noted for his putting ability, says he practices for feel rather than putting for a particular object. Paul Runyan and Ben Hogan were also great advocates of this theory. The underlying thought is that if you can get the solid feel of a well-struck putt in your fingers prior to play, you are more likely to continue such a feeling throughout the game. When you practice at a target such as the cup you tend to forget feel for the moment and tense slightly in your effort to get the ball in the hole. If you miss several makable putts starting out you can get even more tense. Then the uncertainty as to the reason why you missed increases your frustration and detracts from "feel" which is the primary requirement for good putting.

There will be times you will be able to use your putter off the green on the fringe area. If the ground between the ball and the green is fairly level and the grass is not too high, it is advisable many times to use the putter rather than chip. Treat the shot just as you would a putt of the same distance. You can also use your putter out of a flat bunker if you have a good lie and don't have to cross too much sand.

A good putting stroke is attained by holding the head still, taking the clubhead back slowly and smoothly, and keeping the blade low and as square as possible.

A firm, short stroke with little wrist movement leaves little margin for error. Eyes must remain fixed over and on the ball. Hold the head absolutely steady.

The best way to line up a putt is by kneeling and studying from behind the ball. One should look at all angles if the break appears abrupt. Your first reading is usually the truest.

Plumb-line method of lining up a putt is used by some players. This system has advantages if employed correctly. Consult your PGA professional for a complete explanation.

In lining up a putt, most players kneel and study their line from behind the ball. Make a habit of studying green conditions before putting. Observe whether the green is moist or dry. A moist green is naturally going to be slower than one that is dry. Studying the green is commonly referred to as "reading the green." It involves scanning the green's contour for dips, rises and slopes over which your ball will travel.

Another factor that will determine how firmly you must stroke the putt is the direction in which the grains of grass are growing. When the blades of grass are leaning toward your ball, they are against you. This can usually be determined by their darker appearance. When the grain is against you, the ball should be stroked more firmly. When the grain is with you (characterized by a lighter appearance), the grass is leaning toward the hole; thus, you need not stroke the ball as firmly. Grass usually grows towards the morning rays of sunlight and in the direction the green drains.

How to Play Trouble Shots

No matter how good a golfer you become, there will be many times when you will be confronted with a trouble shot. Your ball may land in the rough, in a deep bunker, behind a tree or another obstacle, on bare ground, in a divot hole, near a fence or be buried. If you can learn how to play out of trouble, you can save yourself several strokes per round and a lot of aggravation.

Playing Out of the Rough

When your ball is in the rough, it is important to note that although the ball may be nestled in the grass, there is quite likely to be substantial grass under the ball—probably enough so that once you've soled your clubhead on the ground, the lie no longer

looks so discouraging. There's enough cushion under the ball to enable you to get the ball up without much more difficulty than a normal fairway lie. When the ball is nestled in soft grass, there are two things to consider: first, the ball must get up quickly; secondly, it will fly or soar from this type of lie. The reason it will fly or soar is that when grass gets between the clubface and the ball, it eliminates the usual spin imparted by the club and causes the ball to fly with a boring-like overspin. A flying ball will usually go farther than generally expected of any given club. It will also run farther after it hits the ground.

Selection of a club for hitting out of the rough is determined by the distance to the green, the texture of the grass and how badly

When shooting over trees, lower the right shoulder and right side to set up a swing plane that will make the ball rise quickly.

immeshed the ball lies. Many beginners believe that just because their ball has landed in the rough they should use an iron, even though the distance to the target may require a wood shot. If you can possibly use a wood, by all means do so. However, if the distance to the green may require a 3-wood, it is best to play a 4- or 5-wood. Either of them will get the ball up quicker while still providing you with the distance necessary (remembering that a ball hit from this type of lie will generally go as far and sometimes farther than a shot from a good lie).

In using a wood out of the rough, keep in mind that the ball will usually spin to the left because the clubface closes as it is slowed by the grass. Break your wrists a little earlier and make a more abrupt backswing. Then pull the club down and up in a scooping type of action. To assure accuracy it is important to continue the clubhead through the ball as you would in a sand shot.

If you have a short distance to go, use a sand wedge. The heavier clubhead with thick flange tends to cut through the grass more easily while the extra loft on the clubface gets the ball up quicker.

Shooting Over Trees

In shooting over trees, your entire body should be tilted more towards your right side at address, that is, low on the right and high on the left side. This will enable you to swing with an arc that will elevate the ball abruptly. Play the ball farther forward, just inside your left toe. The lower you can drop your right side, the more you can catch the ball on your upswing. Practice this shot until you know the limit of lowering your right side; if you go too far, you could top the shot or hit behind it. Be sure to break your wrists sooner on the backswing; then keep the clubhead swinging on to a high full finish.

Shooting Under Tree Branches

In hitting under tree branches, position your ball back, more toward your right foot. You must hit the ball low, so choke down on the club slightly as this will reduce the arc of your swing and give a punched effect to the shot. Use a less lofted club, preferably a 3- or 4-iron or even a 3-wood if the shot dictates its use. Play the ball back toward your right foot with your weight toward your left side in order to assure catching the ball on the downward part of the arc at impact. Do not break your wrists until the clubhead is at least waist-high on your backswing. Minimize the cocking of your wrists at the top of the swing. Strike the ball with a more descending blow, being sure to hit it first. Hit the ball nearer the top to keep it low.

In hitting a low shot under tree branches, strike the ball with a more descending blow, being sure to hit it first nearer the top of the ball. The head should remain motionless.

Sidehill, Uphill and Downhill Lies

Key factors in playing sidehill, uphill and downhill lies are keeping a steady head position and maintaining your balance. When playing a sidehill lie where you are standing *below* the ball, choke down on your club according to the steepness of the slope. Clearly, if you grip the club normally, you will hit the ground rather than the ball if the ball is higher than where you are standing. On this type of lie, you are likely to pull the ball slightly off target to the left so adjust your aim slightly to the right.

When playing a sidehill lie where you are standing *above* the ball, use a longer club than you would normally need. The longer shaft length is needed to compensate for the distance you are above the ball. Since this shot is difficult because your weight moves toward your toes, it is important to maintain your position as well as balance throughout the swing.

A *downhill* lie is another difficult shot. If the lie is not severe, play the ball more toward your left foot, trying not to let your weight get too much toward the left foot. Compensate for the slope by keeping your weight toward the right heel so that you can elevate the ball more quickly. If the lie is too extreme, play the ball toward your right foot.

When playing an *uphill* lie, you are likely to over-position your weight to the right side. You can compensate for this by moving your weight forward toward the left side—enough to maintain good balance. Because the ball will be elevated quickly, your shot is likely to fall short of the target; therefore, use a club longer than normally necessary. Aim to the right of the target because there is an inclination to pull the ball to the left and make an extra effort to follow through to the target.

Wet Grass Lie

When playing golf in the early morning, you are likely to encounter morning dew or recently sprinkled grass on the fairway, both of which will have a decided effect on the ball's flight. Water on the ball or clubface will make the ball fly farther because it nullifies spin on the ball. Therefore, use a more lofted club. Whatever you may lose in distance will be made up by the soaring effect the wet grass puts on the ball.

Hitting From a Fairway Bunker

If your ball comes to rest in a fairway bunker, don't automatically take out your sand wedge. If it's a good lie and you have plenty of space in front of you with very little bank (lip) on the bunker, you can use a wood. This is a precise shot and should only be attempted if all conditions are favorable. The ball either must be hit clearly or driven down to get it up, depending upon the lie. There should be little body movement. The slightest movement off the ball may cause you to hit behind or to top the shot. To secure your stance, dig your feet deeply into the sand. Play the ball inside your left toe. Although your backswing is similar to your normal swing, break the wrists more than normal to help get the ball up quickly.

Hitting Off Bare Ground

A ball on hard, bare ground can be played with a wood or iron, depending upon the lie. If you have a good lie, you can use a wood, preferably a 4- or 5-wood. Otherwise, use an iron. Your head and body must remain steady throughout the swing; any movement in any direction will result in a mis-shot. The ball should be struck cleanly with a descending blow. Too flat a swing will likely result in the clubhead hitting the ground behind the ball, causing the club to bounce. This usually results in what is known as a "skulled" or "topped" shot.

Playing Downwind

Golfers should always take advantage of a strong wind when it is behind them by getting the ball up into the air stream. If the shot normally calls for a 3-wood, use a 4-wood because the extra loft will get the ball up faster and higher. Set yourself firmly at address and maintain good balance. Brace yourself so the wind doesn't cause you to move off the ball. Play the ball more toward the left foot so the ball is caught more on the up-swing. As you begin your downswing, drop your right shoulder down and under your chin to help elevate the ball quickly. The ball will roll farther after it hits the ground because the wind tends to nullify any spin.

Playing Into the Wind

Shots played into the wind will usually raise the ball more than is normal, preventing normal distance. Distance can be maintained by hitting the ball low and using a longer club. A flatter type of swing will help to keep the ball low. Shorter persons usually play better into the wind because they have a built-in tendency to be flatter swingers. Brace your body at address to make certain a strong gust doesn't knock you off balance. By choking down on the club slightly, it will reduce the arc of your swing and give you a punched shot. Play the ball back toward the right foot with your weight towards your left side to assure catching the ball on the downward part of the arc at impact. It is important not to break your wrists until the clubhead is at least waist-high on your backswing; minimize the cocking of your wrists at the top of the swing.

Hitting a Slice

Hitting a deliberate slice is sometimes necessary to go around trees or other obstacles. In playing a deliberate slice, open your clubface at address. Keep your left hand firm, gripping the club tighter with the last three fingers. Swing the club back more on an outside line away from your body and return it on the same line, drawing it slightly across the ball. The key point to remember in hitting a slice is to strike the ball harder than in any other shot. Even though you may be set up to slice, if you don't strike the ball hard enough your slice just won't happen.

Draw and Hook Shots

The draw shot, that moves the ball gently from right to left, is the result of doing everything correctly. It is commonly used by pros and other good players. A ball drawn or hooked runs farther when it hits the ground but it does not travel as far in the air. It has a lower trajectory because the swing is flatter. Just as you'll need a deliberate slice occasionally, you will also have need to hit a deliberate hook. While pushing your hands more toward the target close your clubhead in the address position. Your body should be more relaxed. It is important that your shoulders roll more fluidly on the backswing and through the ball. Your left wrist should be flexible and must give way to the right hand at impact; let both hands roll over at impact, imparting hook-spin on the ball. Let your left wrist be relaxed at address and again ease it at the top of the backswing.

In playing a deliberate slice, open your clubface at address. Keep your left hand firm, gripping the club tighter than with any other shot in golf. Move the club out away from you on the backswing and return it hard across coming through.

Hitting a deliberate slice is sometimes required when shooting around trees or other obstacles. Give yourself plenty of room by aiming more to the left than you feel necessary.

Playing a deliberate hook around trees requires that your body be more relaxed—particularly the whole right side. Make a fluid, full shoulder and hip turn both back and through the ball.

When needing a quick snap hook, avoid tension in either hand and particularly the right side. The left side must give way fluidly at impact to a powerful right side thrust.

In hitting a hook, it is important that your shoulders roll more fluidly, and the left wrist be eased or relaxed throughout the swing.

The Mental Side of Golf

Anybody who has played golf for any great length of time knows that the mental side of golf is the predominant factor in scoring and makes the difference between winning and losing. By the same denominator, anyone who works on his own mental approach to his game will improve as his concept and understanding improves. Those who ignore the mental side, and stress only the physical aspects of the swing, will remain forever at the level of their physical ability.

If there is anything more devastating to one's approach to the game than being afraid of losing, it's being afraid of winning. There are golfers who, when faced with the possibility of winning or shooting better than they think is possible, suddenly become fearful of success and immediately set about a mental process designed to fail or at least to stay within the logic and limits they long ago set for their game. Worst of all fears is being afraid you can't win at all—not ever. However, you can be so afraid of losing that you will drive yourself to winning.

There are few fearless competitors. All players experience fears of varied degrees at various times. Their main difference in makeup is that they counter fearful thoughts with enough determination and positive thought to overcome their fears before they can be firmly implanted in the mind.

Start building faith in your game with selected goals that you can attain without too much difficulty. Each day, or at the interval of your choice, increase your goals—always keeping them in sight and just within grasp. Then, by strong effort, you will reach them and rebuild the confidence and assurance that you can, indeed, succeed. Start by telling yourself you *can* do something and soon you *will* do it.

Experienced golfers agree that control of the subconscious mind is the secret of better golf scores. They say that if they can control their subconscious minds by not thinking negative thoughts and, instead, visualize each shot the way they would like it to happen, they will indeed play better.

The subconscious mind never fails to express what has been impressed upon it. That's why golfers should not think negative thoughts, such as: "I don't want to hit it into the water," "I don't want to slice here," "I can't putt," or "I can't chip well." A golfer who thinks that way is polluting his subconscious with negative thoughts that will keep him from doing well. The subconscious mind directs muscle movements automatically so that the conscious mind has nothing to do toward achieving the goal. This is commonly referred to as "muscle memory," but muscles do not have memories. Muscles are directed in their action by nerves commanded by the subconscious. "Subconscious feel" (usually referred to as automatic golf) is achieved when a golfer has so thoroughly committed the physical movements of the game to the unerring memory of his subconscious mind that it is impossible to make a mistake—unless the conscious mind interferes.

When a golfer is unable to recapture the same confident feeling in actual play that he had during practice, he is a victim of the mental side of golf. Professional golfers seldom worry about their *physical* movements. Just before a tournament, they wonder how they are going to *feel.*

Beginning golfers are usually confused when they are told that they must *concentrate* and yet be *relaxed* to play good golf. It may seem contradictory until you realize that the *conscious* mind concentrates while learning and the *subconscious* keeps you relaxed as it learns to replay what has been learned.

Tension caused by fear and failure is what causes even good players to freeze at crucial situations on the golf course. Several leading tour pros, including Jack Nicklaus, say the best thing to do when feeling pressure at a crucial moment is step back, take several deep breaths and enjoy the challenge. Many golfers in tense situations will rush into their shots while still in a tense state. A practice swing will help to loosen muscles. Be most careful of the grip; retain a firm, but never tense, grip. Swing within yourself, letting the clubhead do most of the work. Your body and swing must flow back and through the ball, not forcing—just swinging the club. You'll be pleasantly surprised how far the ball will go with so little effort.

Another way to relax is to be sure that your knees and arms are not stiffly locked. Keep them flexed and mobile at all times. Now and then waggle the club freely in any manner that seems most natural to you. By keeping your fingers, hands, arms and feet in motion you prevent tension from setting in while you gather your thoughts and visualize the shot you are about to play. The picture your mind holds is another important key to relaxation. If you can visualize hitting the shot properly, then you will strengthen your confidence and in turn discourage tension.

Still another primary cause of tension is standing too far from the ball. Stretching the arms to reach a ball that is too distant tends to pull you off balance toward your toes and tenses the forearms.

What should one think of when playing under pressure? I try to think about keeping the swing smooth, hitting within myself—not pressing for any shots. Any thought that relates smoothness to you is worthwhile recalling whenever you feel pressured. I sometimes think of a lazy trout stream, believe it or not, and this usually relaxes me and smooths out my swing. If you can picture a smooth swinger, such as Julius Boros, Gene Littler or Tommy Bolt, imagine you're swinging just like them.

Concentration is a vital part of golf. The player who can maintain his concentration harder and longer is very apt to better his rivals week in and week out. In comparison to a tour pro, beginners and weekend golfers give very little concentration to each shot. If a high-handicap player were to think his shots out better and to hold his concentration to one or two simple thoughts throughout the round, he would be pleasantly surprised how much better his score could be.

"The greatest golf players in the world are the ones who are able to apply themselves mentally for the longest period of time," says Tommy Bolt. "The day I shot 60 in Hartford, Connecticut, I was jiving with the gallery all the way. But I never got my mind off what I wanted to do with those clubs and that ball."

What should a golfer think about during a swing? Golfers who try to think of several things at one time during a swing can suffer from what is known as "paralysis by analysis." Thinking of performing several mechanical parts of the swing while playing is bad. Sam Snead says a player should concentrate on only one thought during the swing. He explains that golfers, in trying to cure one fault, often exaggerate another. Pros agree that you must think of your shots creatively and not jumble your mind with a lot of secondary shots.

Start looking your next shot over and thinking about it as you're walking to your ball. Riding in a cart sometimes nullifies this advantage. It rushes you up to the ball before you've had time to contemplate your next move.

What is the best way to go about aiming for a shot? Pick a target in the background that stands out. It could be a tree, a pole, house, etc. Run your eye back and forth from your clubhead to this target. Make sure your clubhead, shoulders and hips are perfectly square to the imaginary line you draw. When you move the clubhead away from the ball, be sure that it moves away *square* for at least six inches. When you follow through, do so with the clubhead traveling extended on out toward and along the imaginary line to your target. Without an imaginary line to follow no one can consistently hit any shot well, and no one can consistently drive well.

As your mind, because of fearful anxiety, often forecasts the worst result possible to your pending shot, it can in the same way forecast the best result possible. You should train yourself to visualize your ball following the imaginary line you picked out to your target.

If you are planning a slice or hook shot to your target because of a dogleg, get squarely behind your ball and see through your mind's eye the executed shot. Keep the same picture in your mind as you address your ball ready to start your swing. Remember, you can't hit the shot unless you can first see it; you must see the shot that fits the hole. You must always try to move the ball the way the hole sets up, i.e., right to left or left to right.

One problem that plagues many golfers is their inability to recover mentally from a bad shot. It bothers them to the point that they make poor shots on successive holes. Even the greatest professionals make a bad shot or two—or even more in a round. The late Walter Hagen, one of golf's all-time greats, said he always accepted the idea that he might hit five or six bad shots a round and didn't let it disturb him. Relax, concentrate, think smoothness and confidence and you'll have lower scores.

Etiquette

Along with learning the Rules of Golf, beginning players should familiarize themselves with the fundamentals of golf etiquette. Golf ethics are a vital part of the game. They help to make the sport more enjoyable and even play a role in getting better scores.

The first thing to learn is that, unlike other competitive sports, there should be no attempt to hamper the play of your opponent. Golf is a gentlemen's sport. And gentlemen are always more popular than those who are rude and disrespectful of the rights of others. Courtesy to others is the key to etiquette on the golf course.

Here are some of the major rules of etiquette you should always be aware of when playing:

—Don't talk, move, make any noise or do anything that may disturb a player about to make a shot. Do not stand close to a player or on a line behind the ball where he can see you when he is addressing the ball.

—Don't offer unsolicited advice to other players.

—Do not use foul language or throw clubs or other equipment. This might offend other players, cause injury or damage the course.

—Avoid slow play. Always be prepared to play when your turn comes. Think out your next shot in advance and decide which club you will use. Carry a spare ball in your pocket in the event you have to hit a second ball. If a search for a ball delays a following group, signal those players behind to play through.

—Allow the player whose ball is farthest from the hole to play ahead of you. In a friendly game, it's okay to play out of turn if it means saving time.

Never stand too close to or behind a player when he is hitting. It's impolite to talk or move when another is hitting.

—If the group behind you is playing faster than your group, invite them to play through.

—Do not drop your bag, pull a golf cart or drive a golf car on the green. Do not drive a golf car on the tee.

—On the green, be careful not to step on the line of anyone's putt; your spike marks can throw the ball off line. Don't stand so that your shadow falls on a player's line of putt.

—Avoid damaging the green by dropping the flagstick or standing close to the cup.

—Repair ball marks on the green.

—Never litter the course.

—Replace divots on the fairway.

—In bunkers (sand traps), rake and smooth out your footprints and any irregularities in the sand caused from playing a shot.

—Do not drag, scuff or twist your shoes on the putting green be-

Rake or smooth out your footprints before leaving a bunker.

cause it will affect a following player's putt.

—Delay hitting until players ahead are well out of range.

—On par-3 holes, after you have reached the green, invite the players behind to hit.

—Do not take practice putts after you have holed out or hit extra shots from the tee; this will delay play.

—Never do your scorekeeping on the putting green. Move onto the next tee.

—Have pride in the course you are playing and show it through your actions.

—In short, on the golf course, do unto others as you would like done unto you, and you will have filled your greatest responsibility as a golfer.

Always repair your ball mark on the green. This can easily be done with a tee by pulling in the edges.

How to Practice

You can never become a good golfer unless you have a regular program of practice. However, most practice done by the average golfer achieves more harm than good. There's a right and wrong way to practice anything.

Most beginners make a big mistake in their practice by hitting ball after ball with a driver and think only of how far they can whale them. All they're doing is working up a sweat and getting some tired muscles. They have done little towards improving their game.

The first thing to have in mind when going to the practice range is a definite idea about what you want to work on. Never set out to practice unless you can think of some kink to iron out or some fault to correct.

I advocate that you don't work on more than one thing at one time. Too much theorizing can destroy your concentration and coordination. Golf is best learned slowly in bits and pieces, like fitting together a giant puzzle. It is virtually impossible to learn everything at once. Most of golf is mental and there are few, indeed, who can concentrate and retain more than two simultaneous swing actions at once.

What should you work on? Perhaps you may want to work on correcting some flaw in your backswing. Stop the backswing at halfway or at the top and check and re-check it; perhaps it's too fast, or maybe you're losing your grip somewhere. Experiment until you find an answer that helps the swing to flow smoothly again. A

Loosen up your muscles by locking three clubs between your back and arms. Then simulate the golf swing.

show immediate results. Even with practicing for one hour three or four times a week, it may take several weeks or a month to correct a flaw. Then, again, you can get flaw happy—striving so much for perfection that you're always tied up in knots.

Before beginning your practice, it's a good idea to warm up with a few exercises and some practice swings. Try swinging several irons at a time or use a weighted head cover on a wood to loosen golf muscles.

It's a good idea never to practice too long at one time. Practice half an hour, rest and then resume. It never does much good to practice when you're tired.

Concentration is vital if you are to get the most out of your practice. You can concentrate more on each shot by buying a small bucket and taking as much time with each shot as though you were playing on a golf course or in a tournament.

A good way to concentrate on each shot is to visualize the practice range as your favorite golf course. For example, perhaps the course you regularly play has a dogleg to the right and requires a slice around some trees to gain proper position for your next shot. Visualize a spot on the range as being the spot where the trees would be situated and try slicing around that spot. Maybe you wouldn't dare attempt that shot on the golf course, so by doing it on the practice range you can gain enough confidence to try it in actual play. You can practice your slice (or hook) until you have mastered the shot.

Continue to use your clubs as you would in playing certain holes from your favorite golf course. Visualize hazards that may require hooks or slices. Pay close attention

practice range is the best place to check it. When you find what works best for you, work on repeating it over and over until what you're doing penetrates your subconscious mind. The golf swing is 100% memory, some good, some bad, so practice until the swing you want becomes automatic.

It takes time and patience to correct flaws; never be discouraged if your practice sessions don't

Become a "regular" on the practice tee. But before you get there, plan what you will practice. Concentrate on one thing at a time. Avoid experimenting with a new thought every swing.

to club selection. If you can visualize a hole, play your shots on the range using the same clubs you would to play that hole. Hit your drive, then your second shot. Now visualize you have come to within 50 yards of the green. Take out the iron you would normally use for the approach, and aim for the 50-yard marker on the range.

Using all your clubs on a practice range affords an excellent way of learning to gauge their distance. You can learn distance by hitting to some object where distance is familiar to you. Use your clubs to hit to different targets until you get a feel for the distance each club has in it.

I repeat, your practice will be considerably more interesting if you use your imagination on the range. It's one of the best ways to familiarize yourself with your clubs.

Imagine holes on your favorite course that require position shots and play your shots on the range to correspond to those positions. Whether it's windy or not, you can even use your imagination to play wind shots. You can imagine the wind behind you and, therefore, practice high shots to take advantage of it. Or imagine the wind blowing against you and practice hitting low shots.

Select a practice range that has a putting green. Putting is 50 percent of a golf score, so give it its due. Practice putting to a tee or a coin on the green to gauge strength and distance. Practice long putts. Practice short ones. Stroke a few off the fringe of the green until you have confidence in every putting situation. That's what is called "touch": ability plus confidence. You can test your stroke by using a striped ball and lining up the stripe with the line to the hole. If you have stroked the ball properly the stripe will roll end over end on a straight line until it reaches the hole.

In selecting a practice range, also look for one that offers a bunker from which you can practice sand shots. Practice sand shots with your sand wedge by playing all types of lies. This will give you much-needed confidence for shots from the trap, a sure stroke-saver.

If you are weak in your short game, anywhere from 125 yards in to the green, chances are you will have trouble breaking 100. A good way to sharpen up your short game is to practice it by playing par-3 golf courses where you will usually only need your 7, 8, 9 and wedge. Play a round or two a week on a par-3 course and it will do much to improve your short game. The thing to do is concentrate on club selection and learn to gauge distance and accuracy. Learn when to pitch and when to chip. In improving your pitching and chipping, you automatically make your putting easier by placing your ball closer to the pin for a one-putt.

Practice sessions should not be confined to ranges or par-3 courses. Considerable practice can be accomplished in your backyard or in your home. You can easily practice your short game in your backyard. Use your lawn to pitch and chip at a target such as a bucket, bushel basket or an old tire. This can also be done indoors in your basement. Use a cocoa mat or a piece of carpet to hit from and try some pitch shots over, under or through various objects such as a chair, table, ladder, suspended hoop, volley ball or badminton net. You can pitch at or into tar-

Putting is precisely half the game. Start by practicing the short ones for feel and confidence.

gets such as a rope circle, basketball hoop, wastebasket, dart board or archery target. Some tarpaulin or an old mattress can serve as a backstop to stop longer shots.

If you wish to take full swings, without worrying about breaking something or losing balls, use a practice net. There are several good ones available on the market, or you can buy your own netting and set up your own backstop.

There are various devices on the market that will make your indoor chipping and putting practice much more interesting. Putting on carpeting is different than on actual turf, but the important thing is that it affords you an opportunity to practice your putting or chipping. At the same time you can experiment with your grip and stance. You can buy also a load of clean sand and box it into an area large enough to practice sand shots in your backyard.

Golf muscles can be kept in condition by swinging a heavy club in your backyard, basement or recreation room. You can purchase a weighted clubhead cover or make a club heavier by adding lead tape to an old club. This will not only tone muscles but will also improve your timing and rhythm.

Many tour pros stay in condition by a regular program of physical exercises to strengthen golf muscles. Sit-ups, push-ups, knee bends, etc., will loosen and tone muscles. Jogging is a good way to strengthen your legs. At home you can do this by jogging in place.

Above everything else, use your imagination in practice. Boredom, next to tension, creates more bad habits in a golf swing than anything else.

Glossary of Golf Terms

-A-

ACE: A hole played in one stroke. Hole in one.

ADDRESS: The position of a player at the ball before he swings.

APPROACH SHOT: A shot to the green on a hole on which the green has not been reached from the tee.

APRON: The grassy area around the green, usually cut shorter than the fairway.

AWAY: The player whose ball is farthest from the hole. He shoots first.

-B-

BACKSPIN: Backward spin on ball imparted by a downward stroke.

BANANA BALL: Slice; shot that starts left and fades right.

BEST-BALL: Term commonly used for four-ball match.

BIRDIE: A score of one stroke under par on any given hole.

BITE: The backspin on a shot which induces it to stop quickly on a green, and sometimes, in pronounced instances, to back up.

BLADE: To contact the ball with the bottom leading edge of the clubface, causing the ball to fly low. Also, a name given to a thin type of putterhead.

BLIND BOGEY: Competition in which players, before teeing off, estimate handicaps required to net them scores between 70 and 80. A "blind" figure in this range is then selected and the player with closest net is declared winner.

BOGIE OR BOGEY: A score of one stroke over par on any given hole.

BOUNCE: The extension below

horizontal on the sole (bottom) of a club. Usually refers to a sand wedge. The bounce prevents the club from digging deeply into the sand.

BRASSIE: Scottish name for 2-wood.

BREAK: The direction and amount that a putt will curve to the side on its way to the cup.

BUNKER: A depression filled with sand; a hazard. Commonly referred to as a "sand trap."

-C-

CADDIE: One who carries a player's clubs.

CAST: To uncock—or straighten—the wrists too early in the downswing, an action that diminishes the power of the swing. Same as "hitting from the top."

CASUAL WATER: Any temporary accumulation of water; not regarded as a water hazard.

CHIP SHOT: Short approach shot of low trajectory.

CLOSED STANCE: The right foot is withdrawn from the intended line of flight.

CLOSE LIE: The ball at rest close to the ground with little or no grass underneath.

CLUBFACE: Striking surface of the clubhead.

COLLAR: The grass around the edges of a green or hazard.

COURSE: The entire playing area where golf is played. Usually consists of 18 holes.

COURSE RATING: A rating system in strokes based on the playing difficulty of a course. Rating is done by an association to provide the basis for uniform handicapping irrespective of course difficulty.

CUP: The hole sunk into the green into which the ball must be played.

CUT SHOT: The ball is struck on an outside-in swing path causing it to spin clockwise to the right.

-D-

DIVOT: The turf uprooted by the clubhead when it strikes the ball.

DOGLEG: A fairway that bends sharply to the right or left.

DORMIE: A player or team is ahead in a match by as many holes as there are remaining.

DOUBLE BOGIE: A score of two strokes over par on a hole.

DOWN: The number of holes a player or side is behind in a match.

DRAW: A shot that curves subtly from right to left.

DUCK HOOK: A shot that curves quickly and sharply from right to left; an exaggerated hook.

DUFFER: A player of little skill.

-E-

EAGLE: A score of two strokes under par on a hole.

EXPLOSION: A shot from sand when the player hits into the sand behind the ball to blast it out.

-F-

FACE: The hitting surface of the clubhead.

FADE: A shot that curves subtly from left to right.

FAIRWAY: The mowed, open, grassy area between the tee and the green.

FLAGSTICK: The marker in the hole on the green.

FLUSH: To hit the ball with a full swing precisely on the clubface.

FORE: A warning cry to persons in danger of being hit by a shot.

FORECADDIE: One who is positioned at the side of the fairway to spot and mark players' drives.

FOUR-BALL PLAY: Two players opposing two other players, each side playing its better ball.

FOURSOME: Four players playing together, each playing their own ball.

FRINGE: See apron. Occasionally called frog hair.

-G-

GRAIN: Flat-lying grass on a green. Putts will tend to roll in the direction the grain runs.

GRASSCUTTER: A low, hard-hit ball that skims grass.

GREEN: The closely cut area which contains the cup and the flag.

GROSS SCORE: A score before the handicap is deducted.

-H-

HANDICAP: A figure indicative of a golfer's skill that enables him to play on fairly even terms against players of greater or lesser ability.

HAZARD: A natural or man-made obstacle of sand or water.

HEAD: The heavy metal or wood part of the club that strikes the ball.

HEEL: The rear part of the clubhead.

HOLE-HIGH: A shot to the green that finishes even with the hole but to one side.

HOLE IN ONE: A score of one stroke on a hole. Also called an ace.

HOLE OUT: To finish putting.

HONOR: The right to hit first on the tee, gained by having the lowest score on the previous hole.

HOOD: To close the clubface.

HOSEL: The part of the clubhead into which the shaft is fitted.

-L-

LAY BACK: To place the hands behind the ball at address, increas-ing the effective loft of the clubface.

LIE: Where the ball rests on the course. Also the angle between the clubshaft and clubhead.

LINKS: A seaside golf course.

LIP: The rim of the cup.

LOFT: Angle at which clubface is set from vertical. Influences the extent to which the ball can be lifted in flight for various clubs.

LOOP: Moving the hands left or right at the top of the backswing, so that the clubhead returns to the ball on a different path than it took on the backswing.

-M-

MASHIE: An old Scottish term, now obsolete, describing an iron club of about 6-iron loft.

MATCH: A contest between two or more players or sides.

MATCH PLAY: Scoring is on the basis of holes won and lost by either individuals or teams.

MEDALIST: Competitor with lowest qualifying score.

MEDAL PLAY: A competition in which the lowest score wins.

MULLIGAN: Second ball sometimes allowed after poor tee shot, usually on first tee. (Not permitted under rules.)

-N-

NASSAU: A competition or bet in which 3 points are scored, one for each nine and for the 18 holes. Believed to have origiated at Nassau (N.Y.) CC.

NECK: Part of the club where the shaft joins the head.

NET SCORE: A player's score after his handicap has been subtracted from his gross total.

NIBLICK: An old Scottish term, now obsolete, describing an iron club of about 9-iron loft.

-O-

OPEN STANCE: The left foot is withdrawn from the intended line of flight. The hips face slightly toward the target.

OUT-OF-BOUNDS: Ground on which play is prohibited.

-P-

PAR: The score an. expert golfer should make on a hole or after completing 18 holes.

PENALTY STROKE: A stroke added to the score of a side or individual player, under certain rules.

PITCH SHOT: A short approach shot to the green.

PIVOT: The turning of the body during the swing.

PRESS: Effort to apply more than necessary power to a swing; an extra bet, usually on the last few holes or on the second nine.

PROVISIONAL BALL: A ball played after previous ball "probably" has gone out-of-bounds, has been lost or is believed unplayable.

PULL: A shot which travels on a straight line but to the left of the target.

PUNCH SHOT: A low shot, usually into the wind, made with a shortened swing and a hooded clubface.

PUSH: A shot which travels on a straight line but to the right of the target.

PUTT: To play a stroke on the green with a putter.

-R-

RAINMAKER: Very high shot with little distance.

ROUGH: The area of a course which is not closely mowed.

ROUND ROBIN: Tournament in which every player meets every other player one time.

RUB OF THE GREEN: When a ball is stopped or deflected by an outside agency—a forecaddie, for instance. The expression is often used to connote hard luck.

-S-

SCOTCH FOURSOME: A common term for competition in which two partners play one ball, alternating strokes.

SCRATCH PLAYER: A player with a zero handicap.

SCUFF: To hit the ground behind the ball.

SHANK: To hit the ball far to the right of the intended line of flight because contact has been made on the neck of the club.

SKY: To hit the ball very high with little distance.

SLICE: A shot that curves from left to right. The slang for a slice is "banana ball."

SOLE: The bottom of the clubhead; also, the act of placing the club on the ground at address.

SPOON: An old Scottish term, now obsolete, describing a wooden-head club with the loft of a present-day 3-wood.

SQUARE STANCE: Both feet are equidistant from the intended line of flight.

STANCE: Position of feet.

STIFF: A shot hit close to the hole.

STROKE: Forward movement of the club with the intention of striking the ball.

STROKE PLAY: Competition decided by the sum of the strokes by a player or his side.

SUDDEN DEATH: When a match is tied at the end of a predetermined number of holes, an additional hole(s) is played until one player wins.

-T-

TEE: The area from where the ball is first hit on a hole; also the small wooden peg on which the ball is placed.

TEE MARKERS: Two objects on the teeing area which determine the front and side limits of the tee-ing ground.

TEXAS WEDGE: A putter when used from chipping distance or out of a sand trap (bunker).

TOE: Tip or end of clubhead.

TOPPED SHOT: Ball is contacted on upper portion of ball.

TRAP: Sometimes used to define bunker.

-W-

WAGGLE: The back-and-forth movement of the clubhead just prior to the swing. Designed to ease tension.

WHIFF: When player misses ball completely.

WINTER RULES: Improving lie of ball, usually allowed in fairway only, by moving it a few inches with the clubhead. Usually played when the condition of the course is unduly wet.

GROSSET'S FAMOUS
Handbooks of Active Sports

BASEBALL RULES IN PICTURES

Through nearly 200 illustrations showing actual playing situations, Little League players, participants in the many other amateur baseball programs, their coaches, umpires, managers, parents and pro baseball fans have a quick and easy way to learn baseball rules and check decisions. Each illustrated play is captioned and keyed to the Official Baseball Rules of play at the end of the book.

GOLF RULES IN PICTURES

This official publication of the United States Golf Association makes the rules come alive in graphic drawings. The perfect antidote for those inevitable controversies over rules that come up during a game.

PRO FOOTBALL PLAYS IN PICTURES

Offensive formations, running plays, passing plays, pass patterns, defensive formations—each illustrated with an action photograph and a diagram and accompanied by a clear and concise explanation. The ideal book for fans, players, and coaches.

THE BOOK OF TABLE TENNIS by Glenn Cowan

A profusely illustrated basic handbook to the international sport of table tennis. Progressing from need-to-know information on table-tennis equipment and directions for holding the racket, this book takes you pictorially through the various forehand and backhand strokes from service to strategy. Also includes: United States Table Tennis Association Official Rules.

FOOTBALL RULES IN PICTURES

New and revised edition containing the official National Football League Digest of Rules, clearly illustrated with drawings explaining the basic rules of the game. Professional and college interpretations of the rules are covered, making this the perfect handbook for the weekend TV viewer or the amateur official.

BASKETBALL RULES IN PICTURES

With the tremendous growth in popularity of this fast-paced sport, an understanding of the rules and of officials' techniques and signals becomes more and more important for the enjoyment of the game. This concise handbook contains a special section on basic plays and patterns.

ICE HOCKEY RULES IN PICTURES

This game of rousing speed, spectator appeal and color is the fastest team sport in the world, and an understanding of the rules is essential to its appreciation. In addition to illustrating the basic rules, this handy volume contains special sections on scoring goals and on defensive hockey.

GROSSET & DUNLAP

Publishers   New York

Secrets of Podcasting

Audio Blogging for the Masses

Bart G. Farkas

Peachpit
Press

Secrets of Podcasting

Bart G. Farkas

Peachpit
1249 Eighth Street
Berkeley, CA 94710
510/524-2178
800/283-9444
510/524-2221 (fax)
Find us on the World Wide Web at: www.peachpit.com

To report errors, please send a note to errata@peachpit.com

Peachpit is a division of Pearson Education

Project editor: Kathy Simpson
Production editor: Lupe Edgar
Compositor: David Van Ness
Indexer: Joy Dean Lee
Cover design: Charlene Charles-Will, with Mimi Heft
Cover photographs: Corbis, Veer; Scott Cowlin (iPod)
Interior design: Kim Scott, with Maureen Forys
Product images are courtesy of their respective companies.

Notice of Rights

Notice of Liability

Trademarks

ISBN 0-321-36929-7

9 8 7 6 5 4 3 2 1

Printed and bound in the United States of America

For Cori, the backbone of the backbone.

Acknowledgments

A book like this cannot be written without a great deal of support. The first round of thanks needs to go to Cliff Colby at Peachpit. Cliff had the vision to pursue this book before podcasting went into the stratosphere, and he worked hard through the entire process to keep things on track. Kathy Simpson, editor extraordinaire, also deserves a huge thank you, not just for her fine work editing the book, but also for acting as a sounding board whilst I droned on and on about RSS feeds.

Thanks also go out to everyone who participated in the book via interviews; their insights and opinions add greatly to the content. To Phil Torrone, thanks for both your expertise and your help in the early going. Phil is as close to "MacGyver" as any human can get! I also need to send a special thanks to Bob Goyetche (of "The Bob and AJ Show" fame) for his extra help and insights in the late going.

For my family, I need to say thanks for supporting me during the entire project. Without Cori (my wife), the entire operation would collapse (and she knows this). Thanks also to my three kids—Adam, Derek, and Natasha—whose constant harassment of me during the long hours was both maddening and humorously uplifting. Last, thanks to my cat, Shadow, for being a warm, fuzzy hot-water bottle.

Table of Contents

Foreword

I'm not sure what it is about Bart Farkas and forewords, but the last time I penned one of these things, it was in the guise of Michel Nostradamus, the 16th century's all-seeing, dyspeptic monk, in the first pages of Bart's and my book, *The Macintosh Bible Guide to Games*. Rib-tickling as that foreword was, we sold something like a baker's dozen worth of the book. Given *TMBGtG*'s less-than-stellar sales, I'm shocked that Bart would risk opening this book with yet another inane foreword penned by yours truly.

Ah, well, such is the ill-considered good nature of your typical Canadian.

The difference between that book and this one, of course, is that—unbeknownst to us at the time—computer gaming was on the wane, whereas the subject of this book has barely begun its assured meteoric rise. With Bart's *Secrets of Podcasting*, you're getting in on the ground floor of the electrifying new technology known as podcasting. /VID cASTING,

The author will go into greater detail on the subject, but allow me to dip my oar in as well and say that podcasting is A Big Deal. It's going to profoundly change the way you consume news and entertainment, as well as give a voice to those who normally work well outside the bounds of traditional media. Follow the techniques in this book, and one of those voices may even be yours.

One of the benefits of writing forewords is that you have the opportunity to read the book while it's still *in utero*—long before some befuddled crank on Amazon issues a one-star rating because he's disappointed that the book fails to address the intimate workings of Orvis's Vortex VO2 Fly Reel. I've taken the time to read the book, and I assure you, you're getting the goods. Not only does Bart clearly show you how to bring podcasts into your life (and onto your computer and portable music player), but he also tells you all you need to know to create a quality (and, one hopes, *compelling*) podcast of your own. Along the way, he speaks with individuals who are creating today's best podcasts and passing along their insights on how to do it right.

You're in good hands. Enjoy the book. Discover podcasts that stir you. And if the spirit moves you, make some of your own.

I'll be listening.

—Christopher Breen
 Editor in chief, Playlistmag.com
 Author of *Secrets of the iPod and iTunes*

Introduction

In late 2004, the combination of the RSS 2.0 specification and audio blogging came together to create what is now known as podcasting. *Podcasting* is the broadcast of radio shows and other audio content over the Internet via compressed audio files such as MP3s. RSS technology makes it possible for these files to be syndicated on the World Wide Web so that anyone can access them easily with one of many simple programs called *podcast aggregators* (or *podcatchers*). The result is a revolution in radio whereby every day, people can create audio shows that are listened to by thousands or tens of thousands of people all over the world.

This book examines the phenomenon of podcasting and its short history, and demonstrates in detail how you, too, can get started enjoying podcast content. I also supply detailed instructions on how to create and publish your very own podcast. From finding the equipment to setting up the software on your home computer, it's all here.

Podcasting has emerged from the fertile soil of Web logs, and in less than a year it has grown from a small curiosity to a major force, altering the media landscape as it continues to grow and change. Indeed, many radio stations now offer podcast content, and one station in particular (in San Francisco) recently announced a move to an all-podcast format.

Where podcasting will ultimately end up is the subject of speculation, but with the proliferation and ubiquity of iPods and other digital media players, it is clear that podcasting is here to stay. This book is a complete beginner's guide to podcasting that includes interviews with software creators, educators, industry experts, and even the hosts of some of North America's most popular podcasts. I know you'll enjoy learning about this fascinating and entertaining new medium.

How to Use This Book

This book has four main chapters, each of which details a different area of the podcasting universe. Podcasting is so new that it is entirely possible that you may have never heard of it—or that you have heard of it but have no working knowledge of what it is. With this in mind, the book is designed as a beginner's handbook for finding, downloading, listening to, and creating podcasts. The book can be divided into two sections. The first section (Chapters 1 and 2) concerns learning the basics about podcasting and how to go out and enjoy the great podcast content that's available. The second section (Chapters 3 and 4) details the process of creating your own podcasts and then publishing them on the Web for the world to enjoy.

Chapter 1 is an introduction to the concept, explaining what podcasting is, how it is being used, and how it may be used in the future. By the end of Chapter 1, the term *podcast* will be firmly established and completely understandable. Chapter 2 is for the person who wants to download and enjoy podcasts without having to worry about how to create them. This chapter explains the process of setting up a podcast aggregator (podcatching software) and details the most popular programs available for this purpose. Chapter 2 also takes a look at a few of the most popular iPods and other digital media players that are best suited for podcast playback.

Chapter 3 is concerned specifically with the process of creating a podcast. This chapter looks at most of the options available today, in terms of equipment and software, and then takes you through the process of creating a podcast from start to finish. Finally, in Chapter 4, publishing a podcast to the World Wide Web via an RSS feed is explained, demystified, and then described in step-by-step fashion.

Because podcasting is so new, this book is designed specifically for the new user, but that said, there are plenty of details that an intermediate podcaster can benefit from. The inclusion of interviews with people from all walks of the podcasting universe helps bring home the incredible effect that podcasting has had on radio, business, and even education in just a few short months.

This book is designed to be useful on several levels. If you specifically need to learn about RSS feeds, Chapter 4 awaits. If you are completely new to podcasting, the entire book is a treasure trove of information. Use this book as much or as little as you need to get exactly what you want out of podcasting. Most of all, have fun!

Icons

The four icons used in the following chapters are:

 Macintosh-compatible

 Windows-compatible

 Unix/Linux-compatible

 Items to take note of and helpful tips

1

Podcasting Basics

Wouldn't it be nice to be able to listen to radio programs, audiobooks and magazines, and alternative broadcasting on your *own* time? Heck, it might even be nice to make your very own broadcasts that others could listen to and enjoy. If you have ever been interested in such a concept, the wait is over.

The revolution is under way, and it's gaining steam. Podcasting, as it has become known, is a very new and exciting form of Web-based (that's World Wide Web–based) broadcasting. This chapter takes a look at just what podcasting is, where it came from, and what effect it has had on media distribution and the public's listening habits since its creation.

What Is Podcasting?

In a nutshell, *podcasting* is a World Wide Web–based form of broad-casting that allows anyone with a computer and/or a digital media device to download and listen to content. Formed by the combination of the words *iPod* and *broadcasting*, podcasting involves the creation of "radio" shows that are not intended to be broadcast over Marconi's invention. Indeed, these podcasts can be downloaded and enjoyed only through access to the World Wide Web. Podcasts can be enjoyed via a media player on your computer (such as RealPlayer or Windows Media Player), or they can be uploaded directly to your digital media device (such as an iPod) for enjoyment anytime and anywhere.

Over the past few years, sales of digital music devices such as Apple's iPod, MP3 players, and even cell phones and Palm Pilots have been soaring to new heights. Indeed, these devices have been finding their way into the pockets and purses of a wide cross-section of the North American public. With these gadgets becoming increasingly cosmopol-itan, it was perhaps inevitable that a mass movement away from stan-dard media broadcast methods would occur. After all, what's on the radio might not be what the customer wants to hear at any given time, and most digital media devices don't even have built-in radios. Enter the podcast.

The concept is simplicity itself: Allow users to listen to exactly *what* they want, *when* they want, and *where* they want. With today's world becoming progressively crammed with tasks ranging from doing the dishes to taking the kids to karate class, the ability to time-shift infor-mation is increasingly desirable. On the other side of the coin are the folks who want to actually produce podcasts. With little more than a computer, a microphone, and some freeware (or shareware), anyone can produce a podcast on any topic under the sun.

It's a new medium, to be sure, and it is still in its formative years, but podcasting is here to stay. From large corporations looking for new ways to get their programs heard, to home-brewed shows covering a diversity of topics ranging from sports to wine tasting to marital issues and beyond, podcasting is proving that it has the power and flexibility to reshape the media landscape. As the Web site Podcast Alley (**Figure 1.1**) says, "Free the Airwaves!"

Figure 1.1
Podcast Alley (www. podcastalley.com) is one of the best places to look for the hottest podcasts.

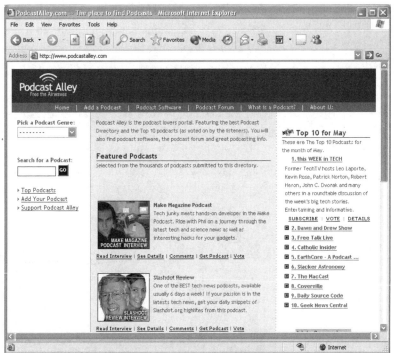

What's in a Name?

Why is podcasting called *podcasting* and not *digital delivery* or *MP3casting*? Well, the emergence of the dominant digital media device has a great deal to do with it. With somewhere around 65 percent of the hard-drive-based MP3 player market, Apple's iPods have taken the niche by storm. It's arguable that iPods are a cultural phenomenon and embodiment of a generation's zeitgeist. With over 10 million iPods on the streets in just a few years of sales, who can argue? For the record, Dannie Gregoire of Louisville, Kentucky, is widely credited with coining the term *podcast*. Who knows—without this gentleman, we might have ended up with a lame moniker such as *Intercasting!*

How It Works

The cutting edge of podcasting involves a set of rules known as *RSS (Really Simple Syndication)*. RSS allows podcast content to be syndicated instantly on the World Wide Web for download and use by anyone who has an interest in listening to it. By using RSS, the creator of a podcast can make his or her material available to anyone in the world (who has access to the Internet) within a matter of minutes.

With the evolution of RSS and associated technologies, podcasting becomes analogous to a TiVo for audio broadcasts of all kinds. Once syndicated, a podcast is disseminated over the World Wide Web to anyone who has subscribed to that content. Via RSS, podcasts are downloaded to users' computers and can be uploaded to a user's digital media player the next time it is connected to the computer.

Although this process may sound complicated and cumbersome, it really isn't. Thanks to incredibly versatile and user-friendly software like Apple's iTunes and Adam Curry's iPodder (**Figure 1.2**), the process of enjoying podcasts plays out like a soft Jamaican breeze.

Figure 1.2

Adam Curry and Dave Winer created iPodder, the leader in aggregator software for the Mac, PC, and Linux.

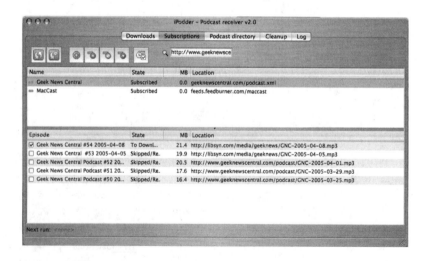

Although syndication is probably the most popular way of obtaining podcasts, there are other ways to get your hands on these audio gems without committing to daily or weekly content. Many podcasts are available as one-time downloads or as streaming content from any of a number of podcasting Web sites (the number of which is sure to mush-room even while this book is at the printer), giving you the option of sampling small bites rather than ordering a four-course meal.

Technically speaking, any media event that is played on a digital media device such as an iPod or other MP3 player is a podcast. Indeed, many weekly magazines, radio shows, and even television shows (such as "Charlie Rose") are available for download in MP3 format for use on digital media devices or home computers. As one might expect, many of these commercial ventures are associated with some small cost, but that is just one small area of the podcasting realm. In fact, 99 percent of all podcast content has no cost associated with it other than the necessary audio hardware and computer/Internet connection.

Why Podcast?

The answer to the above question is simple: Podcasting is so incredibly simple, especially compared with getting your own FCC license, that virtually anyone with a personal computer and an Internet connection can produce a show that could potentially be heard by tens of thou-sands of people. In the United States alone, where freedom of speech is set forth as one of the founding pillars of society, one does not have to take a large leap of faith to imagine that the podwaves are filling with interesting, offensive, humorous, and often inane chatter.

Figure 1.3

Bob Goyetche podcast-ing from his home in Deux-Montagnes.

Photo courtesy of Bob Goyetche

You may ask, "Who is podcasting?" That question can be answered very simply: Everyone is pod-casting. **Figure 1.3** shows Bob Goyetche podcasting out of his home in Deux-Montagnes, Quebec. By *everyone*, I mean people from all geographic loca-tions and all walks of life. If the Internet ushered in a revolution in information dissemination, podcasting has done the same for the audio format. Podcasting is the metaphorical saw that cuts through the chains of radio, be it satellite radio or the old-fashioned AM/FM brand.

The following is a short list of the sorts of topics that are routinely discussed in podcasts available today:

- Wine connoisseurship
- Husband-and-wife relationships
- Suburban life
- Christian fundamentalism
- Geek news
- Science fiction
- Comedy
- How-to shows
- Sports
- UFOs
- Music shows of all genres

Needless to say, this list could go on and on. And on. The number of podcasts is growing exponentially, and by the time you read this book, there likely will be a podcast for nearly every subject that could come to mind. If you can think of a subject that isn't covered, you've found your niche to start podcasting yourself!

Commercial Podcasting

For existing radio networks, individual radio stations, and even television stations, the move to podcasting is an obvious one. These outlets quickly realized that there was a market for their programming to be disseminated in the form of MP3 or AAC files so that individuals could enjoy them on their own time. And while the listener has control over whether she listens to any advertisements during the program, the exposure can only serve to aid in the growth of a fan base for any program. As a result, an increasing number of media outlets are making podcasts available to the public from their Web sites.

Also, several Web sites, including Apple Computer's iTunes Music Store and Audible.com's online store (**Figure 1.4**), sell commercial podcasts of periodicals such as *Scientific American Magazine* and newspapers such as *The Wall Street Journal*. The cost of these podcasts is often less than that of the publications on the newsstand, and they can be purchased through subscription, much like any magazine or newspaper. As time goes on, we can expect nearly every magazine (with the exception of certain sexually explicit rags) to be available in this format, allowing readers everywhere to get in their reading while riding a bike or driving a car.

Figure 1.4

Audible.com's Web site sells audiobooks but also commercial podcasts of popular television and radio shows.

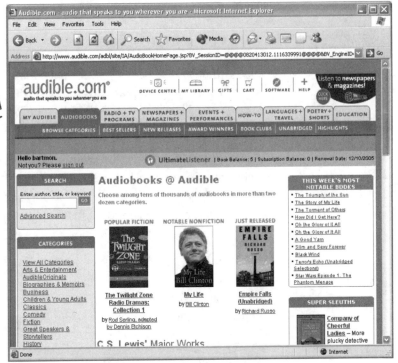

The Podcasting Echo

Exactly what mark podcasting will make on the world is a chapter that is as yet unwritten. Still, despite the fact that podcasting is in its infancy, we don't need a crystal ball to see that the whirlwind surrounding it today will most likely stir up the sand in several established sandboxes. Let's take a look at what might be affected, directly or indirectly, by the rise of podcasting:

Conventional radio. Perhaps the one area that might be most affected by podcasting, traditional radio has a lot to lose. In today's world, most of the people who listen to radio do so in their cars. With an increasing number of cars coming with MP3 players or Apple iPod connections, the ability for a driver to listen to podcast material rather than advertisement-laden radio broadcasts increases. The effects of this on radio are already apparent, with many radio programs offering podcast versions of their shows via station Web sites.

NOTE There are also products on the market that effectively turn any radio broadcast into a podcast. Griffin Technology's radio SHARK (www.griffintechnology.com), for example, will capture any AM or FM radio broadcast and automatically export an MP3 file to iTunes so that the program will be loaded directly onto your iPod the next time you connect it to your computer.

Satellite radio. With less to lose than conventional radio (because satellite radio doesn't include advertising), satellite radio is still in a flat position, because its content is available only at set times. Podcasts are available at any time. Might the satellite-radio fees be diverted to individual commercial podcast subscriptions? It's possible.

Internet radio. Internet radio is perhaps the safest of the radio media, because software already exists that allows the user to time-shift Internet radio shows. The downside to Internet radio is that it is primarily intended to be listened to on a computer and, as such, doesn't have the mobility of a podcast.

Celebrity. In less than a year of official existence, the podcast has already created celebrity. Of course, Adam Curry (former MTV veejay) is the face of iPodder and podcasting in general, but the hosts of the most popular podcasts are also beginning to achieve some measure of celebrity. It's only a matter of time before a podcaster makes the jump from podcasting to mainstream radio.

During the writing of this book, Adam Curry and Sirius Satellite Radio announced that Curry will be broadcasting a four-hour daily show on podcasting over the Sirius Satellite network. Although this broadcast had not premiered at this writing, it is a fair bet that it will give podcasting in general another huge shot in the arm in terms of positive publicity and legitimization.

Television. Television doesn't have a great deal to fear from podcasting. It can, however, profit from the new medium, and some canny producers are already making sure that they have a piece of the podcasting pie. Talk-based shows like "Charlie Rose" and the "BBC News Hour" are available on commercial services like Audible.com (www.audible.com), making them available to an audience that might not otherwise partake.

Advertising. The obvious problem for advertisers lies in placing advertising in a medium that prides itself on freedom: freedom of ideas, freedom from advertisers' pressure, freedom to say what they want. With podcasting's increasing fan base, you can be sure that corporations will want to find a way to advertise, but it's unclear whether the listeners will accept such a thing. Perhaps the most logical path will be for companies to sponsor the production of individual podcasts, thus attaching their names to successful podcasting endeavors.

Education. This is highly speculative, but one can imagine university classes that are digitally recorded and then made available on a Web site as podcast "notes." Students can download the audio of that class and listen to it while they're out drinking beer and eating pizza later that evening. The possibilities for education are huge, and as MP3 players and iPods become ubiquitous (in phones and PDAs, and as stand-alone players), the ability for education to take advantage of this information pathway is increased. Who knows what the future of education will be?

AUDIBLE . COM

Book and magazine publishers. Perhaps at the forefront of podcasting (although some would argue that pay service isn't true podcasting), Audible.com went online in late 1997 and was at the forefront of digital audio content delivery. Audible made its name by selling audiobooks for use on the computer, CD player, or MP3 player, but since its inception, it has been on the cutting edge, offering everything from comedy shows to daily newspapers (in audio format). No doubt the success of Audible.com has spurred more publishers to produce audio versions of their books, thus changing the publishing landscape.

The legal system. Any time there is talk of digital content of any kind, legal ramifications start to rear their ugly heads. Although independent podcasts are free to the world, it's only a matter of time before some conflict arises in this area. How and when are matters of opinion, but one only has to look at the music industry to see how ugly things can become. That said, let's try to be optimistic. Perhaps the spirit of podcasting will prevail, and the medium will thrive without copyright-infringement lawsuits to bog it down.

Commerce. As mentioned previously, Web sites like Audible.com and Apple's iTunes Music Store already sell what are essentially podcast versions of popular radio and television shows, as well as audio versions of periodicals. As podcasting continues to take off, one can imagine compact discs for sale with hundreds of podcasts in a sort of "Best of Podcasting 2005" compilation. No doubt we will see many changes in commerce and e-commerce as a result of podcasting's entrance into the marketplace.

A Brief History of Podcasting

How can I write a history of something that has been around less than 12 months? The answer to that question lies in the truism that just about nothing is created in a vacuum, and just as x-ray photography evolved from radiation tests, podcasting evolved from humbler beginnings. Podcasting's roots actually are planted in the world of blogs (Web logs). Therefore, we must look first at the origin of the blog. Indeed, to see the genesis of podcasting, we have to go back—way back—to the mist-shrouded days of the 1980s.

What is a blog? A *blog*, or *Web log*, is a World Wide Web page where content is added periodically and time- and date-stamped. These additions can be made by one or more people, including the general public. The content of a blog can range from diary entries to news items to opinions on world events. Today, some blogs contain links to podcasts—which isn't surprising, considering that the roots of podcasting are firmly planted in blog soil. As an aside, the Merriam-Webster dictionary announced that by virtue of the number of online lookups, the word *blog* received its "Word of the Year" award in 2004. (For some reason, the word *defenestration* made No. 10 on the list.)

The home computer and Internet

Entire phone-book-size books have been written about the history of the home computer and the Internet, and I'm pretty sure that you don't want me to go down that road in a book about podcasting! That said, I'll cut to the chase and just say that the current ubiquity of the home computer and nearly universal access to the Internet (in one form or another) are the structural underpinnings that make podcasting possible to begin with. Without this technology in millions of homes, this book wouldn't have been written. 'Nuff said.

The blog

While some people feel that the roots of blogging lie in the ashes of pen-pal relationships and ham-radio operation, let's start with the computer culture of the 1980s. By the early '80s, the personal computer was starting to take hold. Apple was still king (in terms of home computers), but others, such as IBM and Commodore, were making significant inroads as the years passed. By mid-decade, many computer users had modems, and they were using these modems to log on to bulletin boards (also known as *BBs*), e-mail lists, or online services such as GEnie and CompuServe (precursors of today's AOL). Many aspects of these outlets and services were essentially early versions of Web logs. People could dial in with their modems, read new messages that had been posted by others, and then enter their own messages.

Clearly, the seeds of blogging were sown in the 1980s, but the real sprouting and growth of blogging occurred in the mid-1990s, paralleling the meteoric rise of the Internet and the World Wide Web. According to Wikipedia, the term *Web log* was coined in 1997 by Web-log pioneer Jorn Barger. By the eve of the turn of the century, *Web log* had melded into the single word *blog*, and the popularity of blogs started to skyrocket. Ultimately, a gentleman by the name of Dave Winer designed a way to inform users when their favorite blogs had been updated with new information, thus making blogging even more versatile and useful to the masses. Today, there are countless blogs, many of which have large followings, such as Jade Walker's "blog of death," shown in **Figure 1.5**.

Figure 1.5
www.blogofdeath.com, the brainchild of Jade Walker, is typical of the modern blog.

Audio blogging

Audio blogging was a variant of the blog that involved the posting of audio files rather than text in its entries. By all accounts, the audio blog was not a resounding success in terms of garnering the kind of world-wide attention that the blog had. Still, the audio blog existed, and files were usually offered in MP3 format, although occasionally, other Web-based formats, like Flash (Macromedia), would be used. It was from the underpinnings of audio blogging that podcasting arose.

In 2004, the RSS format was combined with aggregator software to essentially check RSS-enabled Web pages for new audio content and keep users up to date on content. In English, that means that a combination of software programs came together to enable people to subscribe easily to audio content (podcasts) and have that content delivered directly to their home computers and, ultimately, their digital media devices (MP3 players).

The digital media player

With all the talk about Web logs, blogging, and audio blogging, it can be easy to forget that the digital media player, otherwise known as an MP3 player (**Figure 1.6**) or iPod (**Figure 1.7**), also played a key role in the sudden rise and popularity of podcasting. The lineage of today's digital media players can be traced back to the venerable Sony Walkman from

Figure 1.7

Apple's iPods have taken the world by storm, capturing the vast majority of the market.

Photo courtesy of Apple Computer, Inc.

Figure 1.6

A Creative MP3 player.

the late '70s. A play-only cassette tape machine, the Walkman was small enough that it could be taken virtually anywhere, and it became a huge hit, selling around 3 million units in its first three years of sales. (By comparison, Apple has moved more than triple that amount of iPods in a similar timeframe.)

From the Walkman sprouted plenty of competition, including cassette tape players with radios included. These devices ultimately shrank to near the size of the cassette tapes themselves. In the mid-1980s, the compact disc (CD) hit the market and took it by storm. It wasn't long before portable CD players showed up, and these, too, progressed from relatively bulky devices to very slim and elegant designs that were not much larger than the CDs themselves.

By 1998, the MP3 format was being used to play music on computers (with the help of a piece of software called WinAmp), and during that same year, the first viable MP3 player emerged on the market. Early MP3 players were flash-memory-based (meaning they had a small, fixed amount of space to hold music), but by late 1999, hard-drive-based MP3 players also started to appear. The market for MP3 players was very fragmented until Apple Computer released the first iPod in October 2001.

The iPod has been nothing short of a resounding success, and in the few short years since the iPod's introduction, Apple has gained control of more than 90 percent of the hard-drive-based player market and 65 percent of the total MP3 player market. With Apple's dominance and cultural influence with regard to MP3 players, it's no wonder that the term *podcasting* includes a reference to the iPod.

MP3 players today include software that makes moving music and other audio files from the Internet to computer to player very simple. Apple's iTunes software significantly affected the simplicity of all vendors' software in this manner, making podcasting easier for the average user.

The MP3 file

The MP3 file was developed in Germany by Dieter Seitzer and Karlheinz Brandenburg at a company called Fraunhofer-Gesellschaft and the University of Erlangen. The *MP* part of *MP3* refers to the MPEG roots of MP3 compression. *MPEG* stands for *Moving Picture Experts Group,* which was established in 1988 to set standards for digital encoding. Developed and perfected in the mid-1990s, the *MP3* format, which stands for *MPEG Audio Layer III,* became the standard for digital audio compression worldwide.

MP3 compression is necessary because CD-quality audio files are extremely large—too large, in fact, to fit on digital players of the day. An average song on a CD might consist of 30 MB to 40 MB of information, while that same song in MP3 format could be whittled down nearly tenfold—to 3.5 MB or 4 MB—with minimal quality loss. Obviously, without the MP3 format, the rise of small digital media devices would have been cost-prohibitive and unrealistic.

As another piece of the puzzle, the MP3 format is one of the key elements of the rise of the podcasting phenomenon (among many other things). Although the MP3 format has been eclipsed by AAC (the format Apple uses on its iPods), it is still a viable and frequently used compression method for all Web-based audio content.

Podcasting is born

And so with home computers, the Internet, blogging, audio blogging, the MP3 format, and digital media players all coming together in a roundabout way, the wonder that is podcasting is born. Without all of these elements coming together in just the right way, podcasting as we know it now might not even exist. The connections among all of these diverse technologies could be examined in much deeper detail, but for now, it will suffice to say that podcasting exists. Hooray!

2

Jumping In

OK, so now you know what a podcast is, where it came from, and what sorts of technologies had to come together to make it possible. What's next? Well, you may be champing at the bit to create your own podcast, but before I show you the ropes on that, I suggest that you learn a little more about the podcasting universe in general.

This chapter shows you how to go out and get just the right podcasts for you by examining the various programs that scour the Internet for podcasts of all kinds. This section also touches on podcasting content, resources, commercial podcasting, Internet and traditional radio, and computer and digital music device (MP3 players) podcast players. By the time you finish this chapter, the art of downloading and enjoying podcasts will be second nature.

Getting Started

As mentioned in Chapter 1, podcasts can be found all over the World Wide Web in multiple forms, from audio blogs to daily newspapers (in audio form) to celebrity interviews. The majority of podcasts, however, are home-brewed gems put together by everyday people in an effort to educate, entertain, or even offend. This section examines how to get your hands on just the right podcasts for you and helps you decide which software best suits your needs.

Key podcasting Web sites

Before I get into the nitty-gritty of podcast aggregators and the like, I should point out the top five Web sites that you can surf to get a better understanding of the podcasting community as a whole. In fact, having this chapter open as you look at these sites will help you make connections between my suggestions and what you see on your screen. So if doing is more important to you than reading, take note of these Web sites, and dive straight in.

The sites I recommend here are general enough to answer your podcasting questions and point you toward such fundamentals as podcast feeds and software downloads. The top five Web sites I recommend are:

1. www.podcastalley.com

2. www.ipodder.org

3. www.podcastingnews.com

4. www.podcasting-tools.com

5. www.podscope.com

Podcast aggregators (the software)

The software that goes out and grabs podcasts for you is known as an *aggregator*. An aggregator scours the Web for the exact kind of content (podcasts) you have told it to look for. Many of these programs will go out and get the material at night (or whenever you tell it to), delivering the content to your desktop, iPod, or other MP3 player while you sleep. Because many broadband Internet connections are in an always-on state, aggregator software takes advantage of this situation, grabbing content around the clock.

Aggregators are available for Macintosh computers, Windows PCs, Unix/Linux systems, and handheld devices such as PDAs and SmartPhones.

Although some of these programs are capable of grabbing everything from stock quotes to your daily horoscope, I'll concentrate mostly on the podcasting angle (after all, this *is* a podcasting book).

There are two basic categories of podcast aggregators: highly polished programs that have plenty of features and are easy to use, and quick-and-dirty programs that are meant to be easily accessed and altered by those who desire to do so. It is likely safe to say that the majority of those who like to tinker with actual programming code are more apt to be using Linux than Mac OS X, but of course, there are exceptions to every rule. Therefore, this section looks at many kinds of aggregator software.

Aggregators are not a mystery; for the most part, they are easy-to-use, powerful programs that allow you to get your hands on the content you most want to hear. How they work, their interfaces, their ease of use, and their general suitability for your needs will be examined for each piece of software. The icons detail what systems the software is available for—Mac, PC, or Linux/Unix.

NOTE Many great pieces of software are out there to help you capture podcasts, but for the beginner, I recommend two products. For the Macintosh, Linux, and handheld devices, I suggest iPodder. For the PC, I recommend HappyFish and iPodder; specifically for the Mac, I recommend PlayPod, iPodder 2.0, and iPodderX. Starting out with these programs will ensure a smooth entry into the world of capturing and enjoying podcasts.

BashPodder

Required Software: Xdialog
OS Requirement: Mac OS X, Linux
Price: Freeware

BashPodder (http://linc.homeunix.org:8080/scripts/bashpodder/; **Figure 2.1**) is a very simple (only 44 lines of code) aggregator that was designed primarily to work with Linux but works with Mac OS X as well. Basically, all BashPodder does is download MP3 files that are specified in an RSS feed. If you are not familiar with Linux and programming in general, I recommend that you set aside BashPodder, despite its power and simplicity, until you've learned more about tweaking scripts in Linux.

Figure 2.1

BashPodder is a very simple Linux option for grabbing podcasts.

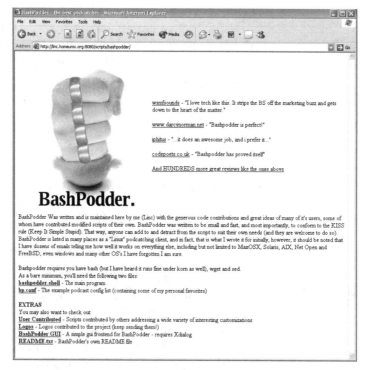

 On the Macintosh, BashPodder requires Xdialog, a program that allows command-line interfaces to appear in dialog boxes rather than just as lines of text in a window.

CastGrab

Required Software: None
OS Requirement: Linux
Price: Freeware

CastGrab (www.fubarpa.com/projects/castgrab) is another Linux-based aggregator that (after you set up your subscriptions file) downloads all the podcasts for each subscription. At this writing, the current version of CastGrab downloads everything in a subscription the first time it is run and only the latest entries in subsequent passes. CastGrab is another example of a very simple and effective script that will do the job in a proper, if unglamorous, way.

FeederReader

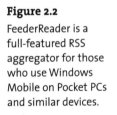

Required Software: Microsoft .NET Framework 1.1, Microsoft ActiveSync
OS Requirement: Windows Mobile
Price: Freeware ($9 donation requested)

FeederReader is a full-featured aggregator for RSS feeds for the Pocket PC crowd running Windows Mobile. One key difference between many home computers and handheld devices like Pocket PCs is that the latter are not always connected to the Internet, which somewhat limits their ability to update podcasts frequently. Despite this limitation, FeederReader (**Figure 2.2**) does an excellent job of managing podcasting feeds for Windows Mobile users.

Figure 2.2
FeederReader is a full-featured RSS aggregator for those who use Windows Mobile on Pocket PCs and similar devices.

FeederReader can be configured to update podcasts only when it is connected to the Internet (obviously) and download the content as quickly as possible so that it can be stored for later use from the Pocket PC. Although FeederReader can be used by the beginner podcast enthusiast, its in-depth functionality and ability to show error messages and scripts in detail make it a better choice for the more seasoned podcast listener.

Following are some of FeederReader's features:

- Can be stored directly on a flash memory card

- Can handle a large number of feeds

- Provides detailed error messaging

- Keeps statistics on all loaded files

- Supports OPML (Outline Processor Markup Language) import and export

HappyFish

Required Software: Microsoft .NET Framework 1.1
OS Requirement: Windows 2000 or XP
Price: Freeware

HappyFish, shown in **Figure 2.3**, is the brainchild of Will Corum and Danny Boyd, and was designed as an RSS Enclosure aggregator (see the note in this section). HappyFish is a very user-friendly piece of software that works on Windows-based PCs and that can be downloaded from http://thirstycrow.net/happyfish/default.aspx.

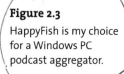

Figure 2.3
HappyFish is my choice for a Windows PC podcast aggregator.

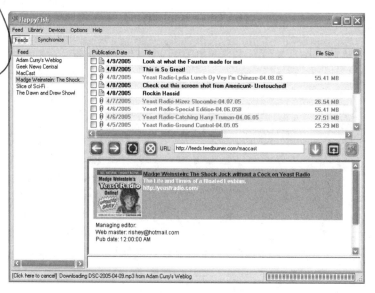

I should note, however, that for HappyFish to work properly, you must have Microsoft .NET Framework 1.1 running on your machine. This is a piece of background software that is published by Microsoft and is available from its Web site. The HappyFish Web site also contains a link to the Microsoft .NET Framework 1.1 site for your convenience.

NOTE **An RSS Enclosure can be any file from a movie to a picture to news headlines to audio files such as podcasts. When I refer to RSS Enclosures, I am speaking of files that are put out on the Internet for anyone to access and download.**

HappyFish is an excellent one-stop aggregator for a Windows PC, giving the user plenty of flexibility, including the following features:

- The ability to add an unlimited number of feeds

- Control over when and how often feeds are checked for new material

- The ability to have multiple devices updated (with different content) from the same PC

- The ability to catalog content so that you can see what's available and choose what to download rather than downloading everything there, which can save on bandwidth considerably

- An easy-to-use interface

- A built-in Web browser, making it easy to obtain RSS feed addresses without leaving the HappyFish program

iPodder 2.0

Required Software: None (iTunes suggested)
OS Requirement: Mac OS X 10.2.3 or later
Price: Freeware

iPodder (**Figure 2.4**), created by Adam Curry and Dave Winer, is arguably the program that got the whole podcasting ball rolling in the first place. Although iPodder is still under development, it is already the aggregator of choice for Mac and PC users.

iPodder is a small program designed simply to download audio files from selected podcasts to your computer, an MP3 player, or an iPod, and is packaged in a way that makes it accessible to all users.

Figure 2.4
iPodder is the grand-daddy of podcast aggregators. It has evolved into an elegant and useful program.

The Macintosh version of iPodder (www.ipodder.org), shown in **Figure 2.5**, is visually more pleasing than its Windows counterpart, but underneath the facades, these two siblings function in much the same way.

Figure 2.5
The Macintosh version of iPodder is also a solid performer.

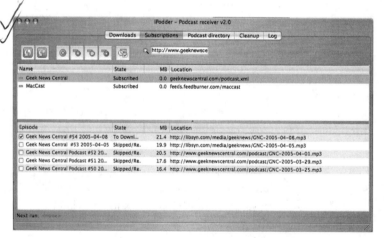

iPodder offers the following handy features:

- The ability to feed subscriptions manually or automatically. (Note that iPodder has a default channel that introduces you to several podcasts and to the iPodderX Top Picks and iPodderX Most Popular directories, instantly giving you access to a world of podcasts.)

- The ability to check for new podcasts ... specific times.

- The ability to hide in the background v. searching and downloading functions.

- Automatic downloading of podcasts to your MP3 play

- Automatic downloading of podcasts to iTunes (Windows or M. and your iPod (if that is your player of choice).

> **NOTE**
>
> **Current Mac iPodder specifications: If you want to run iPodder, you need to have a Mac that is capable of running OS X 10.3 or later.**

iPodder X

Required Software: iTunes 4 or later
OS Requirement: Mac OS X 10.3.5 or later
Price: Free trial, then $19.95

Designed by August Trometer and Ray Slakinski, iPodderX is a Macintosh-only aggregator that goes further than iPodder 2.0 in terms of functionality. iPodderX allows the user to download audio files (**Figure 2.6**), and because it is fully integrated with iTunes, the program makes it easy for Mac users to manage their podcasts.

Figure 2.6

iPodderX is one of my top choices for the Macintosh when it comes to aggregators.

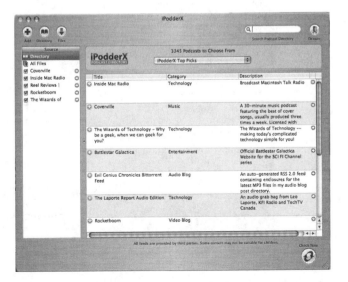

iPodderX also manages images, however, and because it takes advantage of Apple's iPhoto software, it makes managing visual content easy. Finally, iPodderX can go out and grab video footage that you can view with the program's built-in media viewer (**Figure 2.7**).

Figure 2.7

When video media is selected, a flap slides out from the right side of the iPodderX window to allow viewing of the content in the built-in media player.

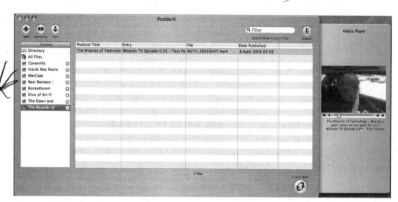

iPodderX is an excellent choice for anyone who wants to stand ready on the frontiers of podcasting. The program contains a Special Directory of podcasts that is continuously updated. At this writing, the directory had over 3,500 podcasts in it (**Figure 2.8**), which should be enough to get even the most voracious podcast listener started.

Figure 2.8

With thousands of podcasts in its directory, iPodderX is a one-stop shop for beginning podcast listeners.

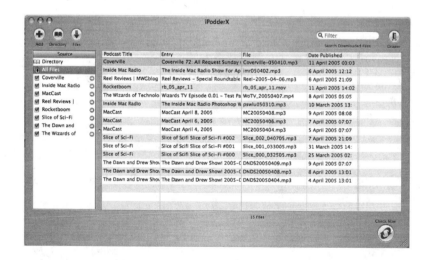

With its built-in media player and its ability to grab virtually any kind of file attached to an RSS feed, iPodderX is a fantastic catch-all program that will likely take care of the immediate podcasting needs of even the most hard-core users.

Some of the features and advantages of iPodderX are:

- The ability to manage audio files, images, video files, and virtually any kind of file attached to an RSS feed

- The ability to deliver content right to your Mac and ultimately to iTunes and your iPod or iPod photo

- Slick, easy-to-use interface

- Easy installation

- Built-in iPodderX Special Directory with thousands of podcasts to choose among

iPodderX Creator Interview

IPodderX is one of the best podcast aggregators for the Mac. It is very popular and has led the way for all podcasting clients. One of the creators of iPodder X, **August Trometer,** agreed to answer a few questions. If you want to learn more about the program, go to http://iPodderX.com.

Farkas: What was the genesis of iPodderX? Whose idea was it, and why did you feel the need to create it?

Trometer: The idea of files included in a regular RSS newsfeed had been around for a while, and it always intrigued me. Some other developers started building bare-bones clients, but they were all command-line utilities and not very friendly. I knew that in order for podcasting to take off, it was going to need a client with a GUI [graphic user interface] that normal people could use. Ray Slakinski had created one of those command-line utilities, and I asked him if I could borrow and adapt his code. He agreed, and several days later, iPodderX was born. It was the very first podcast client to sport a user interface. Soon after, I asked Ray to join me and work together on iPodderX, and we've been at it ever since!

(continued on next page)

iPodderX Creator Interview *(continued)*

Farkas: Was there a specific plan to have iPodderX fit into a particular part of the market, or were you just trying to fill a need?

Trometer: Initially, we were responding to the need of a small group of people. Podcasting in those days didn't even have a name, and there were few listeners and even fewer podcasters. At the time, the community of users was small, and they gave great feedback on how they thought things should work. The foundation of iPodderX was laid then, and a lot of the ideas and input from those early users are still evident.

Farkas: Has the rise of the podcasting phenomenon surprised you? If so, how?

Trometer: The speed of the rise of podcasting has been the most surprising part. It seems almost silly that six months ago, the term *podcasting* hadn't even really been used. That's how it goes in technology, though, and you really need to move fast to keep up.

Farkas: What do you see for podcasting in the next year? In the next five years?

Trometer: Audio, of course, is always going to be a big part of podcasting. But video is going to come into its own as well. Shows like "Rocketboom" are already leading the way for how video will work. I also think you'll see podcasting take on traditional media, much as blogging has taken on the press. In the 2004 election, bloggers had a tremendous impact. Now imagine those same bloggers with microphones and video cameras. It's the complete democratization of the media. Years ago, the cliché was that everyone would have their own TV channel. I think podcasting is the way that's going to happen. You'll get to see mainstream shows right alongside home-grown entertainment.

Farkas: What do you see for iPodderX? What features can you envision being implemented in years to come? What surprises might be in store for the end user?

Trometer: More than anything else, we want iPodderX to be the center of your information flow, not just audio files. Any sort of subscription you have—whether it's audio, text news, movies, or images—iPodderX will handle. Podcasting is much more than just audio, and we have always been moving in that direction.

Managing these files is going to be a big issue for users. We've already implemented a lot of cool technology to get this done. SmartSpace, for example, lets the user set a space limit—say, 2 GB. If that space fills up, we start deleting older files to keep your disk space usage low. You'll see more new features like this in upcoming versions.

Look up. Rocket Boom (handwritten margin note)

iPodderX Creator Interview *(continued)*

You'll also see even tighter integration with Apple's iApps. iPodderX already interfaces with iPhoto and iTunes, but we're working on even more ways to share information between applications.

Farkas: Do you see other aggregators as competition or as siblings to your own software?

Trometer: I'd like to think we're all friendly competitors. Obviously, there's a great deal of idea-sharing going on between the different clients, but knowing that there are half a dozen other applications nipping at iPodderX's heels keeps us moving forward and innovating as fast as we can. It's good for us, and in the end, it's good for podcasting in general.

Farkas: Why do you think podcasting is taking off in this way?

Trometer: Right now, all the planets are aligned, and all the technology and ideas have come together perfectly. The average home computer now has the ability to become a pretty decent recording studio. At the same time, XML feeds and podcast clients have given people a way of sharing those recordings. You'd never be able to have one without the other.

Farkas: Were there any particular challenges, technically speaking, to creating iPodderX?

Trometer: Strangely, my background is in Web development, and I had never programmed a Macintosh application. iPodderX was my first try—sort of an experiment in "I can do that." So there was a huge learning curve to get through. Version 3 of iPodderX is the culmination of the past several months of intense study and learning.

Farkas: What do you think about the commercialization of podcasting that is already starting to seep in?

Trometer: Commercialization is inevitable, especially as the major media outlets realize how many share points they're losing to podcasting. But with commercialization comes legitimacy, and that's a good thing for all concerned.

iPodder.NET

Required Software: Microsoft .NET Framework 1.1
OS Requirement: Windows 2000 or XP
Price: Freeware

iPodder.NET (http://ipoddernet.sourceforge.net; **Figure 2.9**) is a simple Windows-based aggregator that is very simple and no-frills in nature but nonetheless gets the job done.

Figure 2.9

iPodder.NET is a simple program for Windows PCs.

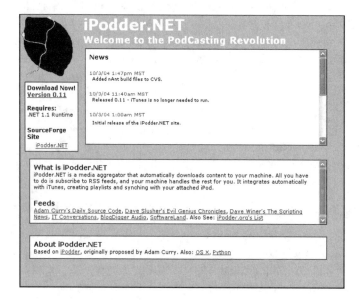

Like HappyFish, iPodder.NET requires that Microsoft .NET Framework 1.1 be installed on your Windows 2000 or Windows XP machine before you can even install it.

In its current incarnation, iPodder.NET is designed to work with iTunes (the PC version, of course), ferrying all downloaded podcasts into the iTunes library, from which they can be transferred to the user's iPod.

Once it's installed and running, iPodder.NET actually functions in the background, and as such may appeal to those who don't want to have to open and close a program repeatedly to complete aggregator tasks. iPodder.NET sits in the system tray, which in most Windows configurations is near the date-and-time area. When you right-click the program's icon in the system tray (**Figure 2.10**) and choose Options

from the shortcut menu, the iPodder.NET Configuration panel appears,
as shown in **Figure 2.11**.

iPodder.net icon

Figure 2.10

The iPodder.NET icon
is a small black lemon
on a blue background
with a pair of iPod
headphones on it.
Right-click this icon to
get at the configura-
tion panel.

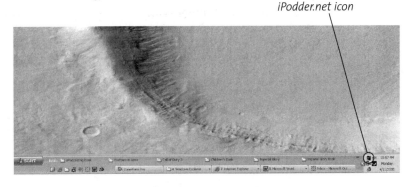

Figure 2.11

The iPodder.NET
configuration panel.

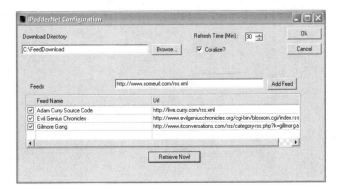

This panel is very simple. Cut and paste the feeds you desire into the
Add Feed box and then click the Retrieve Now! button to gather up all
the podcasts from that feed. In the top-right corner is a spot to set the
refresh time for iPodder.NET to check the feeds for new material; you
can set this option from 1 minute to 999 minutes.

Once the feeds are in place, there is no need to open the iPodder.NET
application and fool with anything. Indeed, the podcasts go directly to
iTunes or to a specified folder on the hard drive, and everything
happens in the background. To add a new feed, you need only right-
click the icon in the system tray to open the iPodder.NET Configuration
panel; otherwise, the program runs entirely in the background.

iPodder.NET is not flashy, but it certainly gets the job done, especially
for those using Apple's free iTunes software to manage their audio files.

iPodderSP/Skookum

Required Software: Microsoft ActiveSync (on PC), .NET Compact Framework (on SmartPhone), Microsoft Windows Mobile 2003 (on SmartPhone)

OS Requirement: Windows 98, 2000, or XP

Price: $9.99

At this writing, the program iPodderSP has been sold, and the new incarnation of this software is known as Skookum. Still, it is not unreasonable to assume that some form of iPodderSP will be circulating on the Internet, so I use both names here.

iPodderSP (**Figures 2.12** and **2.13**) is a podcasting client (aggregator) specifically designed for SmartPhones, although we should point out

Figure 2.12

iPodderSP (also known as Skookum) is a capable program.

that the software installs only on a Windows PC. iPodderSP requires the presence of Microsoft's .NET Compact Framework to be installed on your PC. The .NET Compact Framework isn't the only software that you'll have to have installed first; you also need to have ActiveSync up and running on your machine before you can use iPodderSP to ferry podcasts to your phone.

Figure 2.13

The iPodderSP Browser window.

For those using their SmartPhones to enjoy podcasts, iPodderSP is an excellent choice that offers a solid set of capabilities, including:

- Subscribing to podcast feeds and downloading podcasts directly to your phone

- Playing downloaded podcasts via the SmartPhone's built-in media player

- Importing and exporting podcast subscriptions from and to other aggregators

- Scheduling automatic downloads

- Resuming partial downloads automatically

iTunes 4.9

Required Software: None
OS Requirement: Mac OS 10.2.8 or later, Windows 2000 or XP
Price: Free

For anyone using one of the more than 10 million iPods, Apple's iTunes (www.apple.com/itunes) is the software they are most likely using to manage their digital music and book libraries. It also provides a portal directly to the iTunes Music Store, allowing users to purchase songs for 99 cents a pop and books for varying prices. In late June 2005, however, Apple announced the release of iTunes 4.9 with a built-in podcast aggregator that gives you access to thousands of free podcasts, ranging from ABC News to Adam Curry to Al Franken to the hottest podcasts burning up the charts at any given time. Adding a podcast aggregator to arguably the most complete and functional of the digital audio organizers makes perfect sense, and Apple has risen to the occasion.

To access podcasts, simply click the Podcasts icon directly below the Library icon in the iTunes source window (**Figure 2.14**). iTunes 4.9 also allows you to set the usual parameters, such as how often iTunes checks for new episodes of your favorite podcasts and how many

Figure 2.14
Click the Podcasts icon in iTunes, and the podcast area comes up in full color.

Figure 2.15

Specify your podcast-
ing preferences here.

episodes of each podcast to keep,
as well as preferences for how
these podcasts are transferred (or
not) to your iPod(s) (**Figure 2.15**).

jPodder

Required Software: Java Version 1.4 or later

OS Requirement: Windows 98, 2000, or XP; Linux

Price: Freeware

One of the early entries in the aggregator software derby, jPodder
(**Figure 2.16**) is a solid candidate with a very full set of features.
Installing jPodder can be a bit of a headache, however, because it
requires that you have Java Version 1.4 or later. That said, the software
bundle contains all the information you need to install all the requisite
software and program files to get yourself up and running on your
Linux box or PC.

Figure 2.16

jPodder is a capable
and useful aggregator
for the Linux crowd.

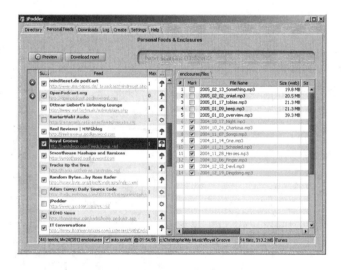

jPodder has a very complete feature set, including the ability to
incorporate detailed information (such as images, artist information,

and bit-rate data) about each podcast or file. Here is the feature set for jPodder:

- Because it is Java-based, jPodder can be installed on multiple systems.

- jPodder has a built-in user manual.

- On a Windows PC, jPodder can sit in the system tray (like iPodder.NET) to work in the background.

- Subscription feeds can be given detailed information (**Figure 2.17**).

- The program has drag-and-drop functionality.

- jPodder includes a built-in media player.

- The program supports transfers to iTunes and WMP (Windows Media Player).

Figure 2.17

If you choose to identify your podcasts or MP3 files with images and technical details, jPodder has an extensive information panel available for each file.

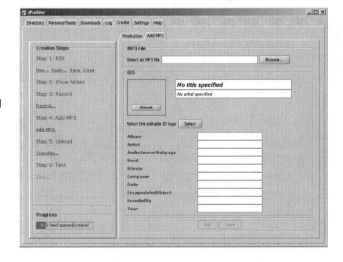

Nimiq

Required Software: Microsoft .NET Framework 1.14322
OS Requirement: Windows 2000 or XP
Price: Donationware

Nimiq is another solid podcast aggregator for the Windows PCs of the world. Like many of the other PC aggregators, Nimiq requires that

Microsoft .NET Framework 1.1 or later be installed on your machine before you can install and run it. That said, installing Nimiq and getting the podcasting ball rolling are a breeze, although the feature set is somewhat limited compared with those of its contemporaries.

Nimiq has two main sections: the main screen, where subscriptions and enclosures can be viewed and accessed (**Figure 2.18**), and the OPML Browser (**Figure 2.19**).

Figure 2.18

Nimiq is very basic, but it's easy to use and very stable.

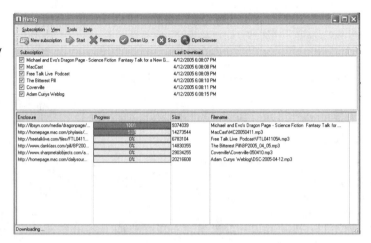

Figure 2.19

Nimiq's OPML Browser functions much like iPodder's directory area.

OPML stands for *Outline Processor Markup Language*, a format for outlines. (An outline refers to the structure of the file, which looks something like an outline with various layers; see Chapter 4 to see an RSS file in this format.) Outlines using OPML are very flexible and are well suited for RSS feeds. Nimiq's OPML Browser allows users to navigate many RSS feeds and then subscribe to those feeds or download them from directly inside the browser.

Nimiq has the ability to import and export files, and it has a History area where the podcast file transactions are logged. To set up schedules for checking RSS feeds, you use the Options panel (**Figure 2.20**), which you access from the Tools menu. Like other aggregators of this sort, Nimiq lets you choose where file downloads are saved, how often Nimiq should check for new files to download, and how long to keep the downloaded podcasts.

Figure 2.20

Despite its simplicity, Nimiq has plenty of useful features.

Nimiq doesn't interact directly with iTunes, and it doesn't have a media player built in; however, it is more than capable of playing your podcasts through Windows Media Player (**Figure 2.21**). It goes without saying that you need not use WMP to play the podcasts; indeed, you can simply save the podcast files to a specific directory and then move them manually to an MP3 player whenever necessary.

Figure 2.21

Windows Media Player (WMP) is the default player for Nimiq's downloaded podcasts and other audio or video files.

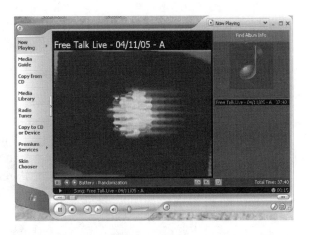

In summary, Nimiq is a fine podcast aggregator, but if you are using an iPod and iTunes, it will behoove you to look at other programs, such as iPodder 2.0 and HappyFish.

Microsoft .NET Framework 1.1

Microsoft's .NET Framework is a *development environment* (a set of tools that allows programmers to develop software) that allows different programming languages to work together to improve the way in which Windows-based software works for the end user. The .NET Framework is a collection of five kinds of development tools: Web services, client-to-server, service-to-service, server-to-server, and client-to-client tools.

Entire books have been written about the .NET Framework, but for the purposes of this book, you simply need to know that this Windows tool helps such disparate devices and concepts as cell phones and podcasts come together through software running on a Windows-based PC. The result is fantastic pieces of software (like the ones I'm examining here) that improve your interaction and experiences with the Internet and World Wide Web, as well as any electronic devices you may connect to them.

Now Playing

Required Software: iTunes or Windows Media Player
OS Requirement: Windows 2000 or XP
Price: Freeware

Designed by Brandon Fuller, Now Playing (**Figure 2.22**) is a podcast aggregator that is distinctly different from the others in that it is not a stand-alone program, but a plug-in for Windows Media Player or an iTunes PC. A *plug-in* is an add-on program that requires the presence of another program to function. Plug-ins are usually designed specifically to add features or functionality to a particular program, and Now Playing is no exception to this rule.

Figure 2.22

As a plug-in rather than a stand-alone program, Now Playing isn't fancy, but it gets the job done.

One excellent feature of Now Playing is that it also acts as a podcast server, getting podcasts (or other audio files) you've made out to the kind folks on the Internet.

Because Now Playing is an iTunes plug-in, any podcasts that are downloaded are placed directly in iTunes and then on your iPod. Entering feeds in Now Playing is a breeze. When you start iTunes after installing Now Playing, a prompt shows up with a panel that allows you to enter the feeds for your favorite podcasts and set the parameters for checking those feeds (**Figure 2.23**). One of the unique features of Now Playing is the Amazon tab, which allows you to connect with one of Amazon.com's Web sites to coordinate album art and other data.

Figure 2.23

Podcast feeds are added in this window.

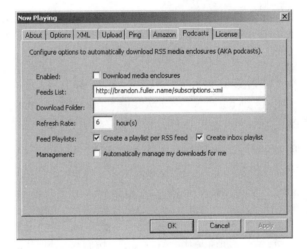

Because Apple's iPod has swept through the world and has become the dominant digital music device, many users rely on iTunes to manage their MP3 collections. Still, there are many who have not joined the iPod generation, and for those folks, Now Playing also exists as a plug-in for Windows Media Player.

Interview with Now Playing Creator Brandon Fuller

Brandon Fuller, the author of Now Playing, is also a software engineer with Cisco Systems. Visit him online at http://brandon.fuller.name/.

Farkas: What was the genesis of Now Playing? Why did you feel the need to create it?

Fuller: Many users desire to have their blogs be more interactive. Some users add webcams, while others add information about the weather in their area. It's fun to add these live personal data feeds to your site so that some of your content is always fresh. Obviously, you wouldn't write a blog post every 5 minutes that says what the weather is!

Since music is such a passion for people, the idea of posting what audio you are listening to just makes sense. Now Playing started out as a way to show people what was currently playing on your computer. As podcasting came about, I saw a great fit inside Now Playing. Given that it's already a media player plug-in, why not have it do some work so that you have more content that you can listen to and then share the fact that you are listening to it? With podcasts (as opposed to copyrighted music), you can actually post a link to the content so others can see it and download it themselves.

Farkas: Was there a specific plan to have Now Playing fit into a particular part of the market, or were you just trying to fill a need?

Fuller: A bit of both, actually. Now Playing is different in that it works inside your media player. I found that this was a great fit because it gave an integrated experience. Competitors have developed podcasting clients that are stand-alone, and they now find themselves building media players inside those clients. Instead of doing that, I chose to leverage the world-class media players from companies like Apple and Microsoft and to attach to those, thus reversing the process.

Farkas: Has the rise of the podcasting phenomenon surprised you?

Fuller: Not really. This has been going on for quite some time in various degrees. It's nice to see the Internet continuing to change distribution models.

Farkas: What do you see for podcasting in the next year? In the next five years?

(continued on next page)

Interview with Now Playing Creator Brandon Fuller *(continued)*

Fuller: The problem in podcasting land is the content. Initially, I found myself listening to all kinds of podcasts just because I could. Now that I have started to cut back due to time, I haven't found as many podcasts that I feel I need to keep up with regularly.

Farkas: Did you have the creation and syndication of podcasts in mind specifically when you designed Now Playing?

Fuller: No. Now Playing was designed a year before podcasting was around. I added podcasting abilities once podcasting started catching on.

Farkas: What is in the future for Now Playing?

Fuller: I have about 1,000 registered users, and they are always sending me ideas on things they would like to see.

Farkas: What MP3 player do you personally use?

Fuller: iTunes.

PlayPod
Required Software: None
OS Requirement: Mac OS X
Price: Free trial, then $16.99

Designed specifically for Mac OS X, PlayPod is a very slick, powerful podcast aggregator and news reader that is an excellent choice for newbies and experts alike.

One of the most impressive features of PlayPod is its built-in tutorial, Getting Started with PlayPod (**Figure 2.24**). This mini-tutorial covers the main bases of podcasting's background and function, making it easy for first-time users to get a handle on the key concepts involved in this new medium.

Figure 2.24

Although it's not an in-depth course on podcasting, the built-in tutorial is very helpful to users who are just exploring what pod-casting has to offer.

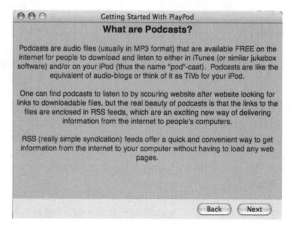

PlayPod comes with an easy-to-use master window that includes three main windows: a general directory window, a directory file window, and a media player window that functions as both a media player and a source of information for the individual podcast that has been selected. **Figure 2.25** shows the PlayPod master window in action, with Adam Curry's "Daily Source Code" playing in the background.

Figure 2.25

Like other polished aggregators, PlayPod is as easy on the eyes as it is to operate and enjoy.

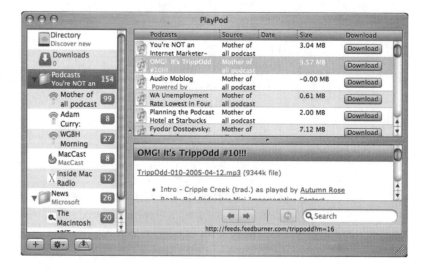

PocketRSS
Required Software: None
OS Requirement: Windows Mobile
Price: Free trial, then $5.95

PocketRSS (**Figure 2.26**) is an aggregator for Pocket PCs that was designed by HappyJackRoad, a company that has been around since 2001. PocketRSS (up to Version 2.0.18 at this writing) is a Today Screen plug-in and stand-alone application that allows the movement of podcasts and other RSS data to the Today Screen. (Those with Pocket PCs will know what that means.)

A solid aggregator for Pocket PC users, PocketRSS offers the following features:

Figure 2.26
PocketRSS is a solid choice for Pocket PC users who want access to advanced options.

- Simple RSS feed content management

- Namespace/XML mapping features for advanced users

- Full feed item control

- Ability to download when connected to Internet and store for offline viewing/listening at a later date

Pod2Go

Required Software: None
OS Requirement: Mac OS X 10.2.7 or later
Price: Free with registration

Pod2Go is a podcast aggregator, but it's also much more. Pod2Go includes feeds for a wide range of other handy information that is available on the World Wide Web through RSS. In fact, when you first run Pod2Go, there will likely be a moment of shock when you see all of the things it can do. The list includes:

- News

- Weather

- Movie times

- Stocks

- Horoscopes

- Lyrics

- Text

- Driving directions (**Figure 2.27**)

- Applications

- Backups

- Podcasts

- Launcher, a built-in utility that makes it easy to open applications and documents from inside Pod2Go

Figure 2.27

Talk about versatility! Among other things, Pod2Go offers driving directions.

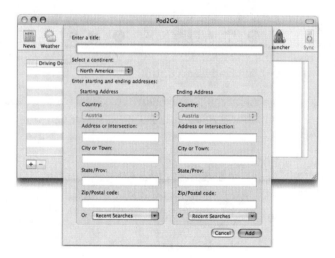

Pod2Go is truly an amazing piece of software, with everything you need built right in. In fact, the only thing you really need to make Pod2Go sing is a broadband Internet connection.

Many people have speculated about where podcasting will go in the future, and although that is open for debate, the future of podcast aggregators is here with Pod2Go (**Figure 2.28**), because there is just so much available information funneling through one place. If getting information other than podcasts turns you off, I recommend that you steer clear of Pod2Go. But if you want to have access to the maximum amount of data and services, this piece of software is worth a closer look.

Figure 2.28

As a podcast aggregator, Pod2Go works very well.

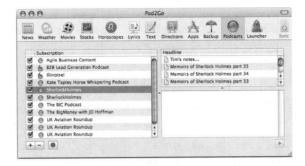

PoddumFeeder

Required Software: None

OS Requirement: Mac OS X 10.3

Price: $4.95

NOTE The $4.95 is a suggested donation to If Then software. If you do not donate this small amount of money, you are limited to subscribing to three podcasts.

PoddumFeeder (**Figure 2.29**) is a straight-up, Macintosh-only podcast aggregator. It is very simple to install and use, and has most of the features we have come to expect from quality software.

Figure 2.29

PoddumFeeder is a quality Macintosh aggregator.

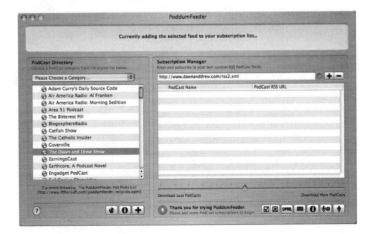

As a bonus, PoddumFeeder has a couple of unique features that allow
it to stand out from the crowd a little. The first of these features allows
you to e-mail a podcast. When you click the Email a Podcast URL
button, you can send podcast feed URLs directly to your friends
without having to leave the cozy confines of PoddumFeeder's interface.
The other handy feature is a long slider bar labeled Download Fewer
Podcasts at one end and Download More Podcasts at the other end. By
moving this slider, you can adjust the number of podcasts that will be
downloaded from each particular feed. Although not particularly
concrete, it's an easy-to-use, enjoyable feature.

Starting with iPodder on the Mac

After you have downloaded iPodder onto your Mac, click the iPodder
icon (it looks like a fresh lemon), and the program will be installed on
your Mac. When you run iPodder, you will automatically be connected
with a couple of welcome messages, including one from Adam Curry
himself. To get started with iPodder, you can click the Subscriptions
button and then click the Add a New Feed button to enter your own
RSS feed address, as shown in **Figure 2.30**.

Figure 2.30
Add a new feed.

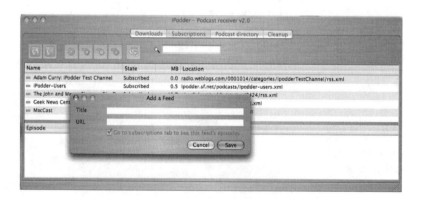

As mentioned earlier, Podcast Alley is an excellent place to find a
podcasting feed. Just click the Subscribe to Podcast link of the podcast

that interests you to see the address. **Figure 2.31** shows an example of a subscription address that has been pulled up on Podcast Alley's Web site. Once you have a feed URL cut and pasted (or typed) into the window, click the Save button to save the feed in the iPodder library.

Figure 2.31

Podcast feeds from Podcast Alley look like this.

Podcast Feed For: The MacCast
Please add the entire URL Below to your Podcast Software:

http://feeds.feedburner.com/maccast

How to Listen to this Podcast:

1. Download a Podcast Aggregator from here.
2. Copy the entire link in the box above to the "URL" or "feed" field in your software.
3. Listen to, and enjoy 1000's of Podcasts!

If you want to see the RSS or XML file, click here

Next, you can check for new content by clicking the Check for New Podcasts button (the green button with two arrows on it), and iPodder will do the rest. It will find the new podcasts; download them to your machine; and place them in iTunes (**Figure 2.32**), which will ultimately place the podcasts on your iPod the next time you connect it to your Mac to update its contents.

Figure 2.32

iPodder places podcasts directly in iTunes for you.

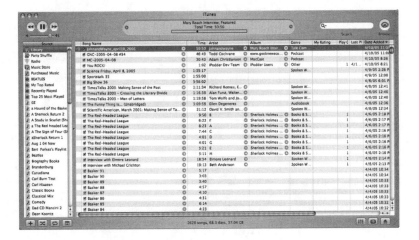

There are five separate iPodder tabs, and each has a distinct function.

The Downloads tab contains up-to-the-second information about just what is being downloaded and from where (**Figure 2.33**), whereas the Podcast Directory tab contains a series of folders with various headings (**Figure 2.34**), each of which contains a list of pertinent podcasts. You can add podcasts to the directory simply by clicking the Add button after you've entered the podcast feed URL. Not surprisingly, you can also add or remove folders and subdirectories as you see fit.

Figure 2.33
This window contains download information.

Figure 2.34
iPodder's podcast directory is impressive.

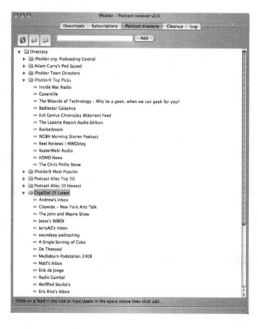

The Subscriptions tab shows you at a glance exactly what podcasts you have subscribed to and which podcasts are already being checked for new material.

The Cleanup tab is for managing files specific to each podcasting feed that you are subscribed to. This allows you to see what files are taking up space on your hard drive so that you can decide whether to keep them or turf them (**Figure 2.35**).

Figure 2.35

The cleanup window allows you to keep your hard drive free of unwanted podcasts.

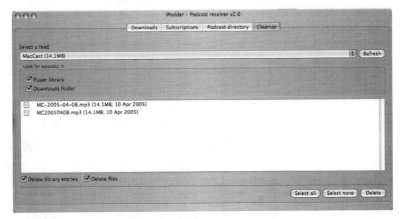

The last tab is the Log tab, which quite simply logs every action undertaken by the iPodder software. For example, if you wanted to check to see whether a particular podcast downloaded successfully, a quick look at the Log area will answer your query.

Starting with HappyFish on the PC

To begin with, ensure that your machine has Microsoft .NET Framework 1.1 before you install HappyFish. Once Microsoft .NET Framework 1.1 is installed, and you have downloaded HappyFish, you can run the installer to place it on your machine. Then start it up, and you'll see the basic program front end, shown in **Figure 2.36**. By clicking the Feed menu and dragging down to the Add Feed selection, you can add any RSS feed your heart desires. RSS feeds look just like the URLs you've come to know and love when using the World Wide Web.

Figure 2.36

HappyFish is a great place to start on Windows PCs.

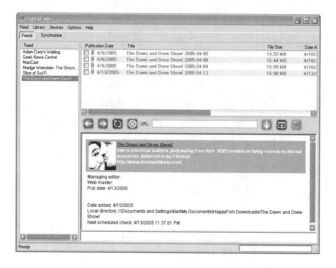

There are several fantastic reservoirs of RSS feeds, not the least of which is Podcast Alley. Find the podcasting feed that you want to use by clicking the Subscribe to Podcast link (on Podcast Alley's Web site; it may be different on other sites). To attach a feed to HappyFish (or any similar aggregator), just cut and paste the feed's URL into the Add Feed window, and voilà! As soon as you complete this task, HappyFish goes out and gets the files available from that feed, as shown in **Figure 2.37**.

Figure 2.37

Add a new podcast feed.

Next up, you can adjust how often the HappyFish software goes out and checks for new files on each feed. After you click Feed and then click Global Feed Settings (**Figure 2.38**), a window pops up, allowing you to select how often and when you want HappyFish to go looking for content. After all of your feeds are set up, you need only let HappyFish do the work while you sit back and enjoy the podcasts it brings to your electronic doorstep.

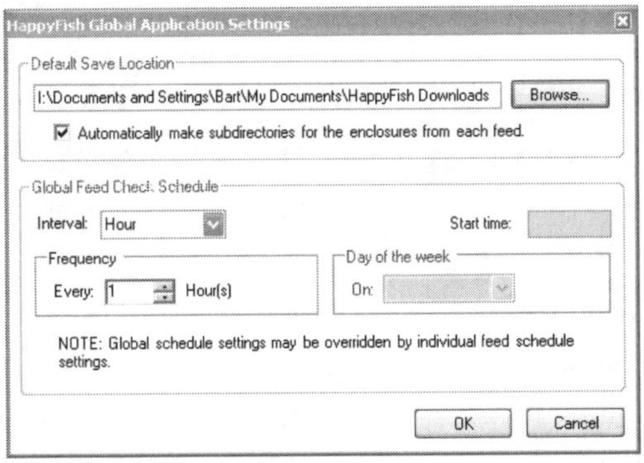

Figure 2.38

In Global Feed Settings, you can decide how often HappyFish should look for new podcasts.

Now that you've got HappyFish downloading all of the great podcasts you want to listen to, you may want to set the program up to download the podcasts automatically to your digital music player device, such as an iPod or any other MP3 player. When you click Devices and then Add Device or Device Management (**Figure 2.39**), you can configure as many digital music player devices as you want to designate as destinations where HappyFish places downloaded podcasts.

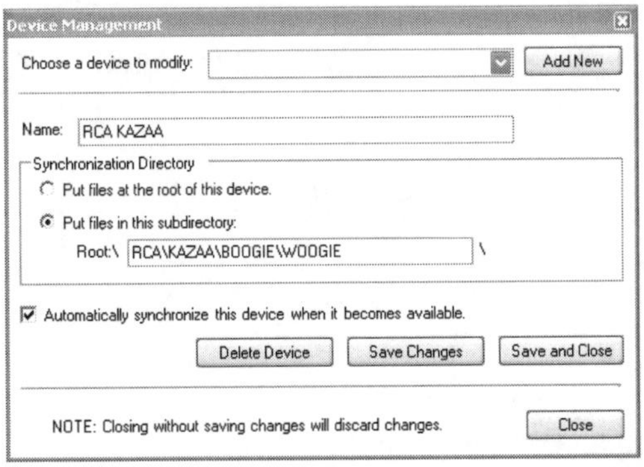

Figure 2.39

Set up HappyFish to work with your particular MP3 player.

Look Here.

Table 2.1 compares all the podcast aggregators presented in this chapter. With this table, you can establish the best aggregators for you at a glance and disregard programs that you cannot run due to the computer or OS you use.

Table 2.1: Podcast Aggregators

	OS	Extra Software Needed?	Stand-Alone Program?	Built-In Media Player?
BashPodder	Mac OS X, Linux	Yes	Yes	No
CastGrab	Linux	No	Yes	No
FeederReader	Windows Mobile	Yes	Yes	No
HappyFish	Windows	Yes	Yes	Yes
iPodder 2.0	Windows/Mac/Linux	No	Yes	Yes
iPodder X	Mac	Yes	Yes	Yes
iPodder.NET	Windows	Yes	Yes	Yes
iPodderSP/Skookum	Windows Mobile	Yes	Yes	Yes
iTunes 4.9	Mac OS X, Windows	No	Yes	Yes
jPodder	Windows, Linux	Yes	Yes	Yes
Nimiq	Windows	Yes	Yes	No
Now Playing	Windows	Yes	No	No
PlayPod	Mac	No	Yes	Yes
PocketRSS	Windows Mobile	Yes	Yes	No
Pod2Go	Mac	No	Yes	Yes
PoddumFeeder	Mac	No	Yes	Yes

Podscope: Google for podcasts

During the writing of this book, a very cool technology emerged for helping folks find the exact podcasts they want to find. You don't need a podcast aggregator to get this material; indeed, you need only a connection to the Internet and a World Wide Web browser to take advantage of this powerful tool. Podscope (www.podscope.com; **Figure 2.40**) allows you to search podcasts for specific words or phrases; then it displays the results (as shown in **Figure 2.41**) on the screen, complete with audio clips from each podcast that contains the phrase you were looking for!

Podscope is a one-stop search engine that is (currently) exclusively for podcasts. Developed by a company called TVEyes, Podscope uses proprietary technology to listen to each podcast and then convert that information to text strings that can then be searched. Currently, Podscope is available on the World Wide Web, and although it's in beta form, it is still an amazing technology that is already the best nonaggregator way to find podcasting content of all sorts.

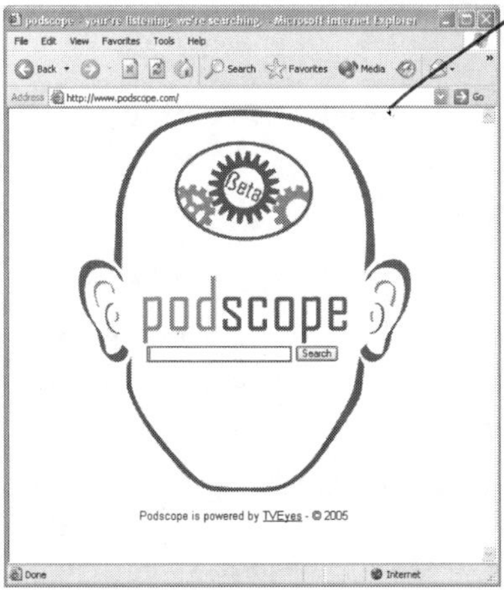

Figure 2.40

Podscope is a very powerful, easy-to-use tool for finding anything under the sun when it comes to podcast content.

Figure 2.41

When you search for a phrase on Podscope, a list of all the podcasts containing that phrase quickly appears on your screen, including short audio clips that include the spoken portions of the phrase you are looking for.

Finding Commercial Podcasts

OK, so you have used your podcast aggregator software to scour the "airwaves" of cyberspace for the content that tickles your fancy the most. But the world of so-called free podcasts is just one portion of the equation. Although some people would disagree, I'm inclined to fit audiobooks into the podcast category, as well as periodicals that are routinely converted to audio format. As mentioned in Chapter 1, Audible.com is one of the forerunners of commercial podcasting, but if you look hard enough (and often, you don't have to look very hard), you can find commercial podcasts all over the place.

Following are locations where you can purchase podcasts and audio-book materials online. Although some of the content available at these sites is free, the majority is not. The upside is that the quality of what you are getting is professional, and the price is very reasonable compared with that of traditional purchasing pathways. (Audiobooks, for example, are much cheaper online than they are in a bricks-and-mortar store.) This section takes a look at the top five Web sites/stores/locations for pay-for-play commercial podcasts and audio entertainment.

Audible.com

www.audible.com

Around since the late 1990s, Audible.com (**Figure 2.42**) is the dominant audiobook and commercial-podcast-content vendor on the World Wide Web. Audible's principal role is to supply audiobooks in MP3 format for users to listen to on their favorite MP3 players, iPods, or desktop media players. Voted one of the best sites on the Web in 2003 by CNET.com, Audible has well over 30,000 hours' worth of content for you to explore. Although most of this content has a cost associated with it, Audible offers various subscriptions that lower the effective cost of an audio-book to less than $10.

Figure 2.42

Audible.com is a great source for commercial podcasts.

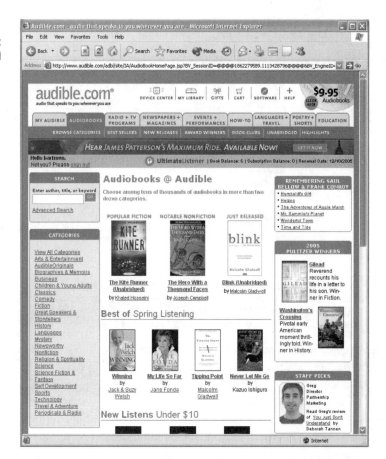

Certainly, some people would argue that commercial audiobooks are not truly podcasts, but I maintain that any audio program that can be easily downloaded and enjoyed on a digital music player such as the iPod should be considered in the same breath with so-called free podcasts. The number of available audiobooks has skyrocketed, and because the majority of them are now unabridged and often read by the author, it's hard to argue that the original content (or intent) of a book is lost in the conversion to the aural format. In fact, even though I'm an avid podcast enthusiast, I have more than 150 audiobooks on my 40 GB iPod (**Figure 2.43**).

Figure 2.43

Nearly every new mainstream book is available in audio format.

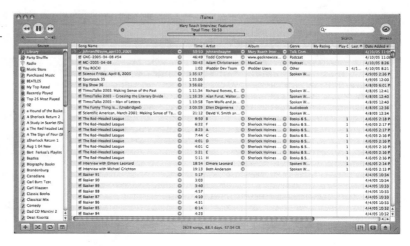

Dealing with Dead Time

I really enjoy reading magazines and books. I love to read to learn, reading magazines like *Archaeology, Discover,* and *Wired*. But I also enjoy reading to escape; there's nothing like a good fiction yarn to take me to another place for a few enjoyable hours. Once I got into my 30s, however, the amount of reading I did dropped off rather precipitously. Not very surprisingly, this dropoff coincided with the birth of my first child. The subsequent addition of two more rugrats hasn't exactly made finding a quiet corner to read any easier!

When Apple's iPod was released in 2001, and a friend introduced me to Audible.com, I realized that large swatches of my day were effectively dead time. *Dead time,* as many people define it, is time when you *could* be reading, studying, or learning if only you didn't have to concentrate on the mundane task at hand. Those mundane tasks include driving, exercising, walking anywhere, riding a bike, riding public transit, vacuuming the house, cleaning the toilets ... and the list goes on!

I got to thinking. What if I could read books and magazines during this dead time? Would I still enjoy the act of reading if someone was reading it to me via a pair of headphones? The answer to both those questions was an emphatic yes, and I am here to tell you that the arrival of this technology has allowed me to cover a large amount of ground that I would otherwise have never even set foot on. If you are like me and enjoy reading but find that your busy life is getting in the way, you can still digest a lot of material in the so-called dead time that occurs every day.

The periodicals and subscription shows better fit the traditional podcast mold, however. Indeed, the amount of podcastlike content on Audible has expanded greatly in the past year; it now includes audio versions of popular newspapers, magazines, and radio shows, and even custom-made podcasts such as the fantastically funny "RobinWilliams@Audible.com" show (**Figure 2.44**).

Figure 2.44

Robin Williams's show is exclusive to Audible.com and is absolutely hilarious. The show has a different celebrity guest every week.

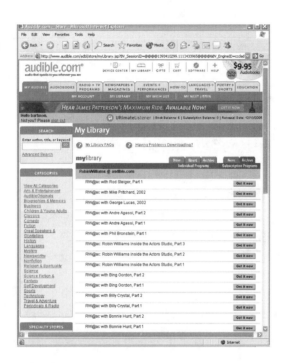

Following is just a fraction of the commercial content available on this site (and elsewhere):

- National Public Radio's "Science Friday" (weekly)

- *Science News Magazine* (weekly)

- "Charlie Rose" (television show; weekly)

- *Scientific American Magazine* (monthly)

- National Public Radio's "To the Best of Our Knowledge" (weekly)

- "SoundMoney" (syndicated radio show; weekly)

- "RobinWilliams@Audible.com" (comedy; weekly)

- *Harvard Business Review* (monthly)

- *Forbes* magazine (monthly)

- "Inside Mac Radio Show" (weekly)

- "Speaking of Faith" (weekly)

- "The Troy Aikman Show"

- "Car Talk" (weekly)

- "BBC Newshour"

iTunes Music Store

Apple's iTunes Music Store (**Figure 2.45**) opened on April 28, 2003, and in slightly more than two years since it opened, more than 300 million songs (yes, you read that correctly) have been downloaded. The store itself is now available in 15 countries, and by the time you read this book, that number will likely have grown.

Figure 2.45
The iTunes Canada Music Store. Already, 300 million music downloads have occurred, and the amount of podcast material in the store is always increasing.

Why does this matter to podcast enthusiasts? As the iTunes Music Store has evolved, an increasing number of podcast-type downloads, such as audiobooks and comedy shows, have become available for purchase and download. Although the iTunes store doesn't have the selection that Audible.com does, I suspect that this groundbreaking Web site will continue to add podcast content as the phenomenon continues to grow.

Audiobooks Online

www.audiobooksonline.com

Audiobooks Online (**Figure 2.46**) is an online merchant that sells (at this time) audiobooks only. The company claims that it will be offering audiobooks in MP3 format for download in the near future, but the one intriguing product it does sell is MP3 CDs of classic books. These files cannot be downloaded—indeed, you must have the CDs shipped to a real mailbox—but they're available for a bevy of classic titles, from Jules Verne's *20,000 Leagues Under the Sea* to Leo Tolstoy's *Anna Karenina*.

Figure 2.46

Audiobooks Online is a source for classic audiobooks.

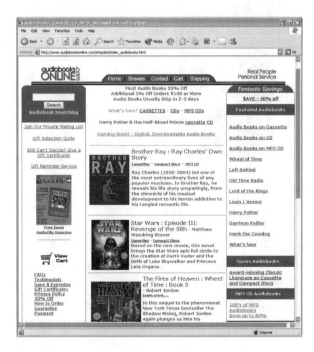

Blackstone Audiobooks

www.blackstoneaudio.com

Another of the audiobook Web sites, Blackstone Audiobooks (**Figure 2.47**) is unique in that it is an actual producer of audiobook content. You'll find a fair amount of crossover between what is available on Audible.com and what's on BlackstoneAudio.com. Still, this is another good source for audiobooks that are available for immediate download to your digital media player.

Figure 2.47

Many newly released audiobooks are published by Blackstone Audio.

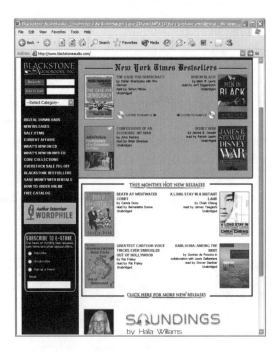

Satellite radio

www.xmsatelliteradio.com and www.siriusradio.com

Satellite radio is a novel approach to broadcasting radio. The idea is that a satellite receiver in a home or car gains access to potentially hundreds of radio stations, in categories ranging from classical to children's programming to up-to-date traffic reports around the clock! This service has caught on and now boasts more than 3 million subscribers.

Currently, two satellite radio providers are available: XM Satellite Radio and Sirius Satellite Radio.

Like any radio service, however, satellite radio is broadcast live at particular times, making it entirely possible for busy professionals to miss the programming they desire. Not to worry—both XM and Sirius supply streaming podcasts of most of their key shows (**Figure 2.48**), but this is not a free service. If you are already a satellite-radio subscriber, however, the service is included in your fees.

Figure 2.48
XM Satellite Radio offers subscribers live podcast feeds of many of its most popular shows.

 Sirius Satellite Radio recently announced that it is entering the Canadian market, in conjunction with CBC/Radio-Canada. Now Canadians will also be able to get satellite radio!

Finding Free Commercial Podcasts

It has been said that the best things in life are free, and when one looks at the vast array of commercial radio shows and other content available as podcasts at no cost, the old saying may just be true after all.

As the phenomenon of podcasting continues to take hold in the general population, there is increasing pressure for producers to make their shows available online, so that they can stay connected to their core audience. Indeed, doing so may even help expand their audience. At any rate, publishing shows as podcasts on their Web sites won't hurt their ratings!

AudioBooksForFree.com

AudioBooksForFree.com (**Figure 2.49**) is a place where you can grab audiobooks in MP3 format for absolutely no cost whatsoever. How is this possible? The answer lies in the fact that all the books available on this Web site have expired copyrights. Before you become despondent

Figure 2.49

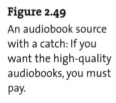

An audiobook source with a catch: If you want the high-quality audiobooks, you must pay.

with disappointment, remember that many fantastic classic pieces of fiction can be had for no cost at all, including works by Mark Twain and Edgar Allan Poe, and AudioBooksForFree.com is an excellent resource.

The catch with this Web site is that the quality of the free books is not exactly what you would be willing to pay for. In other words, there is a reason why it is free. The free books sound like they are coming out of a telephone, but for a small charge of between $3 and $6, you can get high-quality versions of the same books. Either way, it's worth it to see whether the "free" audio quality is bearable enough for you to enjoy.

National Public Radio

National Public Radio in the United States (**Figure 2.50**) is a prime example of free podcasts that are available to the public. Currently, all of the content available for free from NPR is available only as streaming content (audio that streams directly for play on a computer-based media player), but hey, it's free! Many NPR shows are available for a small charge on Audible.com as well, if you are interested in obtaining a self-contained podcast of a particular show.

Figure 2.50

NPR is a pioneer in podcasting, making many of its shows available via this route.

NPR is an excellent example of radio-show content that is made available to the public so that people can listen to specific shows at their leisure. Ideally, NPR shows will be available someday as downloadable podcasts rather than just as streaming content, but beggars can't be choosers.

To listen to an NPR podcast, you need either the RealAudio media player or Windows Media Player (**Figure 2.51**).

Figure 2.51

NPR's podcasts are of the streaming variety.

Canadian Broadcasting Corporation (CBC)

The Canadian Broadcasting Corporation (CBC) has jumped on the podcasting bandwagon, offering podcasts of several of its radio programs, not the least of which is Tod Maffin's "/Nerd" show (**Figure 2.52**).

Figure 2.52

The RSS feed page for Tod Maffin's "/Nerd" show on CBC Radio Canada.

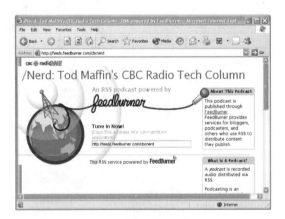

The CBC is a large radio and television network that arguably is the glue that holds the large country of Canada together. Like NPR, the CBC is publicly funded, and as such, the podcasts are available for no cost. The up side to the CBC's adoption of this technology is that Canadians living around the world can keep up on happenings in their home country.

Interview with Tod Maffin

Tod Maffin is an international authority on the future of technology in business and media. He speaks to more than 30 conferences around the world each year. Today, he is the national technology columnist for CBC Television's "Canada Now," as well as a national CBC radio host and producer. I caught up with him in Vancouver.

Farkas: When did you first become aware of podcasting?

Maffin: It was pretty quick. Within a couple of weeks of Adam Curry launching "Daily Source Code" and the iPodder client, I was following the developments with interest.

Farkas: When this happened, did you immediately start forming a master plan for podcasting with regard to your work?

Maffin: Right away. I was in our den in our house, and when I learned about it, I went running into the living room and said to my wife, "I've just found the most incredible technology. It's going to revolutionize radio."

Farkas: Was the idea of podcasting your show on CBC a hard sell?

Maffin: The mandate of CBC is to reflect Canada to Canadians, so we want to do as much as we can do of that, and if podcasting is emerging as a trend, then it behooves us to embrace it. There is cost involved with podcasting, so we're still trying to figure out a cost-effective balance, but since I was already working on a technology column, it made sense to podcast it.

Farkas: How do you think podcasting has expanded your show's audience? Has it?

Maffin: I think it has the potential to expand to a different demographic. Usually, public radio tends to be strong in the upper age demographic. For example, CBC historically is stronger in the 40-plus age range than they are in the under-40 age range, and podcasting helps to open up an entirely new demographic. I think the young people think of public radio as their parents' radio, but if we can deliver it in a medium that they are used to, we can reach them in ways we couldn't before. It is potentially a great way to introduce a younger audience to really intelligent discourse, and secondly, I think it's a way to extend the brand of the public broadcaster.

Farkas: Where do you see podcasting taking the medium of public radio? What effect do you see it having?

continued on next page

Interview with Tod Maffin *(continued)*

Maffin: I think it definitely will have an effect. There are a number of places right now, such as Virgin Radio in the UK, where they strip out all of the music and commercials of a four-hour morning show and podcast just the DJs talking. The result is like a well-produced 45-minute comedy show. If you can take that stripped-down 40- to 45-minute show and present it as what is essentially a marketing endeavor, then I think it's an incredible opportunity for private radio.

Currently, I am consulting with Australia's public broadcasting service, and they have incredible content that's absolutely perfect for podcasting. It's amazing, the kind of content that's out there and how well it fits into the podcasting paradigm. Public radio has 4-minute documentaries, 12-minute packs; their programming is incredible material for podcasting.

Farkas: Do you envision radio moving toward having everything available in podcast format?

Maffin: Absolutely. Why should broadcasters spend money on terrestrial transmitters and regulation from their country's broadcast regulator when they can produce content and distribute it electronically? Every public radio broadcaster from the BBC to the CBC is governed by an act of parliament or government, so they must by definition broadcast in terrestrial radio, but that doesn't mean that they can't offer value-added services in the form of podcasts. Imagine if we could take an award-winning documentary in one country and make it available via podcast to the entire world. This technology will allow the dissemination of fantastic content into countries and across borders in ways that were previously not possible.

Farkas: Is there anything else you want to add?

Maffin: Every single art form—whether it's painting, sculpting, writing—every art form has its moment of revolution. This is radio's moment of revolution. When you think about it, radio hasn't had a moment of revolution; the basic design that Marconi came up with is still being employed today. The realization comes when radio stations realize that they don't just broadcast over radio waves, but they also produce content—content that can be distributed in an ever-increasing number of ways via podcasting.

Internet radio

Internet radio (shown in Windows Media Player in **Figure 2.53**) is a form of streaming audio by which traditional radio stations from around the world broadcast on the Internet for anyone to listen. With hundreds of stations from all over the planet, Internet radio can make for some very interesting listening sessions. Want to listen to a pop radio station from London, England, or possibly want to hear about traffic in Moscow? Internet radio is the medium for you!

Figure 2.53

Internet radio opens the entire world to your ears. As long as you have a connection to the 'net, you're in.

Some would argue that Internet radio is also a form of podcasting, but because Internet radio involves live streaming audio, it is not podcasting per se. That said, there are software packages available, such as Replay Radio (www.replay-radio.com; **Figure 2.54**), that allow you to record any Internet radio show and then turn it into an MP3 file for download to your iPod or other digital music device. At $29.95, the software isn't inexpensive, but if you are a big fan of the programming available on Internet radio, it will be money well spent.

Figure 2.54

Replay Radio is one of the software options for turning Internet radio broadcasts into podcasts.

Radio stations everywhere

Like NPR in the United States and CBC in Canada, radio stations and networks everywhere are starting to jump on the podcast bandwagon and are increasingly making content available for download. One of the countless examples is from CHUM Radio in Toronto (**Figure 2.55**). CHUM Radio recently started podcasting its "Roger, Rick, and Marilyn" morning show so that commuters who may have missed the show in the morning can download it at work and listen to it on the drive home.

Figure 2.55

Radio stations everywhere are turning to podcasts to keep connected to their audience.

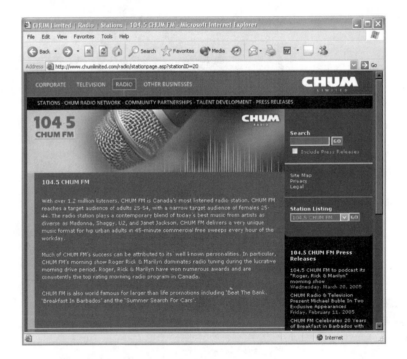

This is just one small example of how radio stations are turning to podcasts to reach and expand their audiences. After all, people who work an evening shift would not normally be out of bed in time to listen to a morning show. But if that morning show is available via podcast, they can catch the show on their way to work in the afternoon via their iPod (or other device). If you have a favorite radio program that you can't always listen to, check to see whether a podcast is available for it. You never know.

The First Radio Station to Go All-Podcast

In the spring of 2005, KYCY-AM announced that it would become the first terrestrial radio station to broadcast an all-podcast format. Now, this doesn't mean that the radio broadcast tower will be torn down and all the content will be distributed over the Internet. In this case, the actual *content* will be podcasts, which will be distributed over the old-fashioned radio airwaves.

With a 3-tower array and 10,000 watts of broadcasting power, KYCY-AM will be broadcasting under the name KYOURadio (**Figure 2.56**). All the content will be available as streaming content and podcasts on the World Wide Web as well, so for those hard-core podcasters who refuse to tune into a radio station, the content will still be there in the format they have embraced with such zeal.

Figure 2.56

KYCY-AM is converting to KYOURadio, an all-podcast radio station in the Bay Area.

The implications of KYCY's move are far-reaching. This announcement means that amateur podcasters have a legitimate chance to be broadcast on a traditional radio station, but it also means that the content of those podcasts will have to conform to Federal Communications Commission rules and regulations, the lack of which has been part of podcasting's appeal. It's an interesting experiment that you can check out at www.kyouradio.com.

Griffin radio SHARK

In the past five or six years, the DVR (digital video recorder) concept has become reality in hundreds of thousands of homes across North America. DVRs, better known by the name TiVo, allow users to pause, rewind, and fast-forward live television. TiVo units (and their cousins) also allow users to record programs very easily, capturing entire seasons of a show with only a few button clicks. The popularity of TiVo has been so significant that network advertising reps are shaking in their boots!

With the DVR revolution sweeping through Televisionland, you may have wondered why it hasn't swept through Radioland as well. A new product from Griffin Technology (www.griffintechnology.com) called the radio SHARK has changed all that. The radio SHARK (**Figure 2.57**) allows time-shifted recording of AM and FM radio signals from your area—that is to say that you can listen to, record, and pause live radio from your listening area.

The radio SHARK, which works on both Macintosh and Windows computers, talks directly to iTunes, turning any new recordings into podcasts that appear in your iTunes window. This is extremely handy; I use mine a great deal to capture local radio shows that I would otherwise not be able to catch. The show is recorded, and within a few seconds, it is transferred to iTunes to be updated onto your iPod during the next update.

Figure 2.57
The radio SHARK from Griffin Technology is an awesome podcast-creating tool.

The radio SHARK is extremely flexible. It can be set up to record radio shows one at a time, daily, and even weekly, as shown in **Figure 2.58**. The software is easy to use and flexible enough to ensure that all the content you want to capture gets captured. The only limitation to the radio SHARK is that you cannot record two programs at the same time. That said, I love mine and recommend it to the world.

Figure 2.58
The radio SHARK software allows you to select which shows to record.

Finding Educational Podcasts

It doesn't take a college grad to see that podcasting can easily play a role in improving education. After all, having an entire semester's worth of lectures available as podcasts could greatly improve a student's chances on the final exam.

In Chapter 1, I speculated about the future of podcasting and how it might affect education in years to come, but Duke University in North Carolina is already deeply involved in podcasting (**Figure 2.59**).

Figure 2.59

Duke University has leaped to the forefront in educational podcasting, giving an iPod to every freshman during the 2003–04 school year.

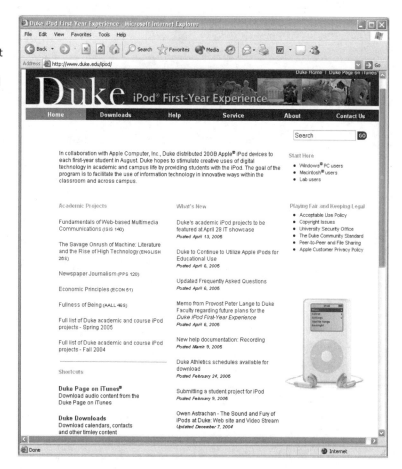

Duke made headlines in the 2003-04 school year by purchasing iPods for every freshman student. These iPods were distributed with an iMic (an iPod accessory that allows for recording, much like an old-fashioned tape recorder) so that students could record lectures as they saw fit. Other classes had lectures recorded as podcasts made available through a special Duke University page on Apple's iTunes Music Store!

This concept intrigued me so much that I contacted Professor Richard Lucic, associate chair of the Department of Computer Science at Duke University, and asked him about this pioneering podcasting project.

Farkas: What was the genesis of Duke's iPod program?

Lucic: It was an outgrowth from discussions that the Information Sciences and Information Studies Program at Duke was conducting with Apple to explore incorporating technology in the classroom. The iPod idea came up during these discussions, and was expanded to a campuswide program.

Farkas: In a nutshell, how does Duke's program work? Are there microphones in every class so that each lecture is recorded and then turned into a podcast at a central location? Also, are computers supplied for students to download the pertinent podcasts to their iPods?

Lucic: This first year, all freshmen were given iPods, but faculty could also make a request to have any course designated an official iPod course, with loaner iPods given to all students. The freshmen get to keep them; the others have to return them at the end of the class. Students were given an iMic in addition to the iPod so that they could record lectures. Duke's Center for Instructional Technology (CIT) would, on request, come and make a recording of the class, but I think most faculty just made the recordings themselves. Duke made a site available to upload class audio content, and Apple also made a Duke-specific iTunes portal available.

Farkas: What has the impact of this program been in terms of both objective data and subjective feedback? Have the students taken well to this new educational medium?

Lucic: Apparently, the response from both students and faculty was very positive. Duke concluded that incorporating the iPod technology into the classroom did in fact enhance the learning experience. The faculty of the official iPod classes were required to provide feedback from surveys or other vehicles used to poll the students and instructors. Several round-table discussions with faculty and with students were also conducted to assess the subjective feedback. A couple of the key conclusions of the experiment are that the iPods made learning portable, reaching beyond the confines of the classroom; increased student enthusiasm and work quality; and facilitated the learning process.

Farkas: What is the current status of the iPod/podcast project?

Lucic: They feel the program has been expanded, no longer being limited to freshmen. Any class, including graduate classes, can now be eligible for iPod use designation. In the expanded program, called Duke Digital Initiative, Duke will also experiment with other classroom technology in addition to the iPod, such as tablet computing, digital video, and collaboration technologies. For example, we have currently installed a system called iLecture in three classrooms to assess its ability to automatically audio- and video-record a class session at high quality

Farkas: How do you see the concept and implementation of podcasting affecting education in the future? Are there any ideal educational paradigms that podcasting can help educators move toward?

Lucic: One use I am very excited about is giving students audio assignments in place of written reports. I have found that field-recorded notes are much superior when the students use the iPod versus hand-written notes. Another experiment I conducted was to replace written research reports with assignments to record a group (four students) discussion of the research subject. In both cases, I found the work superior to that in old-style written reports.

Farkas: What has the inclusion of podcasting meant to you personally as an educator?

Lucic: It has meant an increase in class-preparation overhead. It takes planning to incorporate iPods effectively. Audio files must be processed and uploaded. I found I had to listen to audio assignments at least a couple times before I felt capable of grading them, and grading itself is an issue, because I did not have a paper report to write on. I eventually concluded that I would record my grading remarks and e-mail them to the students. Even with this increased overhead, I feel the improvement in the learning environment has made the effort worthwhile.

Farkas: Have there been any surprising results from the podcasting experiment?

Lucic: I think something that surprised the students the most was when they realized that they could turn "dead time" (like commuting) into productive learning time. Another thing they really came to appreciate was the ability to re-review a lecture in preparation for a test and report assignment. They eventually stopped taking notes during lectures and paid more attention to the speaker.

The biggest surprise for faculty and Duke admin was the wide variety of classes that participated in the iPod experiment. I think the initial perception was that audio-based classes, such as music or languages, would be naturals, but we found that very positive uses of the iPods occurred in engineering, environmental sciences, computer science, etc.

Podcasting specifically is a very exciting technology for education. Because it automates course-content delivery and student response to supplied content, I find that there is much more interaction between students. In the past, the paradigm was essentially a one-way transfer of knowledge from instructor to student. The new paradigm involves the student much more actively in the learning process and brings a new student-to-student learning process into play. Students like podcasting. They relate to it in ways similar to instant messaging. I think there is definitely an important role for it in education.

Farkas: Are there any limitations of podcasts that you have noticed?

Lucic: About the only thing that comes to mind is the quality issue. Podcasts of poor quality are going to turn off students. I have invested in pro audio hardware and hardware to ensure that the audio I podcast is of as good a quality as possible. Listeners tire very quickly when the audio is not of good quality. I also make this equipment available to students so that they can respond to course podcasts with their own good-quality podcasts.

Listening to Podcasts

So now you know where to find and how to obtain your podcasts. How are you going to listen to them? Several options are available to you, depending on what software you are using. First, if you are using a program with a built-in media player, you can enjoy the podcasts on your PC using said player. If you want to use a digital music device, such as an iPod or a Nomad, you must get the podcast downloaded onto your player. There are many ways to do both, as you'll see in this section.

Software-based (computer) players

For those who like to listen to their podcasts directly on their home (or work) computers, a software-based media player is the answer. If the podcast aggregator you are using does not include a built-in media player, and you are not using a program like Apple's iTunes for Mac or PC, you will need to ensure that you have some other form of media player installed on your computer so that you can to listen to the podcasts at they arrive.

Many media players are available in cyberspace. Just about every sound card ever made comes with a media player, as do most video cards, be they from Matrox, NVidia, or ATI. In fact, there are so many media players for Windows-based machines that I could write an entire book on them. Not to worry—despite the vast array of media players floating around, the ubiquity (and utility) of the "big three" means that I need to discuss only those three options: Windows Media Player, RealPlayer, and QuickTime.

Windows Media Player (WMP)

www.microsoft.com/windows/windowsmedia/default.aspx
Operating System: Windows, Macintosh

Windows Media Player is the default media player from Microsoft Corporation (**Figure 2.60**). Because the vast majority of home PCs run Windows software, this means that nearly everyone has Windows Media Player (or some version of it) installed. Because this software is free, updates for it can be downloaded at no cost so that users can keep up to date with the latest advances in media-player technology.

Figure 2.60

The current version of Windows Media Player is available at Microsoft's Web site for free.

The current version of this software is Windows Media Player 10 (**Figure 2.61**), which is available for download at Microsoft's Web site. Windows Media Player can play MP3 files, video files, picture slide shows, and Internet radio, making it a fantastic one-stop basic media player. Of course, don't forget that WMP also plays compact discs, DVD movies, audio DVDs, and MP3 CDs. For Windows users, I recommend Windows Media Player if for no other reason than that you probably already have it on your machine.

Figure 2.61

Windows Media Player 10 in action.

NOTE If you update your Windows software regularly with the Automatic Update feature, your version of Windows Media Player will most likely be current.

RealPlayer

www.real.com

Operating System: Windows, Macintosh, Unix/Linux

RealPlayer (**Figure 2.62**) is the main cog in RealNetworks' wheel. First released in 1995, RealPlayer has long been a favorite of many users, and it arguably has driven many of the innovations in media players. The latest version of RealPlayer, Version 10.5, can play CDs, DVDs, audio DVDs, video, and audio, and also allows users to burn CDs. As a bonus, RealPlayer has a TiVo-like feature that allows you to buffer streaming content, like Internet radio broadcasts. If you dislike Windows Media Player and feel like being closer to the cutting edge, RealPlayer is a good choice.

Figure 2.62
RealNetworks'
RealPlayer is a very
respectable media
player.

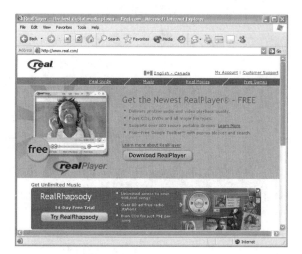

 NOTE The complaints with regard to RealPlayer revolve around the playback quality of the media (although this is entirely a matter of taste and opinion) and the installation process. If you want to get the latest and greatest from RealNetworks, for example, you must pay for it. We're not against this, but compared with WMP's free status, there are decisions to be made: cutting-edge technology versus cost.

QuickTime

www.apple.com/quicktime

Operating System: Macintosh, Windows

The granddaddy of all media players, QuickTime (**Figure 2.63**) is Apple's entry into the media-player sweepstakes. Introduced in late 1991, QuickTime has evolved and constantly pushed the envelope in doing so. Today, QuickTime is the media player of choice for movie studios when they want to put their trailers out on the World Wide Web. Indeed, QuickTime boasts the highest quality of any of the media players.

Figure 2.63

QuickTime is what the movie studios use when they put their trailers out on the 'net.

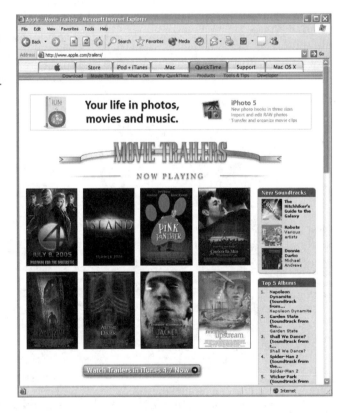

Perhaps the biggest bonus that QuickTime offers is that it is seamlessly integrated into iTunes. Because the majority of digital music devices are iPods, it makes sense that iTunes and QuickTime will be oft-used software in the world of podcasting. The basic version of QuickTime is free (**Figure 2.64**), and it does everything a podcast enthusiast needs. The other main factor with QuickTime is quality, and although this is open for debate, few people will dispute that QuickTime is the hands-down winner when it comes to image and sound quality.

Figure 2.64

QuickTime's dynamic Web page.

MP3 players

Although you can listen to podcasts on your computer, the main thrust of the podcasting movement is to make podcasts portable, allowing them to be played on iPods and other digital music devices, including SmartPhones and PDAs. There are more digital music players, SmartPhones, and PDAs on the market than you can shake a stick at, so I will stick to the top one or two in each category to give you an idea of what is out there and what the feature sets are.

Before I delve into examining various digital music players, however, I need to point out the utter dominance of Apple's iPod. At this writing, the hard-drive-based iPods had more than 80 percent of the market in North America, and with the flash-memory-based iPod shuffles selling like hotcakes, it is reasonable to assume that the flash-based market will fall to Apple as well. Currently, Apple controls more than 65 percent of the total digital music player (MP3 player) market, so I'd be remiss if I didn't focus heavily on these players.

Please note that although I have included prices for the MP3 players in this section, the market change so frequently that both prices and model features are likely to have changed (and improved) by the time you read this book. This section is intended just to give you a feel for what's out there.

iPod

Photo courtesy of Apple Computer, Inc.

Manufacturer: Apple (www.apple.com)
Price: $299
Memory Type: Hard drive
Memory Size: 20 GB (5,000 songs)
Weight: 5.6 ounces
Screen: Yes
Battery: Internal/rechargeable
OS Compatibility: Macintosh, Windows

This is the unit that started it all. The original 5 GB iPods, however, are long gone from store shelves, replaced by fourth-generation machines that have been refined considerably. At this writing, there is only one iPod proper for sale: the 20 GB model. The U2 Special Edition 20 GB iPod can still be had, but there is no doubt that before long, it will no longer be available.

With a very easy-to-use interface that has been copied by its competition, the iPod combines impressive styling with user-friendly features that have propelled it to the top of the heap. The basic features of the iPod are:

- Built-in calendar, clock, games

- The ability to make playlists on the fly

- Simple, elegant menu system

- Easy-to-use, multifunction touch wheel

- Rechargeable built-in battery

- Easy plug-and-play compatibility with iTunes on Windows and Macintosh computers

- Full integration with Apple's iTunes Music Store (in conjunction with iTunes)

- Storage of text files so that the iPod can be used like a PDA for retrieving addresses and other information

- FireWire and USB 2.0 connectivity

- Compatibility with Audible.com

- Full-function wired remote control

- Capability to be used as a hard drive on Mac and Windows computers

iPod photo

Photo courtesy of Apple Computer, Inc.

Manufacturer: Apple (www.apple.com)
Price: $349/$449
Memory Type: Hard drive
Memory Size: 30 GB (7,500 songs)/60 GB (15,000 songs)
Weight: 5.9 ounces/6.4 ounces
Screen: Yes (color)
Battery: Internal/rechargeable
OS Compatibility: Macintosh, Windows

The iPod photo is an iPod with the added benefit of a color screen and the ability to store thousands of photographs (in digital form) as well as music on the iPod's hard drive. Before you scratch your head wondering why anyone would want to combine these two things, let me point out that the ability to listen to music while a slide show of your latest vacation pictures zips by is surprisingly compelling and enjoyable. With the video/audio output cable, the iPod photo can be turned into a portable slide-show machine, displaying pictures while serenading viewers with music of the operator's choice.

The iPod photo can hold up to 60 GB—more than enough to store a couple hundred CDs and a few thousand of your favorite pictures.

iPod mini

Manufacturer: Apple (www.apple.com)
Price: $199/$249
Memory Type: Hard drive
Memory Size: 4 GB (1,000 songs) /6 GB (1,500 songs)
Weight: 3.6 ounces
Screen: Yes
Battery: Internal/rechargeable
OS Compatibility: Macintosh, Windows

The iPod mini is a hard-drive-based player with a much smaller hard drive than we have come to expect from iPods. The tradeoff is that the mini is very tiny, yet still sports the backlit iPod screen and menu system that consumers have come to love.

The iPod mini is the iPod for those folks who value space above all else. Only slightly larger than a credit card (although much thicker), the iPod mini is a joy to tote around when traveling or exercising. The only limitation of the mini is its relatively small hard drive. If keeping your entire music collection on hand is important to you, the iPod mini shouldn't be your first choice. The mini, however, is the coolest digital music device, in my book.

iPod shuffle

Manufacturer: Apple (www.apple.com)
Price: $99/$149
Memory Type: Flash
Memory Size: 512 MB (120 songs) /1 GB (240 songs)
Weight: 0.78 ounce
Screen: No
Battery: Internal/rechargeable
OS Compatibility: Macintosh, Windows

The iPod shuffle is Apple's newest foray into the MP3 player market, and it raised a lot of eyebrows, because the iPod shuffle is a flash-memory-based player rather than a hard-drive-driven device. Add to that the fact that the shuffle doesn't have a built-in screen, and it would seem that Apple took a very big risk. Risk or no risk, upon its release, the public immediately fell in love with the iPod shuffle, and waiting lists to buy it were in the six- to eight-week range!

Despite lacking a view screen, the iPod shuffle is an outstanding digital music device that is arguably smaller than a seven-stick pack of chewing gum. The shuffle has the following functions: play, rewind, fast-forward, previous song, next song, pause, volume up/down, and play songs in order or shuffle songs. Although using an MP3 player without a screen as a podcast player may seem strange, I use my iPod shuffle for just that. In iTunes, I transfer two or three podcasts to the shuffle; then it's off to the gym. I strongly recommend that you use iTunes if you are going to purchase a shuffle; only when these two products work together does the iPod shuffle really sing.

Song-count disparity: Why does a Creative Zen Touch with 20 GB of hard-drive space boast that it can hold 10,000 songs when an Apple iPod with the same-size hard drive offers half as much? The answer lies in the details. The number of songs or podcasts that can fit on a digital music device depends entirely on the quality of the recordings you are storing. If you don't mind your songs sounding like they are coming across two tin cans with a wire between them, a 20 GB iPod could hold about 50,000 songs. So remember—look at the size of the hard drive and not the boasts about the number of songs a player can hold. In the case of the players discussed in this chapter, all of them have 20 GB hard drives, and even though the various manufacturers predict that each player can store a certain number of songs, one player will not store more than another, with everything else being equal.

Zen Touch

Manufacturer: Creative (www.creative.com)
Price: $250/$329
Memory Type: Hard drive
Memory Size: 20 GB (10,000 songs)/40 GB (16,000 songs)
Weight: 7.05 ounces
Screen: Yes
Battery: Internal/rechargeable
OS Compatibility: Windows

Claiming 24 hours of battery life on one charge, the Creative Zen Touch is perhaps Apple's toughest competition in the hard-drive-based MP3 player market. Although Creative has a complete lineup of MP3 players, the Zen Touch is its high-end digital music player, and as such, it comes packed with a wide selection of features, including:

- The ability to create playlists on the fly

- Search function

- USB 2.0 connectivity

- Optional FM radio and voice recorder via wired remote control

- AudioSync button for quick syncing between the Zen Touch and PC

The Zen Touch was designed primarily to work with Windows PCs, so I recommend that only Windows users consider it when shopping for a digital music device. With both a 20 GB and 40 GB configuration, the Zen Touch is a solid digital music player with an adequate included software package. If you intend to use a Zen Touch, ensure that you have USB 2.0 on your computer; otherwise, the time it takes to transfer large numbers of files becomes prohibitive.

iRiver H320

Manufacturer: iRiver (www.iriver.com)
Price: $299
Memory Type: Hard drive
Memory Size: 20 GB (10,000 songs)
Weight: 7.16 ounces
Screen: Yes (color)
Battery: Internal/rechargeable
OS Compatibility: Windows

iRiver has a complete lineup of digital music players, but I chose to discuss the H320 because it is widely acknowledged to be a competent unit, and its price point and feature set are comparable with those of the other devices discussed in this section. Weighing in at just over 7 ounces and sporting a color screen, the H320 offers direct competition to the iPod Photo. The iRiver Web site boasts that the H320 can store up to 600 hours of music, as well as thousands of digital pictures.

Available only for Windows PCs, the iRiver has an impressive array of features, including:

- Capacity for 600 hours of music

- Color display

- The ability to store and display JPEG and BMP file formats

- Built-in FM tuner

- Built-in voice recorder

- USB 2.0 connectivity

When you're shopping for a Windows-based digital music device, you cannot ignore the iRiver H320. The inclusion of an FM radio and a built-in voice recorder automatically save money compared with Apple's iPods, for which those features are available only as add-ons. That said, the H320 is larger than the iPod, and the interface and software package are not the same as those in the Apple suite.

 NOTE **Beauty is in the eye of the beholder. Nowhere is that more true than when choosing a digital music player. Because everyone has a different opinion of what looks good and what is easy to use, I strongly suggest that you head to your nearest electronics store and test these units head to head before making a decision.**

Rio Carbon

Manufacturer: Rio Audio (www.digitalnetworksna.com/rioaudio)
Price: $200
Memory Type: Hard drive
Memory Size: 5 GB (160 hours of music)
Weight: 3.2 ounces
Screen: Yes
Battery: Internal/rechargeable
OS Compatibility: Windows

Rio Audio has been in the MP3 player market for a long time; in fact, the company was one of the pioneers. Rio Audio has a full line of digital music devices, including the Rio Carbon, a 5 GB hard-drive model that is roughly the equivalent of the iPod mini. Coming in nearly half an ounce lighter than the mini, the Carbon is sure to turn heads with its size and built-in microphone for on-the-fly voice recording.

Although the interface is arguably not as slick as the iPod's, this little player is still worth looking at for Windows-based users. Features include:

- Built-in microphone for voice recording

- Drag-and-drop functionality

- USB 2.0 connectivity

- Ability to play Audible.com audio files

iAudio U2
Manufacturer: COWON America (http://eng.iaudio.com)
Price: $180
Memory Type: Flash
Memory Size: 1 GB
Weight: 1.2 ounces
Screen: Yes
Battery: Internal/rechargeable
OS Compatibility: Macintosh, Windows

COWON America's iAudio U2 digital music player is an excellent flash-based player for both the Mac and Windows operating systems. One of the distinct benefits of the U2 over the iPod shuffle is the inclusion of a screen, although admittedly, the U2 is also larger than the shuffle. The U2 comes with a built-in, rechargeable lithium battery that should give you 18 to 20 hours of playback before the device needs to be recharged.

The U2 comes not only as a 1 GB model, but also in 128 MB, 256 MB, and 512 MB flavors. Following are the prime features of the iAudio U2:

- LCD display

- Personalized logo on LCD display

- USB 2.0 connectivity

3

Creating a Podcast

Now that you know what a podcast is, what's it's used for, and how it can affect your life, you may be inspired to create your very own podcast for distribution over the world's podwaves. Perhaps you would love to create a podcast but feel that the technology obstacles preclude you from ever doing so. Or perhaps you aren't worried about the technology but are unwilling to take the time to learn the ropes. Not to worry. Before you succumb to the fear of podcasting technology and crumple up in a fetal position while moaning gently about RSS feeds, have a look at this chapter; it'll change your point of view.

In this chapter, I take a look at the process of creating a podcast, from the nuts and bolts of recording techniques to the software that can help you edit and manipulate the podcast. I also include some tips and interviews with podcasting pioneers and aficionados whose hard-won experience will be to your benefit. After covering the equipment and the software needed for podcast creation, I walk you through the creation of a podcast from start to finish, using basic equipment and popular software.

Choosing Content

Before you get the ball rolling on creating a podcast, it is critically important to figure out what will be said (or not said) during the show. What limits are there when it comes to choosing content? In short, there are almost no limits to what can be included in podcasts. Podcasting allows you to create shows, dramatizations, vignettes, commentaries, documentaries, and any other content imaginable. Indeed, podcasting is limited only by individual podcasters' imaginations. The sky is the limit, and I encourage you to exercise your creative muscle when brainstorming podcast ideas.

 I say there are "almost no limits" on podcast content because some laws dealing with pornography, threatening political leaders, and other such nastiness would preclude anyone from including such material in a podcast. Despite the fact that podcasting is a new medium with a wide-open feel, it is not a license to break the law. It's only a matter of time before someone crosses a legal line with a podcast; just make sure that someone is not you.

Before the Podcast

This section deals with everything relating to the creation of podcast content, from outlining a show's content to booking guests and formulating questions for them. Although it is possible for a podcaster just to pick up a microphone and create a "show," it requires a much larger effort to ensure that the podcast sounds professional while being a compelling listen. In this section, you see what you can do *before* the tape is rolling to maximize the quality and enjoyability of your podcast.

Some podcasts are clearly created by the seat of the host's pants, with little regard to a structure or plan for entertaining or educating the listener. But the "amateur" moniker that is attached to podcasting doesn't mean that the content of podcasts needn't be professional. With a little bit of background work, one can turn amateur hour into something that is respectable and highly listenable.

There are four key elements to a successful preproduction process for a podcast:

- Draft a document that establishes the general tone, taste, and attitude of the podcast.

- Establish the topic of the show, the length of the show, and any guests who will join you.

- Create a general outline for the show, breaking content into blocks no longer than five minutes each.

- Construct a detailed script to keep the show well paced and to ensure that the host(s) and any guests who are being interviewed always have something to talk about. (If you are good at speaking on your feet, this step may not be necessary.)

Mission statement

The first thing to do is write out a mission statement or design document that sets out rules for the tone and overall structure of the show. This document should spell out the boundaries of taste with regard to language, touchy topics (politics, abortion, favorite ice creams), and the overall attitude the host(s) should exhibit.

Although this process may seem rigid for an amateur podcast, the act of going through it goes a long way toward solidifying the overall feel of the podcast in your mind. Remember, this document is not set in stone; you can change it as much or as little as you want. The important thing is to establish the ground rules before you get your pearly whites in front of the microphone. Knowing the general rules allows the host to be more natural and enjoy the process rather than sweat over the appropriateness or validity of everything he or she is saying.

Telephone Interviews

Recording a telephone interview may seem like an insurmountable challenge, but fortunately, several inexpensive devices allow you to record telephone conversations directly from the phone line. I need to point out that these devices are illegal in some places without the consent of the person on the other end of the phone, so you need to inform your interview subjects at the beginning of the conversation that they are being recorded.

Several phone recorders plug into the phone line between the phone's receiver and base unit; others plug into any phone jack in the house. These little devices often cost less than $10. For the purposes of recording telephone interviews, I suggest the Radio Shack Recorder Control (**Figure 3.1**). At $25, this device will automatically start to record telephone conversations when the receiver is picked up. Keep in mind that this device does not include the recorder itself; it's just the conduit from the phone line to the recording device.

Figure 3.1
The Radio Shack Recorder Control allows you to record telephone interviews.

When recording a telephone conversation, it's best to use a digital recorder that can be attached to your PC so that the file can be uploaded to your PC (or Mac) easily.

Topics, guests, and show length

I'm guessing that you've already established an overall concept for your show, but even though you think "Foot Care for Firewalkers" is a fascinating theme for a podcast, you still need a topic for the first show.

I strongly suggest that you choose a topic for the show and stick to it, keeping as much of the content centered on the theme as possible. If you title your podcast "Navel-Gazing for Experts: To the Hole and Back," be sure to stay focused on the topic throughout. People who "tune in" to the podcast have done so because they have read the title and synopsis of the podcast. It is likely that listeners will be disappointed if the podcast strays too far from the announced concepts. It is advisable to make a reference list of related topics so that in the heat of the podcast, you can keep the show on track with just a glance or two at the topic list.

Double-Ender Interviews

Occasionally, the opportunity to interview someone by phone or even in person will arise before the podcast is set to be recorded. Often, it can be difficult to set up an interview during the podcast recording time, so the interview/conversation is recorded ahead of time. In the realm of radio and television, an interview that is conducted in two parts, with the interviewer's questions being added later, is called a *double-ender*, and this technique can be used successfully by podcasters and professional television reporters alike.

A double-ender may occur when you want an interview with someone in another city, but you prefer for the interview to sound live rather than tinny. as though it were coming off a phone line (which is your other alternative). In this case, you need to get a friend or someone near the interviewee's location to meet with that person and record the interview there with relatively high-quality equipment. Then, when the file arrives, you record your own voice asking the questions, and ultimately put the two together to make it seem like a live interview in which you are directly asking the interviewee the questions!

In the world of podcasting, the practice of recording double-ender interviews is usually done to improve the quality of the interview. After the interview is recorded, you can re-record your voice asking the questions, and you can even choose not to run some of the guest's answers during the podcast. In short, using double-ender interviews gives you more control of the quality and content of his or her podcast.

Next up, you need to choose who, if anyone, will be a guest on your show. Guests are fantastic; they provide instant content, and you can bounce ideas and humorous anecdotes off them. The important thing to remember when getting a guest for your podcast is to have at the very least a crude list of questions before the podcast begins. A guest might be a good friend whom you can chat with for hours, but once the mikes are on, it's a different ball of wax. Having a nice list of eight or ten questions at the ready will ensure that even if your stressed-out mind draws a blank, the show will go on!

Last, you must decide on a length for the show. Initially, shorter is better; you would be surprised how hard it can be to fill even one half-hour the first time you attempt to create a podcast.

Outline

Now that you know what the podcast is about, what the tone of the show is, and how long the podcast is, it's time to put together an outline that breaks the show into segments no greater than five minutes long. As shown in **Figure 3.2**, the outline should be set up in such a way as to help you fill every minute of your podcast with entertaining and/or interesting content.

Figure 3.2

An outline is a valuable tool to help keep you on track during a podcast.

> **Our Balls Are Bigger!**
> Canadian Football League Fan Podcast Outline
>
> Introduction (2 Minutes)
> - brief introduction of Bart and Adam
> - Quick review of the topics for today's show
>   o Goalposts, are they necessary?
>   o Interview with Doug Flutie
>   o Statistical Roundup
>   o Media Mayhem – Guest, Walter Cronkite
> News Roundup (2 Minutes)
> -News item #1
>   - discussion
> -News Item #2
>   -Discussion
> Goalposts, are they necessary? (2 minutes)
>   -discussion
>
> Interview with Doug Flutie (4 minutes)
>   -Are you happy in the NFL?
>   -Do you like cheese?
>   -What's the capital city of Rwanda?
>
> Statistical Roundup (1 minute)
>
> Media Mayhem (4 minutes)
>   -open discussion with Walter

If your outline for a 20-minute show is broken into two 10-minute segments, there isn't much point in constructing it. On the other hand, if the outline is broken into 10 two-minute segments, the flow and content of the show will be easy to maintain. Even if you have a detailed outline and a guest takes five times longer to answer a question than you thought she would, the outline is still valuable, because all of the show segments are in front of you, allowing you to decide at a glance which ones to drop.

In summary, an outline helps remove any indecision during the recording of the podcast. When the host has a written schedule sitting on a desk in front of him during the recording, any unexpected happenings don't have to fluster him or cause other problems.

 If your show is meant to be a spontaneous affair, a script is most certainly not for you. That said, even if your podcast is meant to be spontaneous, packed with seat-of-the-pants observations, an outline is still worth the effort.

Detailed script

If the outline is complete enough, a detailed script may not be necessary. The need for a script depends on the host's ability to talk on the fly and keep the flow of the show going. If the host is the kind of person who has difficulty with idle banter while maintaining the flow of the podcast, however, a detailed script will be in order.

A script can be so detailed that it contains every line that is to be said during the show, but if you go to this extreme, you must be careful not to make what's being said too rigid. We have all seen movies in which the lines seem scripted, as though they are just being read and not formed naturally by the actors. In radio, you want a similar feeling—a natural feeling that gives the illusion that everything that's being said is spontaneous.

Equipment

One great thing about podcasting is that you can do it at home with a basic Mac or PC and an inexpensive microphone (which may come with the computer). High-end equipment is nice, to be sure, but many of the best podcasts out there are recorded and edited with basic equipment and widely available software.

Still, there are several ways to set up a podcast recording "studio," from using nothing more than a computer with a microphone to having high-end microphones, preamps, digital recorders, and the like in a sound-dampened room.

For serious podcasters, the list of necessary equipment is as follows:

150 • Microphone 150

200 • Preamp

500 • Digital recorder (or computer)

150 • Headphones

• Sound-editing software

This section examines the equipment you need to get up and running (software is covered a little later on). I need to point out that many devices that can make podcasting easier or higher quality, but I cannot cover every one of them in this book. Instead, I examine several key pieces of equipment in each category.

Microphones

Arguably the most important device in the creation of a podcast, the microphone stands between your voice and the podcast file. As such, it behooves you to ensure that the quality of the recording is as good as it can be based on your budget and expectations.

Two main types of microphones are used for podcasting: condenser microphones and dynamic microphones.

Condenser microphones use a capacitor to capture sound. This works when the pressure from the sound changes the space between the thin membranes in the capacitor. The advantage of a condenser microphone is that it has a very broad frequency response; the down side is that it requires a source of power (like a battery) to charge the capacitor so that it can work.

 Condenser microphones require external power to function. This power often comes from a preamp device and is referred to as *phantom power*.

Dynamic microphones work by measuring the movement of a wire coil around a magnetic field as the sound waves agitate the wire. The advantages of a dynamic microphone are that it is cheaper to make than a condenser microphone and can be miniaturized more easily.

Popping Ps

One of the major problems for first-time podcasters is that any time they say the letter *P*, it comes across as a popping sound. This sound is created when the exhaled air used to form the *P* hits the microphone, temporarily overwhelming it. Unfortunately, this sound is not something that you can remove or doctor with editing software; once it's recorded, it's there forever. Not to worry, however. If podcasting is becoming a major part of your life, there are two relatively simple solutions:

1. Run out and buy a pop filter like the Onstage ASVS6GB Microphone Pop Filter ($25.94), shown in **Figure 3.3**.

2. Get some pantyhose, and stretch it over something that is hollow and roughly circular in shape. An old coat hanger that has been bent into a circle will do just fine. Tod Maffin suggests using an embroidery hoop for this purpose, and at a cost of about $2, it's not a bad alternative!

Figure 3.3
The Onstage ASVS6GB Microphone Pop Filter is an inexpensive way to avoid popping your *P*s.

When the pop filter/screen is ready to go, you must set it up so that it is right in front of the microphone. If you have purchased a commercial pop filter, there is likely a clamp that does this for you. If you have made your own pop filter, you must come up with your own creative solution. A pop filter can be hung from the roof; it can be attached to a small lamp; heck, it can even be placed around your neck on a harmonica holder so that no matter where you are, the pop filter is always there!

No matter how you solve the problem, getting a pop filter in front of the microphone ensures that the sound entering the microphone is clean and unaffected by the "wind" forces associated with normal speech.

The down side is that the frequency response isn't as good as that of a condenser microphone, making the sound quality inferior.

NOTE

Condenser microphones sport significantly better fidelity than dynamic microphones, but this also makes them more prone to crackling, background noise, and *P*-popping (the tendency for the words starting with the letter *P* to make a popping sound when spoken). Fortunately, there are ways to eliminate these problems (see the

Omnidirectional or Cardioid?

Although the decision to go with a dynamic or condenser microphone may be easy, that isn't the only decision that faces the buyer. Most microphones are either *omnidirectional* (sound enters the microphone equally from any direction and can be picked up with equal fidelity no matter where it comes from) or *cardioid* (sound is picked up mostly from in front of the microphone).

As a general rule, cardioid microphones are used for radio, but an omnidirectional microphone will do the job admirably for podcasting, especially if the podcasts are recorded with several guests all gathering around one microphone.

sidebar in this section). **Condenser microphones also require power, which often must be supplied by a preamp device (which adds around $100 to the cost).**

If the frequency response (quality of sound) is important to you, I recommend a condenser microphone. Most microphones that come with computers are dynamic microphones, and although they are acceptable, you will eventually have to purchase a quality microphone if you want your podcasts to sound professional.

Behringer C-1
Frequency Response: 40 Hz–18,000 Hz
Power: Phantom

The Behringer C-1 (**Figure 3.4**) is a professional-quality condenser microphone that uses a cardioid pattern to accept sound. At around $55, the C-1 is an outstanding microphone for the beginning, intermediate, or even expert podcaster. The real bonus is that the quality is high but the price is surprisingly reasonable for a product of this caliber.

(Photo © Copyright 2005. BEHRINGER Spezielle Studiotechnik GmbH.)

Figure 3.4
The Behringer C-1 condenser microphone is an awesome value and can more than do the job.

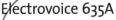

Electrovoice 635A

Frequency Response: 40 Hz–18,000 Hz

Power: Phantom

The Electrovoice 635A microphone (**Figure 3.5**) is probably the best-known microphone in the TV and radio business. A very dependable (some would say nearly indestructible) microphone, the 635A is a mainstay in the radio business and will serve any podcaster well, especially if recording on the road is in the cards.

Figure 3.5

The Electrovoice 635A is a mainstay microphone and, according to Tod Maffin, is the "best microphone you can buy when starting out."

Stageworks CC12

Frequency Response: 40 Hz–18,000 Hz

Power: Phantom

The Stageworks CC12 (**Figure 3.6**) is a more-than-suitable condenser microphone that is comparable to the Behringer in many ways. The CC12 uses a supercardioid pattern to accept sound and, as such, produces very clear sound capturing. Although it lists at $99, the Stageworks CC12 condenser microphone is widely available for around $50.

Figure 3.6

Like the Behringer microphone, the Stageworks CC12 offers high quality for a low price.

MC01 Professional Condenser Microphone
Frequency Response: 30 Hz–16,000 Hz
Power: Phantom

The MC01 (**Figure 3.7**) is the microphone for the high-end user (relatively speaking). At $180, the MC01 is designed for studio use and can be used to record both voices and musical instruments. The MC01 comes with a shock-mount system and a carrying pouch that makes it easy to tote around.

Figure 3.7

The MC01 Professional Condenser Microphone is my choice for a high-end microphone.

Audio Technica ATM73A-SP
Frequency Response: 25 Hz-17,000 Hz
Power: Battery

This headset cardioid condenser microphone is best used by those who want to create podcasts as a one-man (or one-woman) show. At $120, the ATM73A-SP (**Figure 3.8**) isn't inexpensive, but it is a high-quality microphone that you can clip to your head so that you don't have to worry about being directly in front of it all the time.

Figure 3.8

A headset-based cardioid condenser microphone is a great choice for a lone podcaster.

DT 234 PRO Headphone

Frequency Response: 20 Hz–18,000 Hz
Power: Phantom

This headset cardioid microphone costs around $99. Made by Industrial Audio Software, the DT 234 (**Figure 3.9**) contains a dynamic transducer, meaning that the quality is ultimately not as robust as that of a condenser microphone. That said, the DT 234 is a comfortable and reasonable performer best used by podcasters who do their work alone and don't have to share their microphones frequently.

Figure 3.9
The DT 234 headset-based cardioid dynamic microphone

Logitech USB Headset 200

Frequency Response: 100 Hz–16,000 Hz
Power: USB port

Priced around $45, the Logitech Stereo USB Headset 200 (**Figure 3.10**) is a good choice for those who are willing to forgo the highest sound quality in exchange for mobility and ease of use. The Headset 200 plugs into the USB port of your computer and is easy to set up. The microphone is a dynamic noise-canceling device that strives to filter out background noise. The result can be a mellowing of the user's voice, but it is a small price to pay, considering what you are getting for your money with this product.

Figure 3.10
A low-cost but effective headset microphone, the Logitech USB 200 is a solid option.

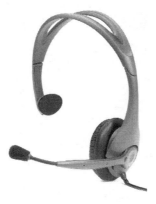

Logitech (www.logitech.com) has one of the largest selections of microphones for computers offered by any manufacturer. If you are looking for a microphone specifically for your PC, and you don't want to shop around, Logitech offers a huge variety.

Labtec Desk Mic 534

Frequency Response: 100 Hz–16,000 Hz
Power: 1.5 V DC (supplied through connector cable)

I include this microphone because it is a very common device that is included with many PC computer bundles. As a result, many readers may already have this microphone sitting on their desk. Although it's not a high-end condenser microphone, the $14.99 price tag makes it an excellent choice for those on a budget.

Apple Computer built-in microphones

Frequency Response: Varies
Power: Internal

Many Apple computers come with a built-in microphone. iMacs have a microphone in their screen, and many older Macs come with an external microphone that can be plugged in. Although these microphones do not offer super-high quality, and although there can be some issues with the computer's fan sound getting picked up, these built-in microphones can do the job in a pinch.

Radio Shack (www.radioshack.com)also has a wide selection of decent microphones that can be used for podcasting. Two examples are the Pro-Unidirectional Dynamic Microphone and the Headset Microphone with Gooseneck Boom. Both of these are very good microphones (for the price) and retail at $49.99.

Audio interfaces/preamps

Many of the microphones mentioned in this chapter require phantom power—that is, they require a device to supply power to them so that they can work. These devices can't be plugged straight into the computer; instead, they must be connected to a preamp device that acts as an input controller between the sound input devices and your computer.

Although these devices add another layer of cost to your podcast setup, they are not terribly expensive, and they also allow access to several extra features you probably didn't even consider. Preamps offer the ability to input any sort of sound into your computer, including inputs from a musical instrument (like an electric guitar) or even inputs from an old eight-track tape that you want to convert to an MP3 file. In short, a preamp computer device allows the input of virtually any kind of audio signal. For everything from making podcasts to recording an acoustic guitar track for GarageBand (a music-creation program for the Macintosh computer), a preamp is a wise investment.

Behringer Tube Ultragain MIC200

The Behringer Tube Ultragain MIC200 (**Figure 3.11**) is a preamp that's perfect for live and hard disk recording applications (such as creating a podcast). The great thing about the MIC200 is that it uses vacuum tubes, which create a warmer sound and make the device a great match for condenser microphones. The MIC200 includes 16 distinct preamp effects that are designed for everything from drums to vocals. At $60, the price is right. The one caveat about the functionality of this powerful device is that it does not have a USB connector, making it more difficult to connect to a PC or Mac than other preamps are.

Figure 3.11

The Behringer MIC200 is a solid preamp that uses old-fashioned vacuum-tube technology.

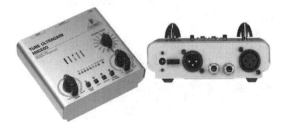

Griffin iMic

The iMic (www.griffintechnology.com; **Figure 3.12**) is a USB device that functions as a universal audio adapter for both the Mac and PC. With the iMic, you can connect any sound input (including microphones) to any Mac or Windows computer with a USB port. Because the iMic is so easy to use and also supports line-level output for speakers or an external recording device, it's the perfect match for podcasters. At $39.99, it is one of the best—and least expensive—units available.

Figure 3.12
The iMic is a low-cost, yet effective, solution.

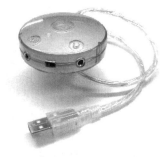

The benefit of USB audio input devices (preamps) comes from the fact that the inputs are isolated from any electronic "noise" that might otherwise be picked up from a computer's sound card. How much of a difference a USB device makes isn't entirely clear, but in the case of the iMic, it works like a charm.

XPSound XP-202

The XPSound XP-202 (**Figure 3.13**) is the Cadillac of USB audio preamps. Workable on both the Mac and PC, the XP-202 includes a phono preamp as well as a Mic preamp for recording voice and other live performances. Manufactured by XPSound, the XP-202 includes a USB connection and a built-in sound card for processing information right on board.

Figure 3.13
The XP-202 is the high-end preamp for podcasters who want the best.

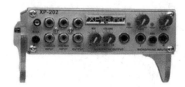

At $199, this is not the inexpensive alternative, but for anyone who wants more control of the sound input process, the XP-202 is the right machine for the job. The feature list includes:

- USB interface

- 24-bit operation

- 2 microphone inputs

- 1 headphone amplifier (onboard)

- Mix/balance control

- Powered by the USB port

Although I tout the XP-202 as a high-end preamp, there are plenty of very-high-end preamps on the market that cost hundreds and even thousands of dollars.

M-Audio MobilePre USB

At $159, the MobilePre USB from M-Audio (www.m-audio.com; **Figure 3.14**) is an outstanding preamp for both the Mac and PC platforms. The MobilePre USB has two channels, stereo microphone input, a powered headphone monitor, phantom power, stereo line outputs, and a gain switch. It's an easy-to-use, powerful preamp that will more than suffice for most podcasters (in fact, it's what I use).

Although designed specifically for use on laptops in mobile situations, this little preamp is plenty powerful enough to sit proudly in any home studio.

Figure 3.14

The M-Audio MobilePre USB is a solid preamp for both the Mac and PC.

Every preamp device mentioned in this section is capable of accepting any audio signal for conversion to a digital music or data file. For this reason, these are excellent tools for converting old audio tapes or vinyl records to MP3 files or music CDs.

PowerWave USB

With a price tag of $99, Griffin Technology's PowerWave USB (**Figure 3.15**) falls between its sibling, the iMic, and M-Audio's MobilePre USB. Like the other units, the PowerWave USB is capable of receiving input from any microphone while importing it to the PC or Mac it's connected to. The PowerWave also includes an amplifier to drive monitor speakers and is powered by the USB port.

Figure 3.15

The PowerWave USB is Griffin Technology's high-end audio input device.

Headphones

Headphones can be considered a luxury, but when it gets down to brass tacks, you will quickly find that a decent pair of headphones is more of a necessity. You cannot monitor the podcast during the actual recording unless you have headphones, for example. If the podcast were playing back through your computer's speakers as you were recording it, a noisy feedback buzz would be the result. For this reason, it is important to get a pair of headphones that is at the very least comfortable for you to have on your head while creating your podcasting masterpiece.

This section suggests several quality headphones for your consideration, but ultimately, any headphone that you are comfortable with will do. If you already own headphones—even MP3 player headphones—they will do the trick. There are literally hundreds of headphone models out there, so all I can recommend is that you use a set that sounds good to you and is comfortable. Of course, if you already are using one of the microphones with attached headphones, you can skip this section.

Sony MDR-V150 Headphones

At $19.99, these MDR-V150 headphones (**Figure 3.16**) are a quality yet inexpensive option from a well-known manufacturer. They are comfortable over-ear headphones with 30mm drivers and ferrite magnets for exceptional response (for the price).

Figure 3.16

Despite being a very basic set of headphones, the Sony MDR-V150 model is good enough for the beginner.

Sony MDR-V700DJ Headphones

These are a midlevel set of headphones from Sony. The sound quality of the MDR-V700DJ headphones (**Figure 3.17**) is noticeably better than that of the cheaper Sony 'phones, so for those who insist on high fidelity, these are a great choice. The V700DJ is a disk-jockey model with swivel ear cups, allowing the wearer to flick the ears over to permit conventional hearing. Many podcasters like this feature when they are engaging in an interview (they like to have one of their two ears exposed). At $149.99, these headphones aren't cheap, but the sound-fidelity difference is noticeable.

Figure 3.17

These DJ headphones feature swivel ear cups.

JVC HA-G55 Headphones

The JVC HA-G55 headphones (**Figure 3.18**) are a middle-of-the-road choice priced at $55. With a frequency response of 12 Hz to 25,000 Hz, they are capable of delivering a wide range of sounds to your ears. The advantage of the HA-G55s is that they have full-size, deep-base ear cups that allow for a rich sound that encircles the listener. These headphones are another excellent choice.

Figure 3.18

Priced between the two Sony models mentioned earlier in this section, the JVC HA-G55 headphones are a quality option.

Digital recorders

Although it may be tempting to rush out and purchase a digital recorder for your podcast needs, I need to point out that your computer itself is a powerful digital recorder, and the need for one of these devices is certainly not critical as long as you have a Mac or Windows PC. Still, digital recorders do have a certain amount of *je ne sais quoi* that makes them more glamorous.

Of course, there are legitimate reasons to get a digital recorder, not the least of which is the portability these devices afford the user. A digital recorder allows you to record programs virtually anywhere, provided that you have a microphone (some digital recorders have built-in microphones) and power to drive the unit. The only limitation with a digital recorder is its memory size; high-quality digital recordings take up a lot of memory space, so the size of the memory in a recorder is the main limiting factor when it comes to recording.

In this section, I take a look at three digital-recorder options: a high-end digital recorder, a midrange MP3 player option, and an iPod using Griffin Technology's iTalk microphone. The digital-recorder market offers plenty of choice, and it isn't within the scope of this book to examine them all, but taking a look at the cost and features of several units can help fill in the blanks about digital recorders and the need (or lack thereof) to own one.

NOTE Although I suggest a few digital recorders in this section, it's important to point out that virtually any MP3 player with the ability to record from a microphone input and then export the file to a PC or Mac can be used as a digital recorder. If you own an MP3 player, you may already have a portable digital recorder and not even know it. Either way, the selection of MP3 players that can record in this manner is vast, giving the buyer plenty of choice.

Edirol R-1

The Edirol R-1 (**Figure 3.19**) is one example of a high-end digital recorder. Although there certainly are more elaborate (and expensive) recorders on the market, this unit (at a price of around $500) is my choice at the high end. The R-1 is a handheld 24-bit digital recorder that is capable of recording high-quality broadcasts virtually anywhere.

Figure 3.19
The Edirol R-1 is one example of a high-end digital recorder.

The feature list of this product is very impressive:

- 137-minute MP3 (compressed) recording time (with built-in 64 MB memory card)

- 24-bit uncompressed recording

- Dual built-in omnidirectional microphones

- External microphone input

- Line inputs

- 13 internal digital effects

- Built-in equalizer

- Built-in tuner (to tune musical instruments)

- Built-in metronome

- USB 2.0 connectivity

Clearly, the Edirol R-1 is a full-featured digital recorder that exceeds the needs of most podcasters. For anyone who is looking to become a serious podcaster, the Edirol is worth considering. Its many built-in features, the high quality of its recordings, and its portability make it a very popular choice.

iRiver IFP-795

The iRiver IFP-795 (**Figure 3.20**) is a tiny (512 MB) MP3 player that can play for up to 40 hours on one AA battery. At $149, the IFP-795 is reasonably priced for a flash MP3 player, but it is much more than just that. Weighing in at just under an ounce and a half, the IFP-795 is a surprisingly full-functioned digital recorder, complete with a separate line input for an external microphone.

Figure 3.20

The iRiver IFP-795 is an amazingly functional digital recorder that masquerades as an MP3 player.

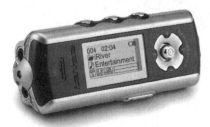

Because the iRiver comes with software that allows easy connectivity to PCs or Macs, its USB 2.0 connection makes connection and export of recorded files a breeze. The device supports recording bit rates between 8 Kbps and 320 Kbps in WMA, MP3, and OGG music formats.

Apple iPod with Griffin iTalk

Not long after the first iPods were released, some iPod owners who were fooling around with the iPod's interface discovered a hidden menu that implied the iPod could be used for voice recording. It turns out that these folks had stumbled onto something that would show up about a year later: devices designed to record directly onto the iPod's hard drive. Today, Griffin Technology offers the iTalk, a small device that attaches to the top of the iPod photo as well as to third- and fourth-generation iPods.

 The iPod mini actually doesn't have recording ability built into its firmware, so the Belkin and Griffin recording devices work only on third-generation, fourth-generation, and photo iPods.

The iTalk (**Figure 3.21**) is an ingenious device that attaches cleanly to the top of the iPod, and after you install the software (which is easy to do), the iPod becomes a competent voice recorder. The iTalk comes with a built-in speaker that allows you to record without any other equipment, but if quality is your goal, I suggest plugging an external microphone into the iTalk.

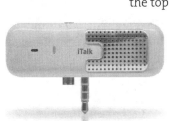

Figure 3.21
The iTalk is a mobile-recording option for iPod users.

The iTalk is a nifty little unit that will record on the iPod's hard drive in .WAV file format. When the iPod docks with iTunes, the file will be transferred to iTunes automatically, making it easy to pull off for editing.

The device does have a down side, in that the user cannot change the recording bit rate. Also, the quality of the built-in speaker, although decent, is not exactly broadcast quality. Still, as a portable recording device, the iTalk is an inexpensive ($49) option for an iPod owner.

 Belkin (www.belkin.com) also sells a voice-recorder attachment for iPods, as well as a microphone attachment for the same purpose.

Software

Part of what makes podcasting so appealing and so popular is the fact that it can be done relatively simply with a user's existing computer and accessories. After the audio podcast file has been recorded, it is still a good idea to use sound editing software to remove any imperfections and insert some appropriate background music. Fortunately, *plenty* of quality shareware and freeware programs are available to help you do just that.

It is also important to note that most sound-editing software can also be used as a digital recorder. In fact, many podcasts are created with a microphone that came with the computer, inputting directly into a program like Audacity or GarageBand. Many sound-editing programs are available, and increasingly, a new type of all-in-one program is showing up. These programs, like iPodcast Producer and Sparks, allow the user to create a podcast from start to finish and even publish the podcast, all from one program!

In this section, I examine several quality sound-editing/recording programs for the Mac, Linux, and Windows environments. I include freeware, shareware, and commercial products, some of which are limited to sound recording and editing; others are one-stop options that allow you to create a podcast and publish it without ever leaving the program.

Ogg Vorbis

Often referred to as just *OGG*, Ogg Vorbis is an open and free audio compression format. Vorbis was created after Fraunhofer-Gesellschaft announced plans to charge licensing fees for the MP3 file format in 1998. It was then that Chris Montgomery began work on the project. The codec was released in July 2002, and the Ogg Vorbis compression format was born.

Slowly but surely, the Ogg Vorbis format is making inroads in the world of audio sound compression. In the past couple of years, it has shown up increasingly on the Internet, in podcasts, and even in some commercial video games. Ogg Vorbis enthusiasts claim that the quality of an OGG is higher than that of an MP3 file, but I can't tell much of a difference. I'll leave that part up to you.

Audacity

Audacity is the program of choice for many podcasters, in part because it is free, but mostly because it's a fantastic, powerful, easy-to-use program. Audacity can be used to record podcasts (with an attached microphone) or to edit existing sound files. Available for Mac computers, Windows PCs, and Linux PCs, Audacity is freeware and is so powerful that it most likely puts a dent in the sales figures of those programs that are for sale. You can download the program from http://audacity.sourceforge.net/download/ for each of the three operating systems (**Figure 3.22**).

Figure 3.22

Audacity is available for most computer users, be they Mac OS, Linux, or Windows inspired.

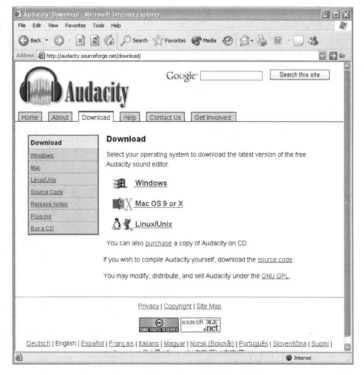

As often occurs in the world of the Internet and computing, this freeware program is superior to some of the for-sale programs on the market. In the realm of podcasting, Audacity has quickly risen to be the top dog for audio mixing and recording (when recording directly on a PC or Mac).

The deep feature list for Audacity includes these items:

- Can record from microphone, line input, or other sources

- Can create multitrack recordings and dub over existing tracks

- Can record up to 16 channels at the same time (special hardware required)

- Can import WAV, AIFF, AU, and Ogg Vorbis files

- Can import and export MP3 files

- Easy editing using cut-and-paste methodology

- Volume fade in/out feature

- Built-in effects generator, including Echo and Phaser sounds

- Can record at up to 96 KHz (more than double a music CD's quality)

- Upgradable with plug-ins

Audacity, shown in action in **Figure 3.23**, is such a complete and easy-to-use recording/editing tool that it is my first choice for all three platforms. There are lots of programs out there, but for someone who is just starting out on a tight budget, free is a great price to pay, and Audacity is also a fantastic piece of software.

Figure 3.23

Audacity is available for Mac, Windows PC, and Linux, and is very powerful.

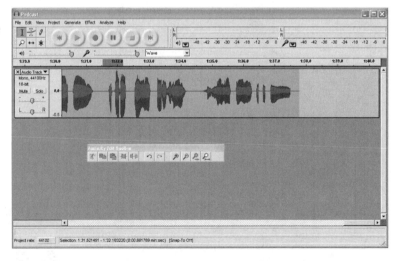

NOTE Because Audacity is such a great piece of software, I recommend that if you use it as your primary editing/recording program, you donate some money to support the development of the next generation of the program. This goes for all freeware software. It doesn't matter whether you donate $1 or $100; if you use the software a great deal, donating to the developer is the right thing to do.

BlogMatrix Sparks! 2.0

 Sparks! 2.0 (**Figure 3.24**) is an all-in-one solution for the Mac and the Windows PC, making it very simple to create a podcast and publish it without ever leaving the program. Sparks! 2.0 is a podcast aggregator as well as an audio recorder, editor, and podcast publisher. It's free for most of the features, but if you want to use the recording feature, you must pay a $10 fee (although the recording feature comes with a 30-day free trial).

Figure 3.24

Sparks! 2.0 has a built-in, multitrack audio recorder/editor.

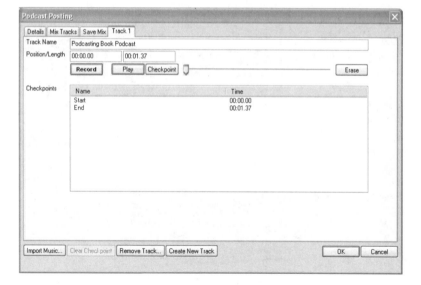

Sparks! is truly a one-stop solution for podcasters and podcast listeners. The feature list for this software is very impressive and includes

- The ability to record and edit podcasts

- The ability to publish podcasts with ease

- Acts as a podcast aggregator (**Figure 3.25**)

- Acts as an Internet radio portal

- Acts as a blog reader

- Allows the creation of podcasts from Internet radio and other sources

- Can use multiple tracks and import music to create podcasts

Figure 3.25

Sparks! 2.0 acts as a very functional podcast aggregator if need be.

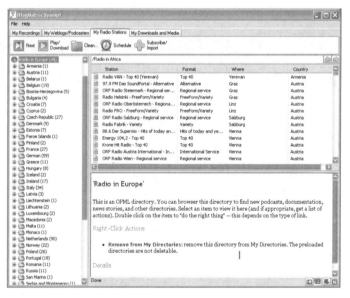

As a one-stop shop, Sparks! 2.0 is an impressive piece of software. For true podcasting aficionados, I suspect that Sparks! 2.0 won't satisfy completely, but for the casual podcaster or the podcaster who just wants to create occasional podcasts, Sparks! is an excellent solution.

NOTE If creating a regular podcast is your goal, BlogMatrix also sells packages for publishing podcasts. These services run between $5 and $100 per month, depending on the level of service one needs. Check out Chapter 4 for details on how to use BlogMatrix Sparks! 2.0 to publish podcasts on the World Wide Web.

Interview with Evo Terra and Michael R. Mennenga

Terra and Mennenga are hosts of the top-15 podcast "Slice of Sci-Fi."

Evo Terra has been involved in various creative and emerging-media products since the early '90s. Author, musician, ordained minister, and herbal therapist, he approaches all of his projects from a point of view that usually sets him far apart from anything resembling normality.

Michael R. Mennenga knows firsthand what "struggling artist" is all about. From fantasy novelist to audio engineer and producer, Mike is the epitome of DIY (do-it-yourself) and tends to rewrite the rules as he goes along. Tenacity and perseverance are his strong suits, and he's never met a problem that couldn't be solved with a big-enough hammer.

Farkas: When did you first become aware of podcasting?

E & M: On October 12, 2004, my [Terra's] partner sent me a link to a page where Doc Searls was talking about DIY radio with this new thing called podcasting. Two days later, and I am neither [kidding] you nor making this up, I hacked our RSS feed and figured out how to use the <enclosure> plug-in in MovableType. My response back to him contained words like "this could potentially change how we do things," and it did. A day or two later, we got listed on Podcast Alley.

Farkas: What made you decide to create your own podcast?

E & M: We've been producing audio content for distribution on the Web and through terrestrial radio stations since February of 2002 and had enjoyed a fair amount of success. But terrestrial radio isn't our best market, and it was frustrating to try and explain what our show was all about and why a station should carry us.

(continued on next page)

Interview with Evo Terra and
Michael R. Mennenga *(continued)*

When we got booted earlier this year from the No. 1 AM talk-radio station in town because we were *too popular* and causing a "speed bump" in their all-right-wing-politics-all-the-time format, we realized there had to be a better way to reach people who wanted to listen to our content, which likely didn't fit in with any radio station's lineup. Podcasting was that method.

Farkas: What has surprised you the most with regard to the impact of your podcast(s)?

E & M: The immediacy, quality, and quantity of the feedback. We reached tens, if not hundreds, of thousands of listeners on our broadcast shows. Maybe once a week, we'd get an e-mail from them. Oh, sure, our phone banks were lit up each time our live call-in show was on, but our syndicated show rarely got us an e-mail or even a comment on the Web site.

However, from the moment we started releasing our show via podcast, the e-mails and Web-site comments stated coming. It's as if the podcatchers feel more of an emotional attachment to our show. Maybe that's because it's still not easy to listen to a show. With that kind of investment, you want the show to be the way you want it, so you're not afraid to let the talent know your feelings.

Farkas: What are your plans for "Slice of Sci-Fi" going forward?

E & M: "SoSF" adds one more element to our science-fiction lineup. "Cover to Cover" handles books and authors (my favorite topic), "Wingin' It!" lets us get a little looser and goofy with the sci-fi stuff, and "SoSF" lets us talk about TV and movies in a dedicated fashion.

Plan on "SoSF" growing. We've got a dedicated team of "professional" sci-fi geeks out there gathering new information for us. With luck, we'll have so much content, we'll have to take the show to multiple times a week. There's already talk of spinoff podcasts, because there is so much to cover! Of course, both of us are excited that XM radio has picked up "Cover to Cover," our syndicated show. I see a great opportunity for us to produce a syndicated version of "Slice of Sci-Fi" as well!

Farkas: Where do you see podcasting going in the next year? The next five years?

Interview with Evo Terra and Michael R. Mennenga *(continued)*

E & M: By the end of summer [2005], nearly all syndicated radio shows will be repurposing their content in podcast form. I predicted that months ago, and it is coming true. That's going to fracture the podcasting community (purists versus "it's just audio content" camps), as well as bring in a lot more listeners who have never heard of podcasting. Additionally, you'll see more large organizations and corporations trying out this podcasting thing, with most of them failing.

Five years from now, personal on-demand content will be the norm. On cell phones, in cars... anywhere you want to go, you can take your content, audio and/or video, with you. Podcatching clients will be embedded in everything. Transferring files will be intuitive and nonissues. Bandwidth will cease to be an issue, and the majority of the information will be free.

Schools will be offering distance learning via podcast. Politicians will try it, and the freedom of information just might change the political landscape significantly. Radio will still be here. TV will still be here. And podcasting will still be here, bringing the best of those two mediums together and putting it in the palm/dashboard/ear/eyeglasses of the masses.

Farkas: Technically speaking, what was the most difficult thing about getting a podcast off the ground (so to speak)?

E & M: Personally, we think listening to a podcast is more difficult than making one. People who want to make a podcast have the motivation to figure it out, but people who might want to listen are quickly turned off by all the hoops. That's the biggest stumbling block right now for the whole movement.

For podcasters, the problem lies in understanding the RSS feed. Recording a show is intuitive. I push the red button and talk, right? FTPing the file isn't hard, as it's no different than moving files from one spot to another on your computer. The challenge is RSS. Yeah, there are lots of tools to automate the process, but inasmuch as some software sucks at what it's supposed to do, RSS feeds need to be tweaked at the code level in order to make them as effective as possible.

GarageBand/GarageBand 2

Folks who own Macintosh computers likely have a copy of GarageBand (**Figure 3.26**) already sitting on their hard drives. If for some reason GarageBand has eluded you, it is included with all new Macintosh computers and can be purchased with iLife '05 for $79.99. What makes GarageBand so appealing to Macintosh enthusiasts is the way in which it interacts with iTunes and Mac OS X. As with most Apple applications, GarageBand's ease of use is very impressive, allowing a first-time user to put together an impressive multitrack recording in only a few minutes.

Figure 3.26

If you own a Mac, there's a good chance that you already own GarageBand, the only sound recorder/editor you'll need.

GarageBand's ease of use comes from simple audio-track creation, drag-and-drop editing, and the ability to add music or other audio files simply by dragging them out of iTunes. Although GarageBand was designed specifically for the creation of music, it is still an elegant solution that works seamlessly with the rest of the software on your Macintosh when creating podcasts.

GarageBand's features include:

- Multitrack recording

- Point-and-click editing

- Compatibility with iTunes

- Multiple voice effects

- Complete control of all aspects of recording, including timing and pitch

iPodcast Producer

iPodcast Producer (iPP; **Figure 3.27**) is a commercial product that runs $149.95 from Industrial Audio Software's Web site (www.industrial audiosoftware.com). iPP is meant exclusively to be a tool for recording, editing, and then publishing podcasts. The product is not as slick as Audacity or GarageBand, but it does contain the features necessary to get the job done.

Figure 3.27

iPodcast Producer is a competent piece of software but a little pricey when one considers what is available for free.

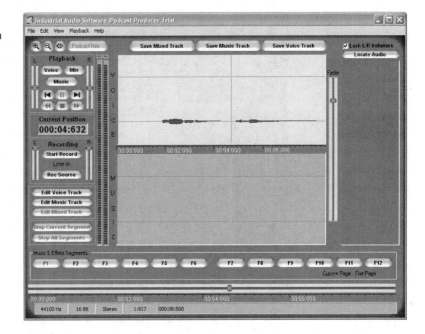

iPP contains a sound/music recorder with two tracks (one for voice and one for music), a fader, and the ability to add up to 12 music or sound effects to keys F1 through F12 on the keyboard. After you assign a sound to one of these keys, you can insert that sound into a recording dynamically by pressing the key that activates it. The recorder also allows for other audio sources in .WAV or MP3 file formats to be imported.

After recording, you can access the iPP Editor (**Figure 3.28**) and edit or modify the sound files with digital effects. You can apply 19 different effects to recordings during this process. When the file is complete, IPP allows the newly created podcast to be syndicated right from the program (**Figure 3.29**). If you don't already have a spot to save your file for the RSS feed, Industrial Audio Software can sell you space starting at $49.95 per month.

Figure 3.28

The iPP Editor allows you to tweak the sound files.

Figure 3.29

You can publish your podcast directly from within iPP.

Adobe Audition 1.5

Adobe Audition (**Figure 3.30**) is a high-end professional sound editing/ recording suite that offers advanced audio editing, mixing, and sound processing capabilities. This software is aimed mainly at professionals, but at $299, it is not priced outside the range of a serious podcaster. It certainly isn't hyperbole to say that Adobe Audition contains myriad features that a podcaster is likely never to use, but for those mavens who want every possible capability at their fingertips, this software is a great value for the money.

Figure 3.30

Adobe Audition is one of the best choices for those who want high-end sound editing when creating a podcast.

Audition's feature list is so long that it might take up several pages in this book, so I'll stick to the highlights as they pertain to the realm of podcasting:

- All-in-one application for mixing, creating, editing, and adding audio effects

- Can be used to edit video soundtracks

- More than 50 digital signal processing tools and effects

- Up to 128 stereo tracks

- Up to 32 inputs with an equalizer on every track

- Record, edit, and mix high-resolution 32-bit files at sample rates up to 192 KHz (double the quality of DVD audio)

- Audio restoration features that allow you to clean up poor recordings

- Multichannel encoder for creating 5.1 surround sound (six speakers: center, left and right front, left and right rear, and subwoofer)

Although it clearly isn't for the weekend podcaster who wants to create relatively simple programs, Adobe Audition 1.5 is inexpensive enough that hard-core podcasters can enjoy its massive suite of features. You can download a trial version at www.adobe.com.

Propaganda

Like iPodcast Producer, Propaganda (www.makepropaganda.com; **Figure 3.31**) is designed to be a one-stop podcast creation station, allowing the user to create, edit, and publish podcasts with relative ease. Propaganda has a free 14-day trial; the cost to keep using it after that is $49.95.

The feature list of Propaganda includes:

- One-touch recording

- Recording from microphone or portable digital recorders

- On-screen VU meters

- Ability to rearrange clips in any order

- Ability to add background music and sounds

- Fade in/out transitions

- Ability to publish completed podcasts directly to a Web site

Figure 3.31

Propaganda is a one-stop podcast creation package for Windows computers.

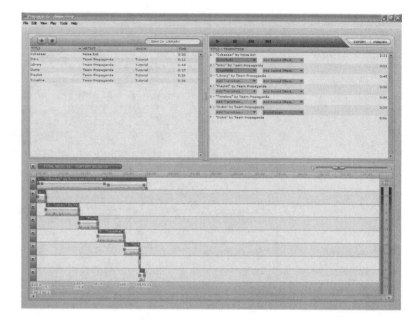

Propaganda allows you to record a podcast from a microphone and to organize and edit the voice file while adding background music and audio effects. When the podcast is complete, Propaganda allows you to upload the show to an RSS feed for distribution on the World Wide Web. If a one-stop piece of software appeals to you, Propaganda is an acceptable alternative for creating and publishing podcasts.

Sound Byte

Sound Byte (**Figure 3.32**) is a bit of a different animal from the other software discussed in this section, because it does not directly help you create podcasts or publish them; instead, it works as a computerized cart machine. In radio stations of the past, a *cart machine* was a device that held a large number of cartridges with short audio blurbs, commercials, sounds, and other such material. When the DJ needed a particular sound, he or she could press a button, and that sound would come off the cartridge and get played on the air. This was a way for radio stations to add unique sounds to broadcasts, and it worked pretty well.

Figure 3.32

Sound Byte allows you to create a palette of sounds that you can access with a click of the mouse.

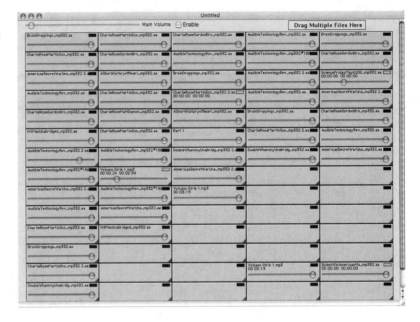

Sound Byte, from Black Cat Systems (www.blackcatsystems.com), costs $24 (after a free trial) and effectively duplicates those old radio cartridge systems with the digital equivalent. The palette comes with 75 slots, each of which is capable of holding a distinct sound byte, piece of music, or sound effect (or whatever you want). When you're recording a podcast, you can simply click one of the sound effects to insert that effect into the background.

For podcasters who like to fly by the seat of their pants and add sound effects as needed, Sound Byte is an outstanding tool. Sound Byte is available only for the Macintosh at this point, but it is a valuable tool that certain podcasters appreciate and use.

Sound Recorder

There are many freeware, shareware, donationware, and commercial sound recorders on the market, but Windows users need not go any farther than their Start menu to find an audio recorder that can do the job. In Windows XP, you can find Sound Recorder (**Figure 3.33**) in this path: Start/Programs/Accessories/Entertainment/Sound Recorder.

Figure 3.33
Sound Recorder is free, and it's sitting right there in Windows.

Sound Recorder is limited in that it records only in mono, in 8 bits at 22 kHz, but for some podcasts, that level of quality is enough to get by. Amazingly, this little utility contains an effects menu that allows you to increase or decrease the clip's speed, add an echo to the clip (**Figure 3.34**), or even reverse the clip's direction. This may be your chance to resurrect the "Paul is dead" controversy!

Figure 3.34
Surprisingly, this little utility has a few tricks up its sleeve.

Sound Recording and Editing Tips

Much of the skill you develop in creating podcasts will come with experience. No matter how much you know about the various terms and aspects of software packages and hardware, in the end, the most important thing is *doing*. That said, there *are* a few important tips that will help you when you are recording, editing, and mixing your podcast:

- When recording, try to use your normal voice. Many people attempt a "radio" voice, and it comes off sounding fake or contrived. Practicing talking in your normal voice will help your first podcast come off better.

- First-time podcasters often speak too loudly into the microphone. It's important not only to speak at a conversational level, but also to be careful not to vary the volume of your voice or the distance between your mouth and the microphone a great deal. Doing either of these things will result in an uneven podcast in which your voice will "drop out" or "explode" during the show.

- Use a pop filter (also known as a pop screen) in front of the microphone to eliminate pops when saying the letters, *P, B,* and *F.*

- When recording, make sure that the levels don't go over the 0-decibel mark on the DB meter. If that happens, the high end of the recording will get clipped off, resulting in very poor sound quality.

- Record at the highest sampling rate possible. CD quality is 44.1 kHz; DVD quality is 96.1 kHz. It's important to record at the highest quality that your recording device will allow. When using a small digital recorder, the size of the memory stick is the usual limiting factor. On a computer, however, there is usually enough hard drive space to record at any level.

- If you are going to use commercial music in your podcasts for any reason, you must get an appropriate license for it (see "Legalities" later in this chapter). Most music is licensed by ASCAP or BMI, and both have licenses for podcasters.

- When interviewing a guest, don't be afraid to rerecord your questions, especially if the questions didn't come off right in the first place (for example, you were coughing or stammering while asking the question). It's easy to rerecord the question and place it over the original question. The listener need never know.

- Use a fade-in and fade-out at the beginning and end of the podcast. This small touch gives a very impressive feel to the show and makes the proceedings come across as being professional.

- Include background music during the podcast (see "Legalities" later in this chapter). Background music can be used in several ways. First, it can demarcate different phases or sections of the podcast, rising in a crescendo to signify the passing of a segment and falling off again to signify the beginning of a new topic or to introduce a guest. Second, music can and should open and close a show, with several seconds of music preceding and following the first and last things said by the host.

Getting Started: Advice from Phil Torrone

Phillip Torrone is an author, artist, and engineer based in Seattle and is associate editor of MAKE. He has written and contributed to numerous books on mobile devices, multimedia, and hacks. He regularly writes for *Popular Science* and *Mobile PC Magazine,* as well as producing the MAKE: audio and video content on the Makezine.com site. Phillip is also an Internet-strategy analyst for creative firm Fallon Worldwide, best known for its award-winning work on BMWFilms.

Farkas: What do you recommend (hardware and software) for the beginning podcaster?

Torrone: If you have a Mac with GarageBand and a Griffin iTalk or a USB microphone, the results will be surprisingly professional. On a PC, any powered microphone and Audacity will get you started. I've found that a portable recorder tends to get you in the podcasting zone more than sitting in front of a computer. If you're going somewhere, actually interviewing someone, there's a lot more context and richness in the audio than the mouse clicks and keystrokes.

Farkas: How has podcasting helped you personally with regard to your career/business?

Torrone: I started podcasting early on, so it's helped a lot in terms of being considered an "expert" in the arena. There have been a lot of opportunities to pursue businesses in podcasting, but I've been more interested in spreading the word about how to create them with writings, how-to articles, and other efforts. To me, that's the exciting thing—turning on tons of people to the self-publishing of audio.

Farkas: What are your top five tips for a beginning podcaster?

Torrone:

1. Get a good microphone. USB; it doesn't matter—something that sounds good will make any podcast a lot better.

2. Try before you buy. A lot of podcasters go out and buy a lot of gear the pros use. Try experimenting with what you have first. In the end, the big spend might not matter.

3. Love or hate your topics. Passion comes across really well in audio; stick to the stuff you care about or despise. Both make great podcast.

4. Break eggs. Make mistakes, try different gear, try different encodings. Don't spend too much time getting it "right"—just get it out there, and the rest will follow.

5. Use Creative Commons (see "Creative Commons" later in this chapter). License your works with a Creative Commons license. Not only is it good for you, but it's also good to get more people aware of the CC.

Music

Music is a very important part of podcasting. After all, many podcasts are like terrestrial radio broadcasts, in that they play a selection of popular music. Even for all-talk podcasts, music is often part of the program in one form or another. Although music plays an important role in making podcasts sound professional, there are issues around the licensing of musical content within a podcast.

Despite the limitations, there are ways (such as licensing or using Creative Commons licenses) to include music in your podcasts. It's a sticky area, however, and it's important to know the lay of the land before you try to walk across it.

Legalities

Few people may realize this, but each and every time a song is played on the radio, on television, or even at a sporting event, a royalty is paid to the rights holder of that song. How much of a royalty is paid depends on where the song is played. For example, the use of a song in a commercial, such as the Rolling Stones' "Start Me Up" (for Microsoft Windows 2000) or the Beatles' "Revolution" (for a Nike shoe ad), can generate hundreds of thousands or millions of dollars. On the other hand, a radio station playing a particular song might require a payment of only 16 cents. Whatever the cost, royalties are designed to reimburse the creative people who wrote and performed this music.

Of course, many songs are owned not by the artists who wrote them, but by large corporations. Either way, the money is owed fair and square.

As one might expect, podcasting can throw a wrench into the royalty situation when it comes to music. Are the many mom-and-pop operations creating amateur podcasts still responsible for paying royalties for the music they may use in the background during their shows? If the podcast contains licensable music, the answer is YES.

Two main bodies manage royalty collection for music catalogs: ASCAP and BMI. ASCAP (American Society of Composers, Authors and Publishers) is a performing-arts organization that acts as a collector and advocate for those artists associated with it. BMI (Broadcast Music, Inc.) is similar to ASCAP in that it represents artists with regard to the collection of royalties for music that is played in public. Surprisingly, despite the sudden appearance and rapid growth of podcasting, both of these organizations have agreements that more or less cover the basics for podcasters.

ASCAP has a contract known as the ASCAP Experimental License Agreement for Internet Sites & Services, Release 5.0. This license costs $288 up front and includes fairly complex fee calculations. This contract is offered on a per-year basis, and the fee is not pro-rated, so if you pay $288 on December 20, 2005, you will have to pay $288 again on January 1, 2006. This is a very dynamic area, however, and any of the above details could change even by the time you read this book. To have a look at ASCAP's license, check out www.ascap.com/weblicense.

BMI has a similar license that appears to be slightly easier to negotiate. The up-front cost of this license is $283, and of course, there are also fee structures, depending on how music is used in the podcasts. To see BMI's license, go to www.bmi.com/licensing/forms/Internet0105A.pdf.

 Adobe Acrobat is required to view both of these licenses; you can download it free at www.adobe.com/acrobat.

Bob Goyetche, of "The Bob and AJ Show" fame, says that when it comes to playing music in his show, the team ultimately looked at two alternatives:

- "We turned to indie musicians. We get specific permission from songwriters and performers, which gives us permission to play their tunes."

- "The background music we use is Creative Common–licensed music from open-source music sites. Usually, the stipulation is that as long as we give attribution, we can use the material."

It is clear that if you want to create a podcast that includes popular music, and you are interested in proceeding in a legal fashion, you will have to obtain licenses from these organizations and follow them to the letter. That said, it is unclear how many podcasters are currently following these rules. It probably won't surprise anyone if these rules change in the coming months or years. Either way, it is important to stay up to date on this issue if you are an active podcaster.

Creative Commons

Created in 2001 by Lawrence Lessig, Creative Commons (http://creativecommons.org; **Figure 3.35**) is a not-for-profit organization with the goal of expanding the amount of creative work available for others to build upon and share legally. Creative Commons licenses were originally designed for the United States, but now, Creative Commons licenses can be obtained in 29 countries.

Figure 3.35

Creative Commons is an excellent place to find music for your podcasts.

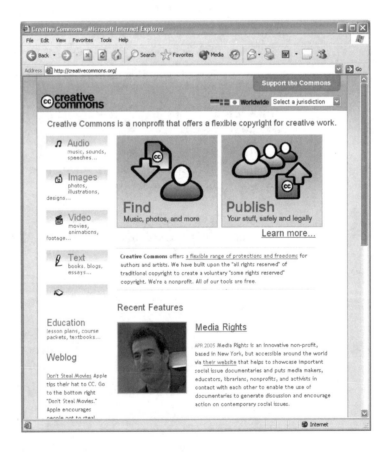

This is a new system, built within current copyright law, that allows an individual to share his or her creations with others and to use music, images, and text online that has been identified as having a Creative Commons license. To learn more about the history of Creative Commons, visit http://creativecommons.org/about/history.

 It's important to note that getting a license with Creative Commons does not mean giving up your copyright. It means instead that you are giving up some of your rights to any taker, but only under certain conditions.

Several of the podcasters I interviewed for this book mentioned Creative Commons as a source for the music they use in their podcasts. If you want to include music in your podcasts, I suggest that you visit the Creative Commons Web site and learn more about what is available. As an artist, you can choose one of several licenses, including:

- *Attribution.* You let others copy, display, perform, and distribute your copyrighted work (and derivative works based upon it), but only if they give you credit.

- *Noncommercial.* You let others copy, display, perform, and distribute your work, but only for noncommercial purposes.

- *No Derivative Works.* You let others copy, display, perform, and distribute only verbatim copies of your work. There can be no derivative works based upon your work.

- *Share Alike.* You allow others to distribute derivative works only under a license that is identical to the license that governs your own work.

The Creative Commons Web site can point you to several excellent sites that contain Creative Commons–licensed sound files and music. One such site is Opsound (www.opsound.com) , shown in **Figure 3.36**. This site is an excellent source of music that you can use in your podcasts provided that you follow the rules of each license. If the idea of reading the license for each song gets under your skin, remember that licensing commercial music is very expensive and requires far more paperwork.

Figure 3.36

Opsound is a great site for Creative Commons–licensed music.

NOTE Most of the music on the Opsound Web site falls under the Share Alike Creative Commons license, which means you are free to download it, share it, and include it in your work as long as you attribute the works to the original authors/musicians. The site also contains some public-domain music.

Interview with Bob Goyetche

Bob Goyetche is co-host of "The Bob and AJ Show."

As the show's Web site says: "If you're looking to listen to two drunk and horny Canadian guys eating potato chips, then there's no better place than 'The Bob and AJ Show.'"

Goyetche is a 36-year-old husband and father whose day job is working as an IT consultant. He's been a musician for 20 years and has always had a passion for broadcasting. **AJ** is a 35-year-old husband and father of two, earning his living as an electrician. Like Bob, he's been involved in music and pirate radio. Bob and AJ have been good friends for 20 years, and that shows no signs of changing.

Farkas: When did you first become aware of podcasting?

Bob: I first heard about podcasting early last fall, through Doug Kaye's IT Conversations site. I had been listening to downloadable programs (weren't called podcasts yet then) for a few weeks when I heard the Bloggercon conference where podcasting was discussed.

Farkas: What made you decide to create your own podcasts?

Bob: As a longtime radio nut, I knew I had to get into this. We used to do pirate radio in the early 1990s, and this seemed like a nice way to recapture the rush of building a listener base. I put out a test show in October, and "The Bob and AJ Show" started the following month. One thing led to another, and now, just a few months later, the "scene" is exploding, and I produce three shows, with possibly more to come..

Farkas: What were the main challenges in creating a podcast?

Bob: Since we record in my home music studio, the only real technical challenges were to decide which pieces of equipment to leave out! We just wanted to be ourselves doing a show. We share a lot of the same values when it comes to what we find funny, the music we like, etc. The main challenge was learning the RSS and related technologies, and that was pretty simple.

Farkas: What are your plans for "The Bob and AJ Show" going forward?

Bob: Honestly, to keep having fun. We have no grand plans for commercialization, though if at some point we hook up with some sponsorship to help defer costs, we're not against it.

Farkas: Are there any copyright issues with playing music on your show? Is that a fear?

(continued on next page)

Interview with Bob Goyetche *(continued)*

Bob: Not at all. We made the decision early on to play only music we had permission and rights to play. This meant no big-label music, but we're very happy with that. Independent music fits better with the vibe of podcasting. It's also opened our ears to lots of great music we otherwise wouldn't have heard. We also get to build relationships with artists, which is very rewarding.

Farkas: Where do you see podcasting going in the next year? The next five years?

Bob: For the next year, I think awareness will be the main accomplishment. We've come so far in seven months. I'm meeting people who I don't have to explain podcasting to, so the medium is on the radar. In the next five years, I think we'll see a buildup to an incredible number of shows. People will jump on this, and some, when they realize the effort involved, may stop. Those who keep going, though, will have found a great outlet and a great hobby. I see more commercial podcasts, much like we're seeing commercial blogs now.

Farkas: Do you have an opinion on the commercialization of podcasting?

Bob: The fact that commercialization is thought to be viable validates what we are doing. Unlike radio, where there is limited space on the dial, the Internet is limitless. We're not limited to 88 to 108 on some little dial. Our show has potentially the same reach as any of these companies. Our production values are equal or superior, and our passion hasn't been smothered by a radio consultant from Toronto.

The way the "traditional outlets" are going to get podcast listeners is to put out programs people want to hear. I see that some Canadian radio corporations are redistributing some radio morning shows via podcast, I think they're missing the point. Podcasting is taking off because people can't stand to listen to another "morning zoo" program. It's too formulaic, too packaged, and too homogenized. I think there will be people who will enjoy the podcasts of these corporations, and more power to them. They probably wouldn't have liked our show anyway.

Tutorial: Creating a Podcast

Now that I've covered the basic equipment and process of creating a podcast, I'll take you step by step through the process of creating a podcast for both Macintosh and Windows PC computers.

In the case of the Macintosh, I used a third-party microphone, a preamp, and GarageBand in OS X to create the show. On the PC, I used a third-party microphone, no preamp, and Audacity for recording and sound editing.

On the Macintosh, I used GarageBand as the recording/editing software, and on the Windows PC, I used Audacity. It's important to note that Audacity for the Macintosh behaves and looks almost exactly like its PC counterpart. Therefore, anyone who wants to use Audacity on the Macintosh can refer to the PC tutorial.

I realize that there are literally hundreds of combinations of software, equipment, and operating systems, so I chose two relatively generic setups for creating the podcasts on each platform. The important thing to remember is that the process is fundamentally the same, no matter what is being used to create the show. It goes without saying that a complex preamp/mixing board and a high-end digital recorder will alter the process, but for the purpose of following from idea to finished podcast, these tutorials do the trick.

Interview with AKG and The Specialist

AKG and The Specialist are hosts of the top-15 podcast "The Specialist and AKG Show."

AKG:

- 27 years old, originally from Boston
- Currently works in the antique-auction industry
- Relocating to Chicago to pursue master's degree in marketing/advertising/communications

The Specialist:

- 27 years old, resides in New York City
- Television producer

The Specialist and AKG were roommates at a small liberal-arts college in the Northeast. It was during this time, they say, that "we realized that we were both fascinated with our own smells, swabbings, and toilet habits."

Farkas: What made you decide to create your own podcast? What were your reasons?

The Specialist: I first heard about podcasting as a phenomenon where everyday people were producing their own Internet radio shows from home. AKG and I had never even listened to any other shows before we started ours, but our initial game plan was just to record a 15- or 20-minute phone conversation between the two of us.

Our normal topics of conversation often focused on the irregularities in our own bowel movements and our other disgusting habits. I felt that the types of things we were talking about with each other weren't being discussed in any other outlets of the mainstream media. I kind of look at our show as the gross underbelly of "Seinfeld," in that we do conversational humor about somewhat taboo subjects. My main motivations for doing the show were to both have something that our friends could listen to, but also to document a period in my life that I could play in 15 or 20 years and have a laugh listening to.

AKG: Ditto.

Farkas: What has surprised you the most with regard to the impact of your podcast(s)?

The Specialist: The two most surprising things for me thus far are that we were approached by individuals like yourself and the Pink Poker Bunny requesting to either interview us or be interviewed by us. I could have never imagined that anybody outside

Interview with AKG and The Specialist *(continued)*

of our immediate circle of friends would give a flying rat's ass about anything we were doing.

Farkas: What are your plans going forward?

The Specialist: We have really enjoyed doing interviews and having guests on the show, and I hope we can continue to talk to even more interesting and diverse people. Also, we feel that with enough support and research, we may one day be able to rid the world of swamp ass.

Farkas: What has made podcasting such a phenomenon, in your opinion?

The Specialist: While we are often baffled by the popularity of some shows, I would have to say that it is because any nitwit with a computer and something mindless to talk about can have their own show, including yours truly.

Farkas: Where do you see podcasting going in the next year? The next five years?

AKG: I don't think podcasting will ever catch on as a mainstream form of communication. It will be useful for freaks, geeks, wasteoids, spotors, and motorheads to spread their messages freely.

The Specialist: I have been discouraged by the direction that podcasting seems to be going in. What started out as an underground alternative to mainstream corporate radio seems to be turning into a marketing tool for big corporations to reach new audiences. Instead of Joe Blow podcasting from his rec room, you have regular over-the-air radio shows converting their content into MP3 and podcast feeds, and you have corporations like Warner Bros. outputting their "Paris Hilton" podcast to promote their rag trash movies like *House of Wax*. My feelings on the group of podcasters banding together to sell advertising and possibly even be broadcast on Sirius satellite radio is mixed. While it is sad on the one hand to see such an indie movement go mainstream, I can't really blame them for wanting to reach a wider audience and perhaps even turn their part-time hobby into a full-time gig.

AKG: I think it is unfortunate if podcasters got into podcasting hoping to get picked up or get signed or make money doing it. Unfortunately, that breeds a cutthroat, competitive environment where podcasters must compete with each other in a way that no longer becomes fun.

(continued on next page)

Interview with AKG and The Specialist *(continued)*

Farkas: Technically speaking, what was the most difficult thing about getting a podcast off the ground?

The Specialist: I bear the brunt of the producing aspects of the show in New York City. Before we started, I had no experience in HTML or Web design, and the biggest initial obstacle was simply creating a Web site that could host the show.

One of the biggest problems for our show is that unlike most co-hosted podcast shows, AKG and I do not sit next to each other in the same room during the show. We record the show over a phone line, with me in New York and AKG in New Hampshire (soon to be Chicago). The biggest challenge I have faced thus far was being able to get a clean signal of AKG's voice from an ordinary phone line without the use of expensive broadcasting equipment.

On top of that, we have many call-in guests, and it becomes tough to get high-quality sound without the use of a professional telephone audio hub. We finally perfected the sound quality around our eighth show, and I am currently very happy with the quality of our broadcast. And the fart sounds are clearer now as well.

Creating a Macintosh podcast

Although other Macintosh programs are available, the fact that GarageBand is bundled with new machines makes it the most ubiquitous sound recording/editing software for the Macintosh. For this reason, I chose to use GarageBand as the software for this tutorial. The list of equipment I used is as follows:

- Karaoke Dynamic Microphone (no joke)

- M-Audio MobilePre USB preamp

- Macintosh G5 dual 2.0 GHz processors, 2.5 GB RAM, OS 10.3.9

- GarageBand version 1.1.0 (26)

It's important to note that though I chose to use a preamp to make this podcast, the G5 Mac has a Line-In jack that allows a microphone to be plugged directly into the machine.

1. Connect the equipment

I am assuming that you came up with the concept for the ...
outline, and possibly even a script before you made it to this ...
That said, the first step is to connect all the equipment properly,
starting with connecting the preamp to the USB port and then the
microphone to the preamp (**Figures 3.37** through **3.40**). When this is
accomplished, ensure that the preamp is receiving power (the lights
are on).

Figure 3.37
Connect the preamp to the computer via
the USB port.

Figure 3.38
Check to see that the power is
active on the preamp.

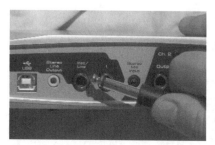

Figure 3.39
Insert the microphone jack into the
preamp microphone input; then set up
your microphone with your pop screen
(if you have one) in front of you.

Figure 3.40
If you have no preamp, the microphone can be plugged directly
into the Line-In jack on the
Macintosh.

podcast, an
int.

the application and OS

is important, because if the correct inputs aren't
stem Preferences, the microphone will not work properly.
o open GarageBand and create a new project for your
e created in. Follow the steps in **Figures 3.41** through **3.48**
traight vocal track (without any effects) so that recording

Figure 3.41

Open System
Preferences, and click
the Sound icon. Then
click the button labeled
Input.

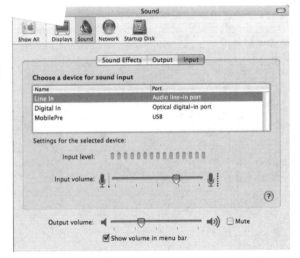

Figure 3.42

In the list box, select
MobilePre. (This is the
M-Audio MobilePre
USB preamp device I
am using.)

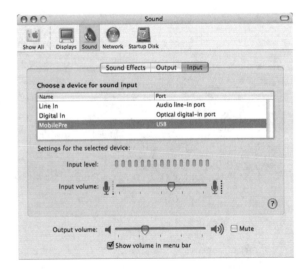

Figure 3.43

Using the microphone, test the Input Level by watching the meter above the volume control. Adjust the volume so that normal speech brings the meter up to about 70 percent of maximum.

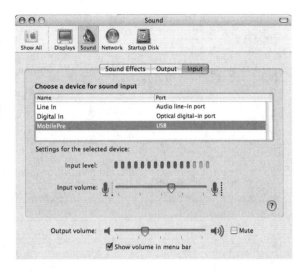

Figure 3.44

Open GarageBand, and select Create New Song.

Figure 3.45

When you select Create New Song, you will get this dialog box, asking you what to name it and where to save it. The Tempo, Time, bpm, and Key settings at the bottom of the dialog box can be left as is.

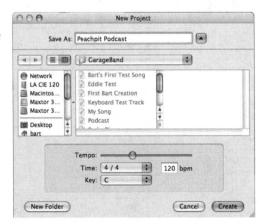

Figure 3.46

When the GarageBand project opens, you will see a Grand Piano track. Choose Track > Delete Track to delete it.

Figure 3.47

Now choose Track > New Track.

Figure 3.48

In the New Track dialog box, click the Real Instrument button and then select Vocals. The default effect position will be No Effects; leave this as is. For these purposes, Mono is also acceptable (although if you have a stereo microphone, you can click the Stereo button). Click OK to continue.

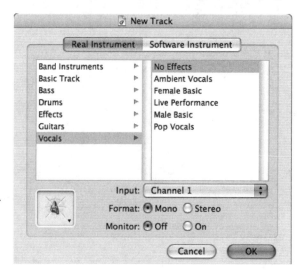

NOTE If you want to add a digital effect to your voice, you are welcome to do it, but for the first podcast, I suggest that you see what your voice sounds like on its own. If you must use an effect, however, the Male Basic or Female Basic effect is recommended. GarageBand add-on modules, called Jam Packs, are available from Apple for $99 each. They contain elaborate effects that give you more options for editing sound files.

3. Record your podcast

Now that everything is set up and ready to go, it's time to record the podcast. Before you start the actual podcast, record the first couple lines of your podcast; then go back and listen to it (**Figure 3.49**). If you feel that your vocal track needs some adjustment, open the Track Info dialog box by choosing Track > Track Info. Here, you can adjust the equalizer, add effects, and manage echo and reverb. After you have set up your vocals just so, get your script out, and click the Record button to start the podcast (**Figures 3.50** and **3.51**).

Figure 3.49

After recording a short test track, if you don't like the sound, you can open the Track Info dialog box (choose Track > Track Info) and make any changes you feel are necessary.

Figure 3.50

Click the Record button, and start talking!

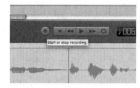

Figure 3.51

If you make a mistake, just pause for a second and then pick up where you left off (the mistake can be edited out later). The other option is to stop the recording and begin a new track.

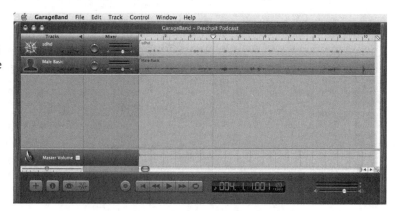

4. Edit your vocal content

The podcast recording is now in the bag. Unfortunately, you made a few verbal flubs and had to repeat yourself in several places to ensure that the material was covered cleanly. This is what editing was made for, and fortunately, it's what GarageBand was made for as well. Using the Track Editor, you can selectively remove (or move around) any portions of the recording that you want (**Figures 3.52** through **3.56**).

Figure 3.52

Begin by selecting the main track (there may only be one); then click the scissor-shaped icon. This brings up the Track Editor, where you can manipulate the recording quickly and easily.

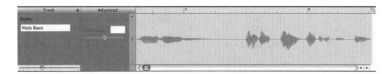

Figure 3.53 In the bottom-left corner of the Track Editor is a slider that allows you to enlarge the scale of the recording strip. Enlarge the scale to between the third and fourth notches.

Figure 3.54 Now move to the areas that you want to cut. Using the mouse, select the individual sections of the recording you want to eliminate; then choose Edit > Cut (Command-X).

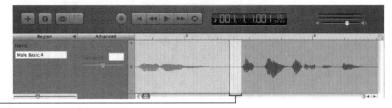

Gap

Figure 3.55 When the portion is cut out, there will be a gap in the soundtrack. Use your mouse to grab the far end of the soundtrack to slide the two halves back together again. In this manner, you can remove any unwanted content and join up the recording again so that the listener never knew anything was cut.

Figure 3.56

Using the simple cut-and-paste interface in GarageBand, manipulate the recording so that it represents the intended broadcast. This usually involves simple cutting of mistakes and rejoining of the audio track.

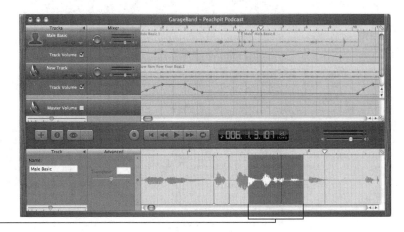

Selected area to be cut

5. Add music and finishing touches

Now is the time to import any music (see "Legalities" earlier in this chapter) into the background and/or at the beginning and end of the podcast. On the Mac, iTunes makes this very simple, because you can drag and drop files directly from iTunes into your podcast (**Figure 3.57**). Similarly, you can drag an MP3 or AAC file from the Desktop into GarageBand. When the music is in place, click the tiny inverted triangle under the track name to open the Track Volume control (**Figure 3.58**). With this control, you can adjust the volume of the track in detail, fading in and out as you please (**Figure 3.59**).

Figure 3.57
Drag files directly out of iTunes and into GarageBand, if you want. Here, an original version of "Row Row Row Your Boat" is being dragged into GarageBand.

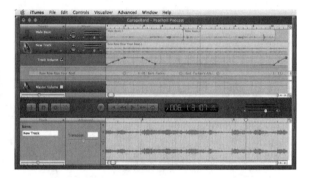

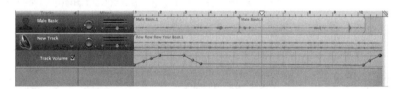

Figure 3.58   When the music is in place, click the inverted triangle to bring up the Track Volume bar. By clicking the volume line in this bar, you create points that you can manipulate to control the volume in minute or heavy-handed ways. Using a series of four points, make your music fade in at the beginning of the podcast and then fade out at the end.

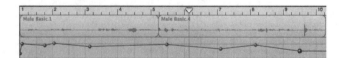

Figure 3.59   Depending on the volume variability of your voice during the recording, you may want to adjust the volume on the main voice track, although I recommend against doing so unless it is absolutely necessary.

6. Export the podcast to MP3 format

The last phase of the podcast creation process is outputting the file in a usable format. Ideally, the MP3 format is the one that can be accessed by the widest range of listeners, so I recommend that you choose that format. That said, GarageBand does not export in MP3 format; it exports in AAC format into iTunes. For this reason, you must export to iTunes first and then convert to an MP3 file in iTunes to complete the process (**Figures 3.60, 3.61**, and **3.62**).

Figure 3.60

To export your podcast to iTunes, choose File > Export to iTunes.

Figure 3.61

When the export is complete, your podcast will show up in iTunes as the latest file added.

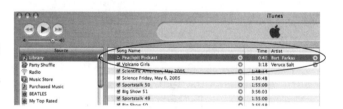

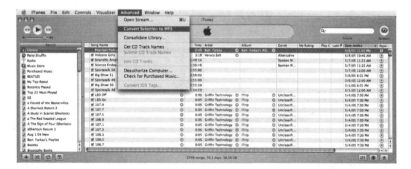

Figure 3.62 In iTunes, select the podcast; then choose Advanced > Convert Selection to MP3 to finish the process. Congratulations—you've completed your first podcast! For instructions on how to publish your podcast, turn to Chapter 4.

Creating a PC podcast

Windows PCs have the largest library of software available for creating podcasts. They also have by far the largest variation in equipment components. PCs have a large variety of motherboards, sound cards, video cards, types of RAM, and even CPUs, and for this reason, it is difficult to present an example of a common PC setup for creating podcasts. That said, the vast majority of PCs have sound cards with microphone inputs, and the lion's share of them run the Windows operating system.

I came up with a process for creating a podcast on a PC that a preponderance of PC users will be able to follow, using the following items:

- Radio Shack PZM omnidirectional condenser microphone

- C-Media PCI Sound Card (in Dell Dimension 4500)

- Dell Dimension 4500 P4 2.4 GHz, 1 GB RAM

- Windows XP (although other Windows configurations are very similar)

- Audacity, Version 1.2.3 (PC version)

1. Connect the equipment

As in the Macintosh tutorial, I am assuming that you came up with the concept for the podcast, an outline, and possibly even a script before you made it to this point. When you are ready to begin, you must make the necessary connections to get the ball rolling (**Figures 3.63**, **3.64**, and **3.65**). In this case, the connections need only be that the microphone is plugged into the microphone or Line-In jack of the sound card on the back of the PC.

Figure 3.63

In the case of the
Realistic (Radio Shack)
PZM omnidirectional
condenser microphone,
check to see that it has
a fresh battery (there is
no preamp to provide
phantom power)
before you plug it in.

Figure 3.64

If your microphone has
a 6.5mm (1/4-inch) jack,
you will likely need an
adapter to turn the
jack into a standard
3.5mm jack that PC
sound cards accept.

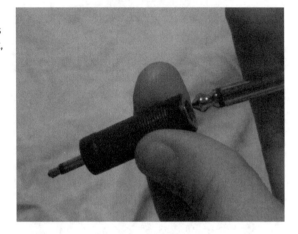

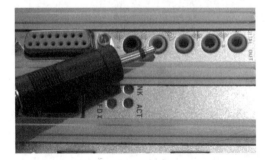

Figure 3.65 Plug the microphone into the microphone input on the sound card
(located on the back of your computer). If you make a mistake and plug it into the
Line-In jack, it won't be the end of the world; you can always change the input in
Audacity later. If you have a pop filter, this is also the time to set it up in front of
the microphone.

2. Configure the application and OS

This next step involves making sure that the microphone is working as an input device in Windows. To do this, you must enter the Windows Sounds and Audio Devices control panel and ensure that the microphone is working (**Figures 3.66** through **3.71**). Then you must open Audacity, create a new file, and test your microphone to ensure that it is working properly with that program (**Figures 3.72** through **3.75**).

Figure 3.66

From the Start menu, choose Settings > Control Panel > Sounds, Speech, and Audio Devices.

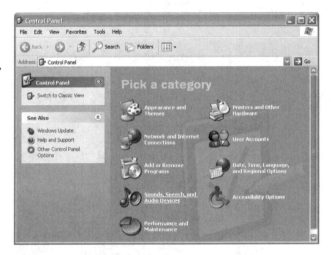

Figure 3.67

Clicking Sounds, Speech, and Audio Devices brings up the Sounds and Audio Devices Properties dialog box. There are five tabs at the top of this dialog box; click the tab labeled Voice.

Figure 3.68

In the Voice Recording area, there is a menu from which you can choose the default recording device. This should already be set to the sound card that is in your computer (in this case, a C-Media card). If you have more than one device available, you can select it here.

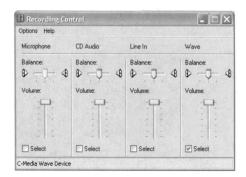

Figure 3.69 While still in the Sounds and Audio Devices Properties window, if you want to adjust the balance or the volume of the various inputs to the computer, click the Volume button in the Default Device window. This brings up the Recording Control dialog box, which allows you to adjust the volume and balance for four inputs: Microphone, CD Audio, Line In, and Wave.

Figure 3.70

If you want to test that the microphone is working properly, click the Test Hardware button. This will bring up the Sound Hardware Test Wizard.

Figure 3.71

After a short time analyzing your system, the wizard shows this dialog box, which allows you to test the functioning of your microphone. When the wizard is complete, the microphone should be working properly.

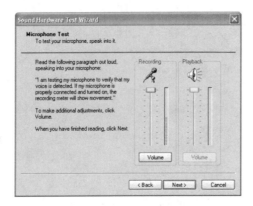

Figure 3.72

Now it's time to launch Audacity. When it's up and running, choose File > Save Project As to name and save your podcast.

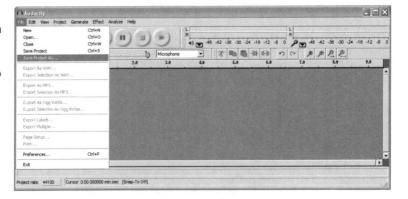

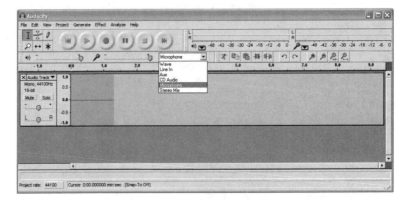

Figure 3.73 In the middle of the main Audacity window is a drop-down menu labeled Microphone. If your microphone is plugged into the microphone jack of your sound card, you're all set. If, however, your microphone is plugged into the Line-In jack, you must select the appropriate input from the Microphone drop-down menu.

Figure 3.74

Next, choose Project >
New Audio Track.

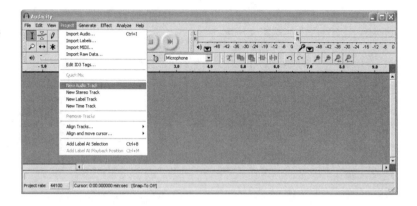

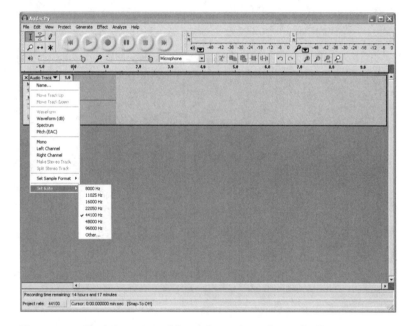

Figure 3.75 The left portion of the Audio Track window will tell you what the recording settings are. These should say Mono, 44100 Hz, and 32-bit float rate. If you are using a stereo microphone, you can click the Audio Track control to select a Stereo input. Likewise, if you want to increase or decrease the sampling rate, you can do that in this menu as well. 44100 Hz is 44.1 kHz, which will produce a CD-quality recording.

3. Record your podcast

Now that everything is set up and ready to go, it's time to record the podcast. Before you start the actual podcast, record the first couple lines of your podcast; then go back and listen to it (**Figure 3.76**). If you feel that your vocal track needs some adjustment, and you want to add an effect to it, you can add it *after* the recording (Audacity doesn't add effects dynamically). When you have completed the practice run, start the recording, and let it rip (**Figures 3.77** and **3.78**)!

Click Play to listen to your recording.

Figure 3.76

After recording a short test track, play back the recording to ensure that it sounds OK.

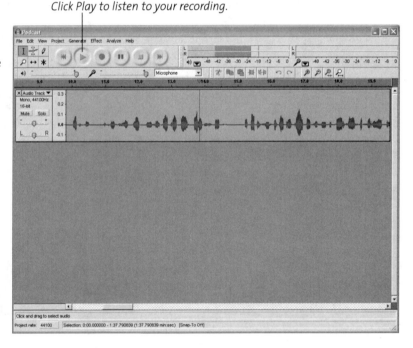

Click this button and then start talking for your podcast.

Figure 3.77
When you're ready, click the Record button, and start talking!

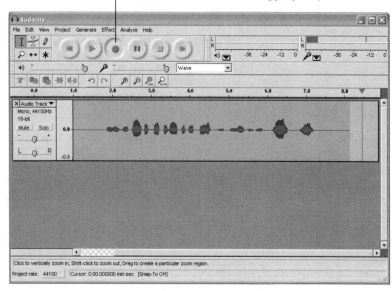

Any highlighted area (such as this one) can be moved, cut, or copied.

Figure 3.78
If you make a mistake, just pause for a second and then pick up where you left off (the mistake can be edited out later). The other option is to stop the recording and begin a new track. I recommend that you pause and then restart at the point where you made your mistake. This way, you will be editing just one track.

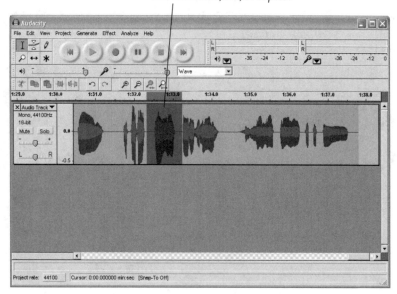

4. Edit your vocal content

The podcast recording is now in the bag. Unfortunately, you made a few verbal flubs and had to repeat yourself in several places to ensure that the material was covered cleanly. This is what editing was made for, and fortunately, the folks who made Audacity have made it easy for us to edit out any verbal mistakes (**Figures 3.79** through **3.82**).

Figure 3.79

Audacity allows you to edit the tracks right in the Audio Track window. To edit a specific portion or add an effect to it, highlight that portion of the track.

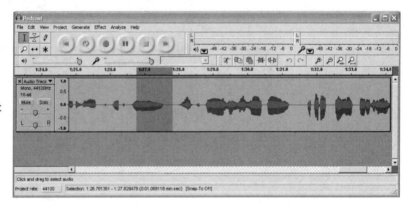

Figure 3.80

When the portion of the track you want to alter is highlighted, click the Effect menu and drag down to the effect you want to apply to the recording. In this case, you are adding an Echo effect to the selection.

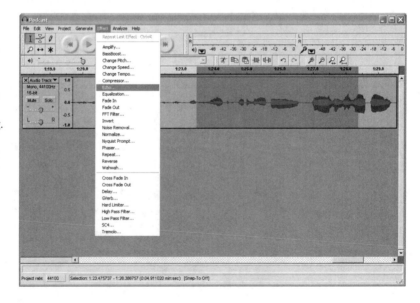

Figure 3.81

If you want to remove a specific portion, select that portion; then choose Edit > Cut. When you do this, the portion you selected will be cut from the recording.

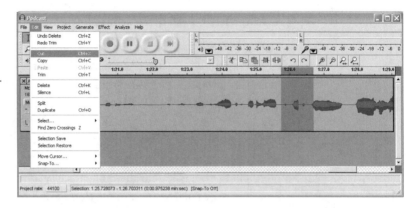

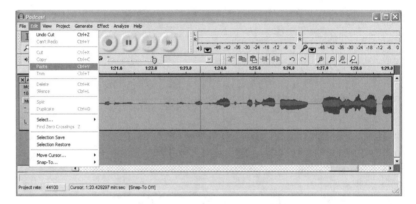

Figure 3.82   To move a portion of the recording around, choose Edit > Cut. Then, using the selection tool, click the place in the recording where you want the cut piece of audio to be placed. When the area is selected (a line will appear in the recording showing the exact point of insertion), choose Edit > Paste.

5. Add music and finishing touches

The voice recording is now just right, but it's just a plain voice recording. Now is the time to import any music (see "Legalities" earlier in this chapter) into the background and/or at the beginning and end of the podcast. Audacity allows for the easy drag-and-drop addition of any MP3 or WAV file. Simply pick up the MP3 file you want, and drag it to the area beneath your main sound track (**Figure 3.83**). The MP3 will be added as a separate audio track. When the music is in place, you can highlight specific sections and adjust the volume or apply effects such as a fade-in or fade-out as you see fit (**Figures 3.84**, **3.85**, and **3.86**).

Figure 3.83

Drag audio files directly to Audacity. When you do, the files will be imported automatically.

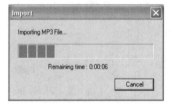

Figure 3.84

When the music is in place, you can adjust the volume control on the bar on the left, or you can select portions of the music and add effects to it. This is where you can add the Fade In and Fade Out effects.

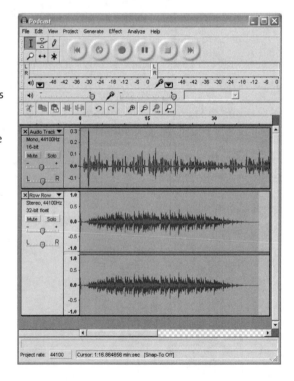

Figure 3.85

Note the (very loud) MP3 recording and how it is tapered at both ends. This file has had a short Fade In and a longer Fade Out effect added to it.

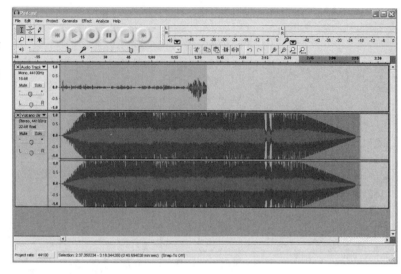

Figure 3.86

If you want to add any effects to any portion of the recording, now is the time to do it. To add an effect, simply select the portion of the recording that you want to alter; then choose the effect you want to add from the Effect menu. You can undo the addition of effects, if need be.

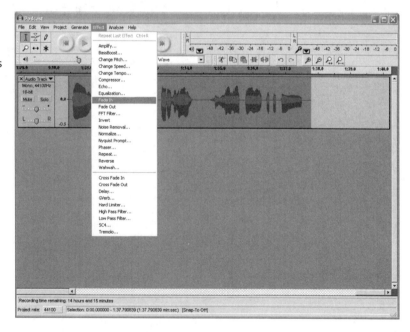

6. Export the podcast to MP3 format

The last phase of the podcast creation process is outputting the file in a usable format. Ideally, the MP3 format is the one that can be accessed by the widest range of listeners, so I recommend that you choose that format (**Figures 3.87**, **3.88**, and **3.89**). Audacity can export files as .WAV files, MP3 files, or Ogg Vorbis files. For the purposes of mass acceptance, the MP3 is the file of choice.

Figure 3.87

When the podcast is complete, choose File > Export As MP3.

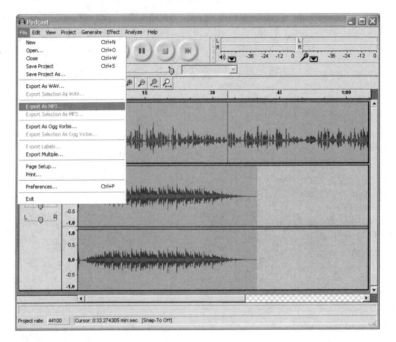

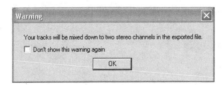

Figure 3.88 When you select the Export as MP3 file, a warning appears that the file will be mixed down into two tracks (a stereo recording). This is fine.

4

Podcasting Distribution

OK, so you have put together a podcast that's going to set the world on fire. You spent hours coming up with witty and erudite discourse between the host and co-host. Important and compelling guests were interviewed at just the right time during the podcast, and everything went swimmingly. Heck, even Peter Gabriel decided that he would allow you to use some of his music in the background. The editing process is complete, and the shiny new podcast is all ready to be heard by the masses!

There's only one catch: Knowledge of how to publish your podcast on the World Wide Web eludes you. Not to worry, because this chapter details the intricacies of using the RSS specification so that your podcast can reach the maximum number of people with the least amount of effort. Although *RSS* actually stands for *Really Simple Syndication,* for a nonscripting or programming newbie, the term "really simple" doesn't exactly jump to mind when learning RSS from scratch. Fortunately, several programs have emerged that make the process of publishing podcasts with RSS a relatively simple process.

This chapter covers podcasting distribution options, from the complex types that appeal to the programmer personality to the all-in-one packages that completely demystify the process. The routes this chapter examines are:

- RSS file construction: building an RSS feed from scratch

- Alternative podcast distribution: MP3 files and streaming audio

- Web-site packagers: companies that charge a fee to do it all for you

- Software packages: software, like FeedForAll, that makes publishing an RSS feed an automated process

The chapter also looks at how to get your podcast out there and noticed (**Figure 4.1**). I've even sneaked in a couple of interviews, including one with the creators of the very popular RSS feed software option, FeedForAll. No matter what route you choose to take with regard to creating RSS feeds, this chapter has all the information you need to make the process second nature.

Figure 4.1
This simple diagram shows the process of creating a podcast, a Web site, and RSS feed to get the podcast out on the podwaves.

Podcast Creation and Publication Process

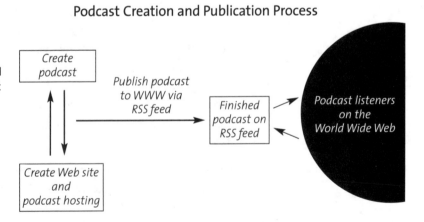

RSS

RSS, or *Really Simple Syndication,* is the engine behind the podcasting phenomenon. The RSS standard is what enabled the relatively simple proliferation and dissemination of podcasts throughout the world. RSS is defined as a standard set of tools for the purpose of allowing frequent updates for content on the World Wide Web. In short, RSS is a XML-based format for content distribution over the World Wide Web. Using RSS, a Webmaster (or podcaster) can place content on a Web log or podcast Web site in such a way that news or podcast *aggregators* (programs that search for new content) can grab the fresh content in a concise manner.

What the heck is XML? *XML* **stands for** *Extensible Markup Language.* **First, you need to know what a markup language is. A** *markup language* **combines text and extra information about the text into a file that can be used to perform a function. A good example of a markup language is HTML (Hypertext Markup Language), which is the backbone of every page on the World Wide Web. Extensible Markup Language (XML) is designed to help mediate the sharing of data across different kinds of systems, such as those present on the Internet. In summary, XML is a type of language that allows information to flow freely through different systems across the Internet without difficulty.**

RSS means that consumers can use programs like iPodder or HappyFish and have them scour hundreds of podcast Web sites in minutes, downloading *only* what is new on those sites. In this manner, RSS has revolutionized the way information is disseminated, and that includes podcasts. For podcasters, RSS allows them to place the podcast out on the Web for millions of people to access. For consumers, RSS allows them to have access to a nearly unlimited amount of content while saving them from having to look for the content one item at a time.

A Brief History of RSS

Really Simple Syndication was originally designed by Netscape back in 1999. Eventually, Dave Winder added features to RSS, including the Scripting News SML format. In 2002, RSS 2.0 was proposed, and that is the standard used today. RSS 2.0 is published under a Creative Commons license at the Berkman Center for Internet & Society at Harvard University.

From an actual line-by-line explanation of an RSS enclosure to a tutorial on how to create your own, this section delves into the nitty-gritty of the Really Simple Syndication standard and how it works. I need to point out that there are entire books (many of them, in fact) that cover just RSS and how it works. That said, I will attempt to give you enough information to feel comfortable with the format and to use it on a basic level for podcast publishing. If you want to learn more about RSS online, check out the Berkman Center site at http://blogs.law.harvard.edu/tech/rss.

In the following sections, I first go through the process of creating an RSS file for a podcasting feed. Then I list the completed file with an explanation of each and every line in the file. By following through these two sections, you will have a decent understanding of how RSS works. The example I set out can even be a template for your own RSS file.

Creating an RSS feed

Anyone who has some experience coding in HTML will likely find RSS relatively easy to understand. By comparison, anyone who has never done any HTML coding will likely find RSS a little cryptic despite what the acronym implies.

 In this tutorial, I refer to RSS files with regard to podcasts and podcasts alone. RSS feeds can be created for many kinds of information, but for the sake of simplicity and the spirit of this podcasting book, everything I discuss refers to podcasts.

Needed: Web Site

To create an RSS file or feed, you need a Web page with space to store the podcast. That page will need to be able to handle the bandwidth if the podcast becomes successful and thousands of people download it. If you are serious about podcasting, setting up a Web site for your show is a necessity, both as a contact point for your fan base and also as a syndication point for getting your podcasts out on the World Wide Web.

Obtaining a Web site is remarkably easy, and many ISP services supply easy-to-construct online tools for creating a Web page without any knowledge of HTML. Conversely, if you are knowledgeable in the ways of HTML, you might want to create a Web site from scratch. Many design tools—such as GoLive (Adobe), FrontPage (Microsoft), and Dreamweaver (Macromedia)—are decent choices for creating a Web site.

If money is no object, plenty of Web-design houses all over the world are champing at the bit to design Web sites of all kinds. Finally, the boom in podcasting has led to the emergence of several podcast hosting Web sites that enable you to publish your podcast on its own Web site for a fee (see "Web-Site Packagers" later in this chapter).

 When your podcast is all set up and the RSS feed is in place, I suggest that you put the RSS and XML icons on your Web site. These two tiny icons tell the world that you have a syndicated podcast feed that can be accessed by a podcatcher program (aggregator).

To begin, I'll explain what an RSS file is: quite simply, a set of *tags* (instructions) that name, explain, and point to a podcast. In addition, these tags set up parameters for other details, such as how often people can check the feeds and whether to allow a failed download of the podcast to restart. There are other elements of an RSS file, of course, but not to worry; I'll go through them in detail one at a time.

Conventions

The RSS language has certain conventions that you need to be aware of:

- All tags are *closed*—enclosed between the characters < and >. The tag <title>, for example, means that all text following this tag will be represented as the title of the podcast.

- Every instruction that you enter must also be closed. In `<title>Bart's Book</title>`, for example, `<title>` means "Start the title here," with the words *Bart's Book* being the title; then the `</title>` tag instructs the program to close the title (**Figure 4.2**). The forward slash before the tag signifies that this is the end of the instruction. Every instruction must be closed after it is opened. In the sample file, notice that `<channel>` at the beginning of the file is closed with a `</channel>` tag at the end of the file.

Figure 4.2

A breakdown of each element in one line of an RSS file

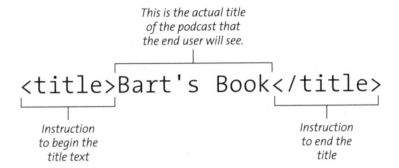

This is the actual title of the podcast that the end user will see.

`<title>Bart's Book</title>`

Instruction to begin the title text

Instruction to end the title

RSS files can constructed with high-end features that can be fairly complicated when the full range of instructions (tags) and features are implemented. It is not in the scope of this book to explore RSS and XML in depth, so I have kept the process as simple as possible. Therefore, for the purposes of creating a simple RSS feed, the following instructions are all that you need:

`<rss version="2.0">` identifies the files as RSS 2.0 files.

`<channel>` is an instruction that sets up an area where information about the feed goes. This information includes the show title, the Web page's URL, copyright information, and several other factors.

`<title>` identifies the title text for the show.

`<link>` identifies the link to the podcast's Web site.

`<description>` identifies the descriptive text for the show.

`<lastBuildDate>` identifies the last time the file was altered.

`<language>` identifies what language the programming is in (English, Spanish, German, and so on).

`<copyright>` establishes the copyright of the podcast content.

`<generator>` identifies who created the file.

`<webmaster>` identifies the Webmaster for the podcast's Web site.

`<ttl>` means *time to live*. This value instructs the RSS readers (such as iPodder and HappyFish) how often they can look to see whether new content is available on this feed.

`<item>` is a podcast feed. It can also be a feed to a text file, video file, or anything else. For purposes of this book, however, it refers to a podcast feed.

`<enclosure>` links to the actual MP3 file and also establishes the file's length and type.

The instructions such as *<channel>* are commonly referred to as *tags*. The proper way to describe them is to call them *elements*, but because the term *tags* is ubiquitous, that's what I use here.

Creating the file

This section takes you through the process of creating an RSS file for the purposes of publishing a single podcast. I assume that you have already set up a Web site and that the podcast is already linked on the site.

The first section of the RSS file contains information such as the show's title, the copyright information, the Web site for the show, and the *ttl* (*time to live*) value. Following is a step-by-step walkthrough of each line of the RSS file.

Note that the file names and links used in this sample are not real links. They are for demonstration purposes only.

1. First, the RSS file needs to be identified. The first line of the code identifies the files as an RSS file.

```
<rss version="2.0">
```

2. The next entry is `<channel>`, which acts as a marker that begins the information about the podcasting feed.

```
<channel>
```

3. The next two lines show the feed (or show) title and the URL of the show's Web site, respectively.

```
<title>Secrets of Podcasting</title>
<link>
  http://www.peechpitpress.com/secretsofpodcasting/
</link>
```

4. Next up is the description text for the show. Note again that the description instruction is started and then closed after the descriptive text.

```
<description>
  The best podcast about a podcast book in the world!
</description>
```

5. The next two lines show the last time the RSS file was edited and establish the language in which the RSS file is written (English, Spanish, and so on).

```
<lastBuildDate>Mon, 9 May 2005 22:19:41 -0400
  </lastBuildDate>
<language>en-us</language>
```

6. The next two lines show copyright information and the identity of the creator of the file.

```
<copyright>Copyright 2005</copyright>
<generator>Bart</generator>
```

7. The next line contains the contact information for the Webmaster of the Web site where the podcast file resides or is hosted.

```
<webMaster>JerryG@bogusaddress.com</webMaster>
```

8. The final line before the nitty-gritty of the actual podcast feed involves something called time to live (ttl). Time to live is important because it tells aggregators (podcast readers) how often they are allowed to check to see whether a new feed is available. I suggest that you set the ttl to at least 60 minutes; otherwise, your server could get hammered by people checking every minute. Setting the ttl to 60 minutes ultimately saves bandwidth as well, which usually translates into cash in your pocket.

```
<ttl>60</ttl>
```

The next portion of the RSS file deals with the actual podcast feed information, which is classified as an `<item>`. If you were placing several podcasts in the feed, each podcast would have its own `<item>` section like this one.

9. The first line is an `<item>` line, which signifies a distinct podcast. If there are multiple podcasts in a feed, each one will have a section beginning with `<item>` and ending with `</item>`.

```
<item>
```

10. The next line is the title of the podcast. In the case of a weekly or daily podcast, this line would contain the name of the episode.

```
<title>Secrets of Podcasts Show #1</title>
```

11. Now you need to show the link to the actual MP3 file (or other type of audio file). A link is signified with the `<link>` tag.

```
<link>http://www.peechpitpress.com/secretsofPC.mp3
   </link>
```

12. The next line describes the podcast (or episode).

```
<description>Learn how to podcast!</description>
```

13. Next up are the publication date and time. The date is self explanatory, and it is worth noting that the time is on a 24-hour clock (22:41 = 10:41 p.m.). The -0600 at the end denotes the time zone—in this case, minus six hours from GMT (Greenwich Mean Time). The most important thing to remember with the time zone is to be consistent from feed to feed with whatever time zone you select.

```
<pubDate>Sat, 7 May 2005 22:41:10 -0600</pubDate>
```

14. The next portion is perhaps the most important. This part is called the *enclosure,* and it is the link that the podcatching software will download. The most important aspect of the enclosure statement is to ensure that the length of the audio file (in this case, an MP3 file) is exactly correct. The length is represented in bytes, and if this value is correct, it allows podcatching software to resume an interrupted download, which can help reduce bandwidth in the long run. Last, the `type` parameter is important because it describes exactly what kind of audio file you are using and, therefore, ensures the proper handling of the MP3 file after it is downloaded by a listener.

```
<enclosure url=
  " http://www.peechpitpress.com/secretsofPC.mp3"
length="38998016" type="audio/mpeg"/>
```

15. That's it. Now that the item is complete, you just need to close out the item, the channel, and the RSS file as follows:

```
</item>
</channel>
</rss>
```

The finished file

Following is the complete file, all ready to go. At a glance, the RSS file in this form can be a daunting thing for someone with no experience in HTML coding. However, after you go through it line by line, reading an explanation for each line, it really isn't that bad. In fact, you could use this file as a template for any RSS file meant for publishing a podcast.

```
<rss version="2.0">
<channel>
  <title>Secrets of Podcasting</title>
  <link>
    http://www.peechpitpress.com/secretsofpodcasting/
  </link>
<description>
  The best podcast about a podcast book in the world!
</description>
<lastBuildDate>Mon, 9 May 2005 22:19:41 -0400
  </lastBuildDate>
<language>en-us</language>
  <copyright>Copyright 2005</copyright>
```

```
<generator>Bart</generator>
<webMaster>JerryG@bogusaddress.com</webMaster>
<ttl>60</ttl>
<item>
  <title>Secrets of Podcasts Show #1</title>
  <link>http://www.peechpitpress.com/secretsofPC.mp3
  </link>
  <description>Learn how to podcast!</description>
  <pubDate>Sat, 7 May 2005 22:41:10 -600</pubDate>
  <enclosure url=
    " http://www.peechpitpress.com/secretsofPC.mp3"
  length="38998016" type="audio/mpeg"/>
</item>
</channel>
</rss>
```

Putting the RSS file to use

Now that the RSS file is complete, you have a couple more things left to get things up and running. The up side is that the hard part is over; this portion of the process is not particularly difficult, but it needs to be reviewed nonetheless. The following steps take the process through to completion:

1. The first thing you need to do is name your file—for this example, Secrets.xml.

The .XML extension isn't actually necessary, but it's fairly standard, so just go with the flow.

2. The next thing is to place the file on your Web site (or wherever your podcasting feed is being hosted).

This will end up looking something like http://www.bogus address.com/Secrets.xml.

3. As a test, try to open that file directly from your browser.

Most likely, a warning will flash across your screen complaining that the file is not a valid HTML file, but that isn't a problem. What should happen is that the file you worked on appears in the window (**Figure 4.3**). This means that the link works!

Figure 4.3

When you use a Web browser to go to the RSS feed link, it should look something like this.

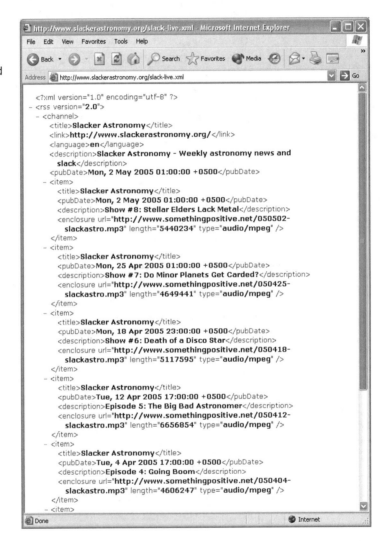

4. Launch a podcast aggregator (a podcatcher program) such as iPodder X, iPodder, or HappyFish, and paste your link into the New Feed box.

If the software goes to the site and downloads your podcast, you've done it!

Telling the world about your podcast

Next up, you must tell the world that your podcast exists. There are quite a few ways to get the word out—so many, in fact, that it's difficult to list them all. That said, there are a few common tried-and-true methods for getting your podcast on the radar of the podcasting community, including using blog advertising channels and using Web sites to aid in your cause.

Audio.weblogs.com

One of the first places to go is a Web site called Audio.weblogs.com (http://audio.weblogs.com). This site is one of the best places to get your podcast listed immediately. The site has a specific page—http://audio.weblogs.com/pingform.html—that allows you to enter the podcast feed link and the URL of your Web page (**Figure 4.4**). After you do this, your podcast will appear on the Audio.weblogs.com page.

Figure 4.4

The Audio.weblogs.com "Ping form" page is an easy way to get your feed out there immediately.

Contact the community

Contact the main podcasting Web sites like www.podcastalley.com, www.podcastingnews.com, and www.podcastbunker.com

(**Figure 4.5**). Each of these sites has an "add your podcast" link that allows you to get your podcast feed out there so that listeners can find it and give your show a listen. Check out the appendix in this book for a list of podcasting Web pages that you can contact to help distribute your podcast.

Figure 4.5

There are scores of Web sites that can help you get the word out on your podcast.

Advertise on your own Web page or on a blog

If you have your own Web page, it is a good idea to put up a banner or a note about your podcast and the feed link. If you have friends or colleagues with Web pages, you can trade with them so that they link to your podcast as well. This technique may net you some new listeners, and if they like the show, their word-of-mouth advertising will be worth the effort.

Interview with Aaron, Pamela, and Travis

"Slacker Astronomy" is a top-10 podcast run by Aaron, Pamela, and Travis—no last names here (**Figure 4.6**).

Aaron has a MS in astronomy and currently is in a Ph.D. program at James Cook University. He has worked for the American Association of Variable Star Observers (AAVSO) for seven years.

Pamela has a Ph.D. in astronomy. She works for Harvard University's Science Center and writes for *Sky & Telescope* magazine.

Travis has a BA in broadcast journalism from Emerson College and is involved in several musical projects in addition to working at the AAVSO.

Figure 4.6 The "Slacker Astronomy" crew: Aaron, Pamela, and Travis.

Farkas: When did you first become aware of podcasting?

SA: Aaron read about it in a newspaper article at the airport while traveling for the holidays. The article talked about mainly the religious podcasts. He thought it would be perfect for astronomy and then invited Travis and Pamela to join him, and it was the first they heard about it.

Farkas: What made you decide to create your own podcast? Was the desire to get the message out with regard to astronomy the driving force?

SA: Our Prime Directive is to have fun. We do this for ourselves first of all. A strong second is the desire to share news of astronomy while respecting the intelligence of our audience (i.e., not "dumbing" it down). Aaron and Pamela are both very active in astronomical education and public outreach. so this was a natural extension for them. Travis is interested in the broadcasting aspect of it as well as astronomy.

Farkas: What has surprised you the most with regard to the impact of your podcast(s)?

SA: Two things. The first is that so many people listen! We were hoping for about 500 listeners, and so far we have ten times that. Secondly, the e-mails we get surprised us—in particular, the numbers and thoughtfulness of them. People have been very kind and supportive, and that keeps us going.

(continued on next page)

Interview with Aaron, Pamela, and Travis *(continued)*

Farkas: What are your plans for "Slacker Astronomy" going forward?

SA: We have lots of ideas. We want to expand our interviews and soundseeing tours. We also have ideas to move it beyond podcasting and into public talks and other media. Finally, we want to work with more professionals and produce podcasts on demand. For example, when a professional observatory has a press release, they can contact us to produce a podcast version of it for release at the same time.

Farkas: Where do you see podcasting going in the next year? The next five years?

SA: The most interesting thing will be to see how the attempts at commercialism play out. We think it has equal chances to succeed or fail.

Farkas: Do you have an opinion on the commercialization of podcasting?

SA: It will depend on whether marketing agents have respect for the audience. If they don't, and they treat [the audience] as one mass, it will fail. They need to tailor their technique for each unique podcast. Our advice to marketers: Pay no attention to what others are doing, and come up with your own plan.

As for our podcast, we do not plan to become a for-profit enterprise simply because it would violate our Prime Directive: to have fun. Freedom is important to us. As soon as we have to self-censor and kiss a brass ring, the show will no longer be fun, and we doubt we could ever make enough to justify that. We did an April Fool's show where we pretended to be shut down by The Man. Our audience loved it.

Alternative Podcasting Distribution Options

RSS is the de facto dominant way to distribute podcasts over the Internet, and for most home-baked podcast creators, this is the way they go about distribution. There are, however, a couple of other ways to distribute podcasts that are used by some commercial enterprises, and that's what this section examines.

MP3 files

Ultimately when a podcast is created, it becomes an MP3, Ogg Vorbis, WAV, or AAC file. In the case of mainstream podcasting, these files are then published via RSS. Some podcasts, however, are not set up with RSS but are instead available as straight downloads in the form of MP3 files (or one of the other compression formats). Although RSS offers the most exposure for a podcast, having a simple downloadable file also has its advantages and uses.

The most common examples of downloadable MP3 files in the commercial realm are audiobooks and periodicals through sites like Audible.com (**Figure 4.7**). These sites sell content and then make the content available as downloadable compressed files that can be played on a number of MP3 players. In the case of Audible.com, the files are also available as streaming content, but a large number of the site's customers use the download feature so that they have a copy of the podcast on their hard drives.

Figure 4.7

Audible.com allows downloading of all the podcasts it sells.

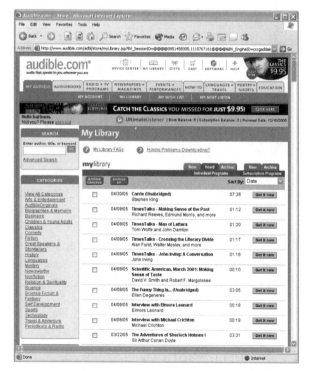

Corporations are increasingly making podcasts available to both the curious public and their employees. In the case of Duke University (**Figure 4.8**), educational lectures are made available as MP3 files for download by the student body. Basically, any audio file that is available as a download from a hyperlink on any Web site is considered to be a podcast.

Figure 4.8

From this portal, Duke University is using hyperlinked audio files to disseminate lectures to its students.

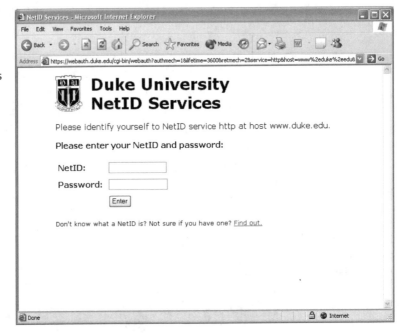

If you are creating a podcast for a company that wants only a select group of people to hear it, placing the podcast in a hyperlink for individual download may be the best route to take. Many companies and organizations include a combination of a hyperlink to the podcast file and an RSS feed and/or a streaming feed. Indeed, some podcasters have begun to make their podcasts available through multiple routes. On the site of the top-10 podcast "Catholic Insider," for example, links are included for download of the podcasts, streaming podcasts, and RSS feeds (**Figure 4.9**).

Figure 4.9

"Catholic Insider" is an example of a podcast that offers multiple access points.

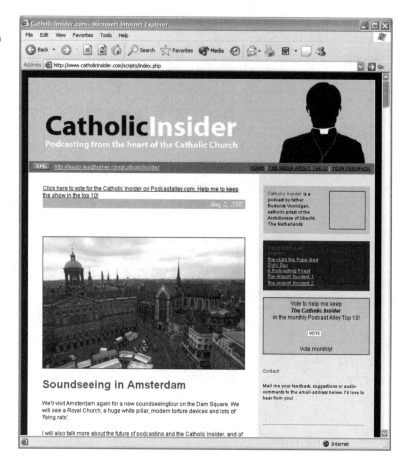

Ultimately, the most compelling reasons to link a podcast file to a hyperlink on a Web site are:

- For corporations to disseminate information to their employees

- As an adjunct to publishing podcasts through RSS

- For educational institutions to make podcasts available to their students but not the rest of the world

- For anyone who wants to control who gains access to the podcast

- For private podcasters who want only people who visit their Web sites to have access to the podcast

Streaming

Until the phenomenon of podcasting reared its head just a few short months ago, much of the audio content on the Internet came in the form of streaming audio. *Streaming audio* is an audio feed that is downloaded dynamically (as you listen to it) from a source somewhere on the Internet to a media player on your computer. Internet radio uses this technology, as do many movie preview sites that show movie trailers. Streaming is also used by commercial Web sites like Amazon.com (where users can hear samples of songs being sold) and Audible.com (where users can listen to entire books).

Ultimately, streaming audio is not the most important pathway for getting your podcasts heard; RSS feeds are by far the best method. That said, if you want to use it, you can provide streaming audio in several ways, including:

- Formatting the file link so that it starts playing the file as soon as the link is clicked.

- Using a flash-based player on your Web site to stream the audio files.

- Using a Web service like Live365 (www.live365.com), which offers packages for hosting your material and stream it out for you (**Figure 4.10**). The costs of sites like this vary depending on the package and features chosen.

Figure 4.10

Sites like Live365 can stream your material if you are gung-ho on having streaming audio of your podcasts.

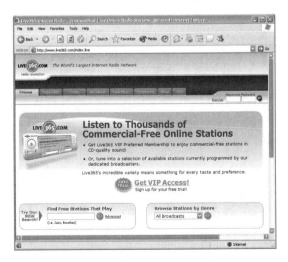

Nicecast

M Available only for the Mac, Nicecast (www.rogueamoeba.com/nicecast; **Figure 4.11**) is an Internet broadcaster that allows users to broadcast MP3 files to the Internet via iTunes. Although it's not practical for large-scale podcasting, Nicecast is a very ingenious way to enable streaming audio from a Macintosh computer running OS X (required).

Figure 4.11

Nicecast allows Mac users to stream podcasts onto the Internet in a limited way.

The feature list of Nicecast includes:

- The ability to broadcast a live event

- Via iTunes, the ability to broadcast podcasts one after another

- The ability to add voice-overs and digital effects to outgoing streaming content

Nicecast is best used by those who want to enable a few select people to stream their podcasts; this is not the answer for large-scale dissemination of a podcast. Still, at only $10, it is a very handy piece of software to have around, and it allows you to broadcast your podcasts over the Internet, if only in a limited way.

RSS Feed Software Options

If actually writing an RSS feed file is something that does not hold much appeal for you, worry not—several software options allow you to create RSS feeds with relative ease. These programs don't create the Web sites or host the space where the podcasts will reside, but they do make the process of creating the RSS file very painless.

FeedForAll

FeedForAll (www.feedforall.com; **Figure 4.12**) is the RSS feed creator of choice right now. With a very simple wizard that asks a few questions about the podcast, the link to the podcast, and the addition of some descriptive text, FeedForAll automatically creates an RSS file that you can set up on your Web site immediately for your podcast to be published. Available for the PC (and currently in beta for the Macintosh), FeedForAll is a powerful tool that allows the user to create, edit, and publish RSS feeds with ease. For those with a deeper knowledge of RSS, FeedForAll allows tweaking of details that novices are likely to avoid.

Figure 4.12

FeedForAll is a great one-stop RSS feed creator.

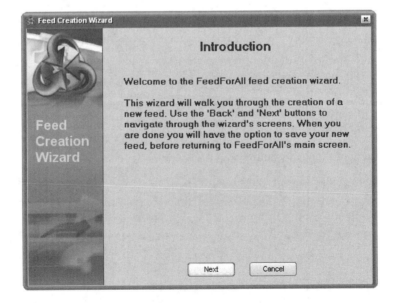

At $39.95, FeedForAll is reasonably priced for anyone who doesn't want to learn how to create RSS feeds from scratch. The features of FeedForAll include:

- Spell checking

- XML editor

- Simple Feed Creation Wizard that walks users through the process step by step

- Image editor for creating RSS feed images

- Automatic feed repair option

- Automatic date management

- Support for an unlimited number of feeds

- Customizable

The most appealing feature of FeedForAll is the Feed Creation Wizard. Using the wizard, you can create an RSS feed simply by answering a few questions, one of which is shown in **Figure 4.13**. For anyone who's serious about podcasting but not serious about spending time learning XML and RSS, FeedForAll is an excellent answer.

Figure 4.13

FeedForAll's Feed Creation Wizard is a snap to use.

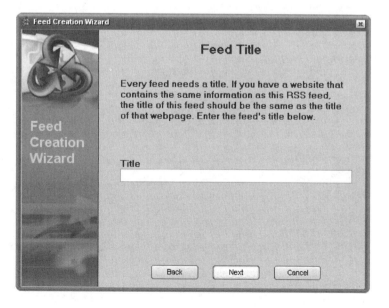

Interview with Sharon Housley

Sharon Housley is vice president of marketing for NotePage, Inc., the creator of FreeForAll.

NotePage, Inc. was founded in 1996 as a software company with a focus on communications software. In the fall of 2004, NotePage launched the FeedForAll product line, which involves RSS feed creation, editing, and publishing. Housley has written numerous articles and tutorials related to RSS, podcasting, and online marketing. She has been marketing online since 1996 and currently manages the content and marketing for more than 100 independent Web sites owned by NotePage.

Farkas: Where did FeedForAll come from?

Housley: FeedForAll was the result of a need that our marketing team had. In their attempts to create RSS feeds for product promotion, they realized the difficulties that an erroneous character or malformed feed could cause. As a result, the marketing team searched for software to create feeds. Unable to find any solutions, our marketers met with our development team and proposed the product. Realizing the need and market opening, our development team worked with our marketers to develop an easy-to-use RSS feed creation application, which has evolved into modern-day FeedForAll.

Farkas: What are the future plans for FeedForAll?

Housley: There are a number of enhancements planned for FeedForAll. I've detailed the enhancements that I can share below:

Improved uploading capabilities

We will be working on a easy way to upload files associated with a feed, all in one simple process. For example, with podcasts, there are audio files referenced in the feed that also need to be uploaded to your Web server. There will be a way to have FeedForAll upload your feed *and* the audio files, images, etc., all with the click of a button.

Interview with Sharon Housley *(continued)*

Importing

We will also be adding a way to import items easily from other feeds into the current feed. One possible use for this feature would be to create a new feed by picking and choosing items from other existing feeds.

WYSIWYG description editor improvements

We are constantly trying to add small improvements to make FeedForAll more powerful without losing any of its ease of use. For example, the next release will allow you to add images to your item descriptions easily by using the WYSIWYG description editor (and even make them into links).

Farkas: How do you see the realm of podcasting changing in the next few years?

Housley: I think the quality of podcasts will significantly improve. Businesses will embrace podcasting as a means to further streamline corporate communications, by finding innovative new uses for both internal and external podcasts.

I think online learning will blossom with the advent of podcasting and that innovative new uses of podcasts will help unify the global marketplace. Obviously, advertising and fee-based podcast will evolve, and quality podcasts will become the standard while the lower-quality casts will fade away.

Farkas: What impact do you think FeedForAll has had on podcasting?

Housley: FeedForAll currently makes it extremely easy for *anyone* to podcast, for very little expense. Some will make a name for themselves and be able to compete with large companies that have deep pockets. Ultimately, professional podcasts, whether made by an individual or a corporation, will survive, but for now, FeedForAll helps even the playing field.

Feeder

Published by Reinvented Software (www.reinventedsoftware.com; **Figure 4.14**), Feeder is a Macintosh RSS feed creator that makes creating an RSS feed as easy as pie. Feeder is an excellent tool for podcasters who are producing multiple podcasts on a regular basis.

Figure 4.14

Feeder is exclusive to the Mac.

The features of Feeder include:

- Templates to edit and create feeds

- Preflight check that checks the feed before it's published

- Quick-start feature for creating, importing, or downloading a feed

- Ability to publish finished feeds to your server via FTP

Feeder uses a very intuitive interface to guide you through the process of creating an RSS feed. After the feed has been created, clicking the New Item button allows you to add subsequent podcast feeds with ease. For Mac users who want a simple way to create RSS feeds for their podcasts, Feeder is the No. 1 option, and at $24.95, it won't break the bank. Feeder has a 14-day free trial built in, enabling you to sample before you buy.

Propaganda

Mentioned in Chapter 3, Propaganda (www.makepropaganda.com) is an all-in-one podcast creation/publishing program that takes you from recording the podcast through editing and finally to creating and publishing the RSS feed. If an all-in-one solution is what you need, Propaganda does the job adequately. That said, there are more elegant individual pieces of software that do what Propaganda does, but the process is not confined to one piece of software.

iPodcast Producer

Also mentioned in Chapter 3, iPodcast Producer is a commercial product that runs $149.95 from Industrial Audio Software's Web site. iPodcast Producer is an all-in-one solution that is acceptable, but again, if elegance and ease of use are your goal, it may be better to put the pieces together piecemeal rather than have this all-in-one package. The one thing that iPodcast Producer does offer is the ability to create the RSS feed for your podcast with relative ease. For those who are looking for all-in-one solutions, this is on par with Propaganda.

Sparks! 2.0

BlogMatrix, the creator of Sparks! 2.0 (also mentioned in Chapter 3), offers a free service for sharing your podcasts via its Web site (www.blogmatrix.com). Remember that Sparks! 2.0 is a podcast aggregator as well as an audio recorder, editor, and podcast publisher. Most of its features are free, but if you want to use the recording feature, there is a $10 fee. (The recording feature comes with a 30-day free trial.)

For all-in-one solutions, it's hard to beat this piece of software, but there are limitations in terms of the free BlogMatrix account and RSS feed publishing. The feed is available to other BlogMatrix users but not to the world at large. Still, this is a viable option for some podcasters.

Web-Site Packagers

If creating your own Web site and managing RSS files are things you would rather not do, several online options can ease the pain of learning RSS. Web-site packagers (as I call them) offer up complete packages for hosting an RSS feed so that your podcasts can be available to the masses with little effort on your part. The rub, of course, is that most of these Web sites charge a fee for this service.

This section looks at a pair of Web-site packagers that offer services to enable you to get your podcast and Web page up and running in a very short period of time with relatively little blood, sweat, and tears. This field is changing so rapidly that a search on Google is likely to yield a large number of companies willing to host your podcasts.

Liberated Syndication

Liberated Syndication (www.libsyn.com; **Figure 4.15**) is a Web hosting company designed specifically for podcasting. Libsyn.com goes beyond simple Web-site hosting; it offers a podcast-specific product that includes storage for media (podcasts) and an easy-to-use interface for publishing your podcast.

Although Liberated Syndication doesn't offer a front-end Web page per se, it does offer an easy solution for publishing your podcast to an RSS feed for a relatively low cost. The costs of the company's services range from $5 per month (100 MB of storage space) to $30 per month (750 MB). Liberated Syndication takes the attitude that it doesn't want users to be penalized if their programs become popular. Therefore, it does not charge for bandwidth use—only for the space that users' podcasts take up on its servers.

Liberated Syndication is my No. 1 choice for this sort of service. The prices are *very* reasonable, and you would be hard pressed to find another service that offers so much for so little.

Figure 4.15

Liberated Syndication is an excellent Web-hosting service that's dedicated to podcasters.

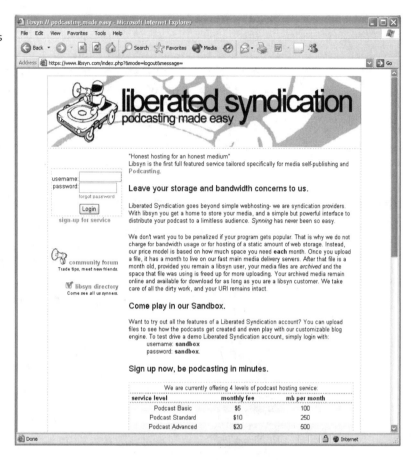

The list of features, as noted on the Libsyn.com Web site, are as follows:

- Unmetered bandwidth

- Easy-to-use interface

- No lock-in (users are not tied to Libsyn.com for their podcasting needs)

- Quickcast feature that immediately creates a podcast feed for an uploaded media file.

Podbus.com

Podbus.com (www.podbus.com; **Figure 4.16**) is another outstanding commercial Web-hosting service for podcasters. For only $4 a month, Podbus offers 300 MB of storage space and 10 GB of bandwidth. For noncommercial podcasters, this is a very good start in terms of both storage space and bandwidth, and at $4 a month, it's not exactly a financial risk. Additionally, if you happen to exceed the 10 GB bandwidth limit, each 10 GB of additional bandwidth costs just $4.

Figure 4.16

Podbus.com is an outstanding service for hosting podcast feeds.

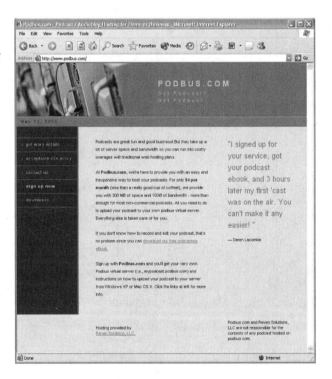

Podbus also includes automatic RSS feed creation. In other words, when a podcast is added to its server, a podcast feed is generated automatically (saving you the pain and suffering of creating your own). The one thing Podbus.com offers that Libsyn.com does not is Web hosting. For a measly $2 per month, Podbus.com allows you to use your 300 MB of space to host your own Web page. Like Liberated Syndication, Podbus is an outstanding service for podcasters, whether they are newbies or seasoned veterans.

A

Appendix: Resources

Podcasting as a known entity is not even a year old, yet in this very short time, it has already woven its way into the world's consciousness, vernacular, and commerce channels. Podcasting as an entity is progressing and changing at a blinding pace. This is partially because of the nature of the Internet and partially because podcasting is a new medium that is still finding its niche in society.

Because of the ever-changing nature of this medium, I recommend that you check out www.peachpit.com/podcasting to get updates on the most up-to-date Web sites and resources available. Despite the continual morphing of the podcasting realm, there are a large number of important Web sites that I'd be remiss if I didn't mention.

Podcasting-Related Web Sites

This section includes links to all Web sites relating to podcasting as an entity. These sites provide information about the community, as well as links to software and podcasts. These are the first sites that a new podcaster should visit to get a feel for the community.

Our podcast

To listen to the podcast made especially for this book, check out:

www.peachpit.com/podcasting

General podcasting Web sites

These Web sites are catch-all reservoirs of podcasting information. Most of these sites contain how-to information, a top-10 list of podcasts, a large bank of podcast feeds, and links to the latest and greatest software for podcasting-related activities.

Audio.weblogs.com: http://audio.weblogs.com

iPodder.org: www.ipodder.org

Podcast Alley: www.podcastalley.com

The Podcast Bunker: www.podcastbunker.com

Podcast Central: www.podcastcentral.com

PodcastExpert.com: www.podcastexpert.com

Podcast.net: www.podcast.net

The Podcast Network: www.thepodcastnetwork.com

Podcasting News: www.podcastingnews.com

Podcasting Tools: www.podcasting-tools.com

General search engines

These are the search engines you can use to scour the World Wide Web for anything related to podcasting. These engines gather data by the minute, so making the same search every day or so often yields different results.

AltaVista: www.altavista.com

Ask Jeeves: www.ask.com

Google: www.google.com

Lycos: www.lycos.com

MSN: www.msn.com

Yahoo!: www.yahoo.com

Podcast search engine

Although any search engine, such as Yahoo! or Google, can come up with all things podcasting, only one currently is dedicated to searching for specific words or phrases *in* podcasts themselves.

Podscope: www.podscope.com

Podcasting-related sites

These Web sites are not catch-all podcasting sites, but they often contain valuable information for some topic that's podcast related.

Engadget: www.engadget.com

Podcasting Avenue: http://podcasters.blogspot.com

Portable Media Expo: www.portablemediaexpo.com

Really Simple Syndication Web sites (RSS)

These Web sites cover everything from the history of RSS to the down-and-dirty details of the specification itself.

Berkman Center for Internet & Society (Harvard University): http://blogs.law.harvard.edu/tech/rss

RSS Digest: www.bigbold.com/rssdigest

Music legalities

These are the various Web sites where Creative Commons–licensed music is available and where you can learn about Creative Commons. I have also included the license links for both ASCAP and BMI.

ASCAP Internet License Agreements: www.ascap.com/weblicense

BMI Web Site Music Performance Agreement: www.bmi.com/licensing/forms/Internet0105A.pdf

Creative Commons: http://creativecommons.org

The Freesound Project: http://freesound.iua.upf.edu/index.php

Opsound: www.opsound.com

Podcasting software: Aggregators (podcatchers)

These are the programs that go out and grab the podcasts for you to listen to. Some of the podcast aggregators listed here are not covered in this book; however, I thought it worthwhile to list them here for your convenience.

Bashpodder: http://linc.homeunix.org:8080/scripts/bashpodder

CastGrab: www.fubarpa.com/projects/castgrab

Doppler: www.dopplerradio.net

FeedDemon: www.bradsoft.com/feeddemon/index.asp

FeederReader: www.feederreader.com

HappyFish: http://thirstycrow.net/happyfish/default.aspx

iPodder: www.ipodder.org

iPodder.NET: http://ipoddernet.sourceforge.net

iPodderSP/Skookum: www.equin.co.uk/ipoddersp

iPodderX: http://ipodderx.com

iTunes 4.9: www.apple.com/itunes

jPodder: www.jpodder.com

Nimiq: www.nimiq.nl

Now Playing: http://brandon.fuller.name/archives/hacks/nowplaying

PlayPod: www.iggsoftware.com/playpod/index.html

PocketRSS: www.happyjackroad.net/pocketpc/pocketRSS/pocketRSS.asp

Podcast Tuner: www.podcasttuner.com

PoddumFeeder: www.ifthensoft.com/index2.html

Pod2Go: www.kainjow.com/pod2go

ppcTunes: www.pocketmac.net/products/ppctunes

Primetime Podcast Receiver: www.primetimepodcast.com/blog/default.aspx

RSSRadio: www.dorada.co.uk

Podcasting software: Creating podcasts

This is the software that you use to create podcasts from scratch. From recording the content to editing out mistakes and inserting music, these are the programs that do it.

Adobe Audition 1.5: www.adobe.com/audition

Audacity: http://audacity.sourceforge.net/download

GarageBand: www.apple.com/garageband

iPodcast Producer: www.industrialaudiosoftware.com/products/index.html

Propaganda: www.makepropaganda.com

Sound Byte: www.blackcatsystems.com/software/soundbyte.html

Sound Recorder (Windows): www.microsoft.com

Sparks! 2.0: www.blogmatrix.com

Podcasting software: Publishing podcasts

These are the links for the software packages I've recommended that can help you create an RSS feed with ease.

Feeder: www.reinventedsoftware.com

FeedForAll: www.feedforall.com

iPodcast Producer: www.industrialaudiosoftware.com/products/index.html

Live365 (streaming): www.live365.com/index.live

Nicecast (streaming): www.rogueamoeba.com/nicecast

Propaganda: www.makepropaganda.com

Sparks! 2.0: www.blogmatrix.com

Publishing podcasts: Web-site hosting solutions

These are the two sites I recommend if you are interested in paying a hosting service that specializes in podcasts to host your files.

Liberated Syndication: www.libsyn.com

Podbus.com: www.podbus.com

Commercial podcast sources

It goes without saying that I can't possibly list every commercial venture that has podcasts available. That said, these are the major sites that you can visit just to get the flavor of what's available.

Audible.com: www.audible.com

AudioBooksForFree.com: www.audiobooksforfree.com

Audiobooks Online: www.audiobooksonline.com

Blackstone Audiobooks: www.blackstoneaudio.com

Canadian Broadcasting Corporation: www.cbc.ca

iTunes Music Store: www.apple.com/itunes/store

National Public Radio: www.npr.org

Other software

These are links to software that is mentioned in the book, from media players to Web-page design programs.

Dreamweaver: www.macromedia.com/software/dreamweaver

FrontPage: www.microsoft.com

GoLive: www.adobe.com/products/golive/main.html

QuickTime: www.apple.com/quicktime

RealPlayer: www.realnetworks.com

Replay Radio: http://www.replay-radio.com

Windows Media Player: www.microsoft.com

Top podcasts

To come up with this list, I went to Podcast Alley and took the top 15 podcasts from its voted top-50 list.

1. **"This Week in Tech":** http://thisweekintech.com

2. **"The Dawn and Drew Show":** www.dawnanddrew.com

3. **"Free Talk Live":** http://freetalklive.com

4. **"Catholic Insider":** www.catholicinsider.com

5. **"EarthCore: A Podcast Novel":** www.scottsigler.net/earthcore

6. **"Slacker Astronomy":** www.slackerastronomy.com

7. **"The MacCast":** www.maccast.com

8. **"CURRY.COM: Adam Curry's Weblog":** http://live.curry.com

9. **"Coverville":** www.coverville.com

10. **"Geek News Central":** www.geeknewscentral.com

11. **"The Specialist and AKG Show":** http://specialistandakg.com

12. **"Slice of Sci-Fi":** http://sliceofscifi.com

13. **"Keith and The Girl":** http://shitecom.libsyn.com

14. **"The Bob and AJ Show":** www.bobandaj.info

15. **"The Bitterest Pill":** www.thebitterestpill.com

Hardware

These links take you to the various companies that manufacture the hardware discussed in this book.

Apple Computer: www.apple.com

Audio-Technica: www.audiotechnica.com

Behringer: www.behringer.com

COWON America: http://eng.cowon.com

Creative: www.creative.com

Edirol: www.edirol.com

Electrovoice: www.electrovoice.com

Griffin Technology: www.griffintechnology.com

iRiver: www.iriver.com

JVC: www.jvc.com

Labtec: www.labtec.com

Logitech: www.logitech.com

M-Audio: www.m-audio.com

Rio Audio: www.digitalnetworksna.com/rioaudio

Sony: www.sony.com

Other interesting sites

These are a collection of other interesting Web sites that are related to podcasts and/or podcasting in some way.

Duke University iPod First-Year Experience: www.duke.edu/ipod

How-To Podcasting: www.engadget.com/entry/5843952395227141

Podcast about the Podcast: http://reelreviewsradio.com/archives/2004/12/27/podcast-about-the-podcast

Glossary

You may not be familiar with some terms mentioned in this book. Although many of these terms will be familiar to those who have experience with the World Wide Web, some terminology may be confusing to newcomers. This glossary should clear up any confusion.

A

AAC: Stands for *Advanced Audio Coding,* a type of digital compression that is used to reduce the size of music files while maintaining quality. AAC, which is the preferred method of digital encoding for Apple Computer and its line of iPod players, is superior in quality to the MP3 format but is still part of the MPEG specification. *See also* MPEG, MP3.

ActiveSync: A program from Microsoft that synchronizes data between a PC and portable devices running the Windows Mobile or Windows CE operating system.

aggregator: A piece of software that scours specific areas on the World Wide Web to find selected content and then deliver it to your computer.

audio blog: A Web log (blog) that contains audio files instead of written text.

B

bit rate: The speed at which bits of data flow through a specific area or connection. The bit rate measures the number of bits over time (bits per second).

BitTorrent: A peer-to-peer file distribution program. Files are broken into smaller chunks, distributed in fragments, and then reassembled on the requesting machine. If a piece is missing, each peer takes advantage of the best connection to find the missing pieces. BitTorrent is a very effective tool for sharing large amounts of data, such as videos and large audio files. *See also* peer-to-peer.

blog: A term formed by the combination of the words *Web* and *log*. A blog is a Web-based page where content is added periodically. The content of a blog can range from diary entries to news items to podcasts.

blogging: The act of contributing to or running a Web log (blog). Depending on the form of the blog, there can be various incarnations of the name, including video blogging, audio blogging, and photography blogging.

C

CPU: Stands for *central processing unit,* the brains of a computer.

D

digital music device: Any hard-drive- or flash-memory-based digital music player. *See also* hard-drive memory, flash memory.

F

flash memory: A kind of RAM (Random Access Memory) that does not lose the data it contains when the power on the device is turned off. Flash memory is limited by the size of the chip used and is generally a fraction of the space available on a hard drive.

flash player: An MP3 player that uses flash memory to hold information.

FTP: Stands for *File Transfer Protocol,* a protocol for transferring large files over the Internet.

H

hard-drive memory: A digital memory medium using a hard drive. In the context of digital music devices, hard drives are not unlike the hard drives used in your home computer. The most significant difference between these hard drives is the size; hard drives in digital music players can be as small as a stack of three quarters!

hyperlink: A word or string of words in a document linking to another resource, such as a Web page or another document.

I

iPod: A hard-drive- or flash-memory-based digital media player from Apple Computer, Inc.

iPodder: A nifty piece of software designed to download audio files (podcasts) directly to your digital media player (such as Apple's iPod).

iTunes: Apple's Mac- and PC-based software for managing MP3s, AAC files, and other audio content among the World Wide Web, your computer, and your iPod.

L

LCD: Stands for *liquid crystal display*, the type of screen used in iPods and many MP3 players.

M

MPEG: Stands for *Moving Pictures Expert Group*, a digital information compression standard that allows large digital files, such as audio or video files, to be compressed nearly tenfold without much quality loss. *See also* MP3.

MP3: A type of digital compression that is used to reduce the size of music files while maintaining quality. MP3 compression is part of MPEG compression.

N

newbie: Slang for someone who is new to a particular concept or discipline.

O

Ogg Vorbis: An open-source file compression format, similar to MP3.

OOG: *See* Ogg Vorbis.

OPML: Stands for *Outline Processor Markup Language*, a kind of programming language that is used to create files for Really Simple Syndication (RSS).

P

peer-to-peer: A computer network that uses the computers on the "edges" of the network rather than a central point or the network itself. In short, peer-to-peer takes advantage of all the computers on the network to speed things up.

plug-in: A piece of software that can be "plugged" into an existing program to modify it in some way.

podcast: A digital broadcast that can be loaded onto a digital music device, such as an iPod or other MP3 player.

podcatcher: A piece of software (also known as an *aggregator*) that goes out on the Internet and finds podcasts for download.

podwaves: An analog to airwaves.

preamp: Stands for *preamplifier,* an amplifier that comes before another amplifier. In the case of podcasting, the preamp usually powers the microphone.

P2P: *See* peer-to-peer.

R

RAM: Stands for *Random Access Memory,* a computer-chip form of memory. Information such as computer programs and data is temporarily stored in RAM while the computer is turned on. As a general rule, RAM is volatile memory, and its contents are lost when power is removed. Flash memory is an exception to this rule.

RSS: Stands for *Really Simple Syndication,* a protocol designed to make it easy for the average person to get podcasts out for the world to hear.

RSS feed: The actual link to the podcast or other file to be syndicated.

S

streaming media: A form of broadcasting in which content is streamed directly from a Web site to a home computer. This content is played "live" on the computer as it is streamed, rather than being saved on the computer's hard drive.

U

URL: Stands for *Uniform Resource Locator,* the address of a Web page, often starting with www.

USB: Stands for *Universal Serial Bus,* a now-standard connection modality for PCs and Macs.

USB 2.0: A much faster form of the USB bus.

W

WAV: Stands for *WAVEform,* Microsoft's audio format.

Webcasting: A form of broadcasting in which the content is downloaded directly off a Web site to a home computer and onto the computer's hard drive.

Web log: *See* blog.

X

XML: Stands for *Extensible Markup Language,* a programming language that underpins RSS.

Index